An Angel
Directs the Storm

An Angel Directs the Storm

Apocalyptic Religion
and
American Empire

Michael Northcott

I.B. TAURIS

LONDON · NEW YORK

Published in 2004 by I.B. Tauris & Co Ltd
6 Salem Road, London W2 4BU
175 Fifth Avenue, New York NY 10010
www.ibtauris.com

In the United States of America and Canada distributed by
Palgrave Macmillan a division of St. Martin's Press
175 Fifth Avenue, New York, NY 10010

ISBN 1 85043 478 6
EAN 978 1 85043 478 8

A full CIP record for this book is available from the British Library
A full CIP record is available from the Library of Congress

Library of Congress Catalog Card Number: available

Project managed by M&M Publishing Services
Warner Road, Ware, Hertfordshire
Typeset in Palatino 10/13 by Cambridge Photosetting Services,
Sturton Street, Cambridge
Printed and bound in Great Britain by MPG Books Ltd,
Victoria Square, Bodmin, Cornwall

For Ben

Contents

Acknowledgements

I want first to record my thanks to American friends who, on my many visits to the United States, have shown me so much warm-hearted and generous hospitality and kindness. I first flew to JFK to join my family in Connecticut in the summer of 1969 when Americans first walked on the moon. I came to know then the warmth of spirit that is so much a feature of American life, which I have wanted and often been privileged to return.

I am grateful to my American graduate student Tristin Hassell, in conversation with whom this book first began to take shape, and to my 2003 graduate class in Christian Ethics, who read an early draft and offered much encouragement. A number of friends commented insightfully on later drafts, including: Marcella Althaus-Reid, Timothy Clayton, Cormac Connor, Duncan Forrester, Stanley Hauerwas, Alastair McIntosh, Jolyon Mitchell, Kevin Reed and Wilf Wilde.

I read a paper from which this book emerged in the Department of Theology in the University of Durham, my *alma mater*, and I am grateful to the insightful comments of David Brown, Douglas Davies, Robert Song and Stephen Sykes. That paper was published in *Political Theology* in April 2004. Parts of it appear in revised form in what follows and I am grateful to Equinox Publishing for their cooperation.

I thank my editor at I. B. Tauris, Alex Wright, who believed in this book before I did, and to the librarians of the National Library of Scotland and New College Library, where most of the research and writing was done. Finally, I am thankful to my family, Jill, Lydia, Ben, Rebecca and Jacob, who remind me that I have no need for the wilder forms of apocalyptic imaginary for they give me a wonderful home in this life – though I do of course hope that God will lend me one in the next. I dedicate this book to my son Ben as he embarks on his own studies of politics and culture.

Introduction

The American invasion and occupation of Iraq in 2003, aided and abetted by the British, was seen around the world as a war without any basis in international law, and as a war that could not be described as just or moral. Political leaders from France and Germany to Russia and Canada were opposed to the war and refused to participate in either the war or the post-war pacification and reconstruction of Iraq. Christian leaders also displayed an unusual degree of unanimity on this point. Pope John Paul II and the Anglican Archbishop of Canterbury, Rowan Williams, both vocally opposed the war, as did the leader of the United Methodist Church, of which President George W. Bush is a member, together with the leaders of world Lutheranism, most Presbyterian churches and most other world communions including Baptists and Orthodox. But this display of official Christian opposition to the war obscures the extent to which millions of American Christians, including not only conservative Southern Baptists but the fast-growing conservative churches and suburban 'megachurches', supported the war. Analogously, the outpouring of patriotism after September 11, 2001 was particularly noticeable in the car parks of conservative churches on Sunday mornings, which were replete with the plastic-masted miniatures of the Stars and Stripes which millions attached to their automobile windows across America.

Thanks to the effectiveness with which the Bush administration sold their deceitful claims about Iraq to the American people – that Saddam Hussein supported Al-Qaeda, that he was in possession of weapons of mass destruction which he could launch against other countries and which he intended to pass on to international terrorists, that his regime was consequently a direct threat to the people of America – and their uncritical adoption by the corporately controlled American media, a majority of Americans came to believe that Saddam Hussein was involved in the terror attacks on America's East Coast. I use the word 'sold' advisedly in relation to the campaign for war, for Bush, Cheney, Powell and Rumsfeld hired a brand consultant, Carolyn Beers, who had been formerly a Madison Avenue advertising CEO responsible for selling Head and Shoulders shampoo and Uncle Ben's Rice, to sell the Iraq war to the American people. The intention, according to Colin Powell, was to brand American foreign policy.[1] So long as the long-planned attack on Iraq could be sold in terms of the new foreign policy brand – the 'war on terror' – they were always guaranteed American support. I say 'long-planned' because plans to unseat Saddam Hussein were discussed in the White House from the first day of the Bush administration, and long prior to that between administration insiders.[2]

Support for Bush was nowhere stronger than among the millions of Conservative Christians who had voted for him as the chosen candidate of the Christian Right in 2000, whose central moral concerns – abortion, 'family values' and Israel – Bush had done much to address in his campaign for the Presidency. This campaigning strategy reflected his long-standing courtship of the evangelical Christian lobby, first in relation to his father's campaign for the Presidency in 1988, and then in his own campaign for the governorship of Texas. Bush experienced a personal conversion to evangelical Christianity under the influence of Billy Graham, Arthur Blessitt and other prominent evangelical figures close to the Bush family. Subsequently as governor of Texas he pursued the agenda of the conservative Christian right in a way no governor had done before. He drastically cut state funding for welfare and education while allowing for the first time state funds to be diverted to religiously organised social services. He rewrote state tort law, making it almost impossible for communities or individuals to take civil actions against private companies for death or injury at work or over pollution or other negligent or harmful activities. Furthermore, he enhanced the reputation of Texas as the most punitive state in the union, where even children may be judicially executed.[3]

Before winning the White House in a disputed election in which his brother, Jeb Bush, had played a notable role in suppressing the black vote as Governor of Florida,[4] Bush confessed that he believed he had been divinely called to serve his country at some great moment of crisis: 'I feel like God wants me to run for president. I can't explain it, but I sense my country is going to need me. Something is going to happen. And at that time my country will need me'.[5]

A Chosen People?

In his Inaugural Address in January 2001, George W. Bush clearly articulated his belief in his own and America's divine calling to lead the world in an apocalyptic struggle between the forces of good and evil, and to shape the world after the American values of liberty, democracy and the free market. The use of religious discourse in inaugural addresses is by no means unique to Bush. Clinton, Reagan and Carter had all used this kind of language. Bush, however, went beyond the usual civil religion of such occasions by inviting Franklin Graham to give a Trinitarian blessing and prayer at the inaugural ceremony. Bush commenced his address with a near-Messianic account of the American story as the pursuit of liberty and of America as the liberator of humanity:

> We have a place, all of us, in a long story – a story we continue, but whose end we will not see. It is the story of a new world that became a friend and liberator of the old, a story of a slave-holding society that became a servant of freedom, the story of a power that went into the world to protect but not possess, to defend but not to conquer.[6]

America in this story is the 'new world' redeemer of the old world from whence it sprang, liberating Europe from the pogroms and totalitarianism that threatened it in the twentieth century. Bush also recalls America's triumph in the Cold War, and the downfall of the

Soviet Empire that American military strength and active resistance to communism around the world were said to have brought about. Defending the story of America as agent of liberty is an act of faith, 'faith in freedom and democracy'. It was America's commitment to this faith which made her 'a rock in a raging sea' and this 'democratic faith is more than the creed of our country, it is the inborn hope of our humanity, an ideal we carry but do not own, a trust we bear and pass along'.[7]

This account of the American story is again not peculiar to Bush or his speech-writers. Americans have a story about themselves as victims of oppression and as anti-imperialists. Many Americans have ancestral histories that tell of liberation – radical reformist Protestant Christians fleeing persecution in Europe in the eighteenth century; Sicilians and Irish fleeing poverty in the nineteenth century; Jews fleeing anti-semitism, Mexicans, Guatemalans and El Salvadoreans fleeing rightist military juntas in the twentieth century, albeit juntas supported by the United States. These waves of refugees in their small towns and urban and rural neighbourhoods would in time constitute a federation. As they passed the Statue of Liberty, and went through Ellis Island, on their way to these often far-flung places they came to understand themselves as having entered a large and spacious land whose government could give them freedom because it had overthrown European imperial power through revolution. At least until the late nineteenth century, this new nation had no ambition to establish an empire of its own beyond its borders, busy as it was consolidating its hold over lands to the West and South which were as yet not American but Spanish and Mexican. In the self-consciousness of most Americans, America is an anti-imperialist nation, a self-consciousness that is clearly reflected in Bush's speech. Recall that at this point in his life Bush had only left the United States on two occasions, and these were on visits to Mexico. Like most Americans who have no passport, before he became President America was the world for Bush.

Combined with this sense of the sufficiency of America – that from the redwoods of California to the Statue of Liberty in New York it is already a world unto itself – many Americans have a sense, which again has deep roots, that they are indeed a 'chosen people'. The Puritans who left England for America in the seventeenth century saw their new colony as the Promised Land gifted them by the providence of God. They had been delivered from religious persecution in England and they sought to build a holy common-wealth in New England free of the corruption of the old country.

At the outbreak of war with the colonial power in the eighteenth century, as the English were shelling Boston harbour, an Episcopal priest, Jacob Duche, read from the 35th Psalm in the presence of George Washington at the First Continental Congress and it was clear from the words he selected that he was putting America in the place of Israel: 'Plead my cause, O Lord, with them that strive with me: fight against them that fight against me. Take hold of shield and buckler, and stand up for mine help'.[8] Duche, like the Puritans, was laying claim to the Exodus story of the deliverance of Israel from slavery in Egypt and of its calling to be God's Chosen People. Duche appeals to the God of Israel to fight on behalf of his new nation against the oppressor, just as God fought on behalf of Israel. As Clifford Longley notes, the reading of this Psalm at the inauguration of this first convention of the new America, in the midst of the revolutionary break with Britain,

> was *par excellence*, the act that founded America upon a specific understanding of God's purposes. Henceforth the Chosen People were to be not the Jews, not the Catholics, not the English, and not just the New Englanders, but all Americans. Henceforth 'being an American', like being a Jew or being a Christian, was to possess a distinct religious status as one of the elect.[9]

This sense of being a divinely chosen people has passed into the American imaginary and the names for it are many – 'the American way of life', 'the American dream', 'Manifest Destiny', 'American Exceptionalism'.

Bush explicitly drew on this imaginary in his Inaugural Address, and in his response to the September 11 terrorist attacks when he recalled the religious roots of what had become a secular America, and called Americans back to the 'sacred origins', and hence the 'sacred calling', of their country. In a speech to religious broadcasters in Nashville, Bush claimed that the United States had a God-given mission to bring the divine gift of freedom 'to every human being in the world'.[10] But there is a twist to this God-given calling which sets it at odds with the vision of the first pilgrims as they fled imperial Europe, or that of the people of Israel as they sought divine protection from the Egyptian Empire. For Bush, America is not only divinely chosen to be a place of safety for the persecuted from other lands, but also to be the instrument that God will use to bring liberty and democracy to the nations of the world. Instead of a refuge from the storm, America becomes the storm, threatening to visit its military might, and its unchallenged supremacy as the sole remaining superpower, on those who would resist its influence: the 'enemies of freedom'. From a liberated people America has become in Bush's mind the liberator. Instead of the plot of the Exodus from Israel Bush has adopted the plot of *Rambo* or *Terminator*:

> We will build our defenses beyond challenge, lest weakness invite challenge. We will confront weapons of mass destruction, so that a new century is spared new horrors. The enemies of liberty and our country should make no mistake: America remains engaged in the world by history and by choice, shaping a balance of power that favors freedom. We will defend our allies and our interests. We will show purpose without arrogance. We will meet aggression and bad faith with resolve and strength. And to all nations, we will speak for the values that gave our nation birth.[11]

The struggle to achieve this vision at home and overseas will require courage and perseverance but ultimately it will be successful because it is 'the angel of God who directs the storm'.[12] Bush's speech-writer adopted the reference to the angel of God from the words of the Virginia statesman John Page who wrote after the Declaration of Independence to Thomas Jefferson: 'We know the race is not to the swift nor the battle to the strong. Do you not think an angel rides in the whirlwind and directs this storm?'

In his 2002 State of the Union address, three months after the terror attacks, Bush finds confirmation of his vision of America serving a larger purpose and destiny. The terrorist attack provided a 'unique opportunity' to bring together nations once at odds in a common global struggle for the free market and deregulated trade as the means for global economic and political progress:

> In this moment of opportunity, a common danger is erasing old rivalries. America is working with Russia and China and India, in ways we have never before, to achieve peace and prosperity. In every region, free markets and free trade and free societies are proving their power to lift lives. Together with friends and allies from Europe to Asia, and Africa to Latin America, we will demonstrate that the forces of terror cannot stop the momentum of freedom.[13]

The battle for 'free markets' and for liberty is with America's enemies who hate the idea that 'in this great country, we can worship the Almighty God the way we see fit. Liberty is God's gift to every human being in the world'.[14] Consequently America is in an apocalyptic struggle between the forces of good – America and those who ally themselves with her – and her enemies, described in a now infamous phrase as an 'axis of evil':

> We've come to know truths that we will never question: evil is real, and it must be opposed. Beyond all differences of race or creed, we are one country, mourning together and facing danger together. Deep in the American character, there is honor, and it is stronger than cynicism. And many have discovered again that even in tragedy – especially in tragedy – God is near.[15]

A year later Bush addressed America and its military as America's Commander-in-Chief from the deck of the Aircraft Carrier *Lincoln* on the day when victory was declared after an invasion that had cost the lives of at least 3,000 Iraqi civilians and many more military personnel, and fewer than 150 US and UK troops:[16] 'Wherever you go, you carry a message of hope – a message that is ancient and ever new. In the words of the prophet Isaiah, 'To the captives, "come out" and to those in darkness "be free"'.[17] During the war, in a speech to troops at MacDill Airbase Florida, the Command Centre for the war, Bush was even more explicit in his account of the sacred role of

America's military: 'The freedom you defend is the right of every person and the future of every nation. The liberty we prize is not America's gift to the world; it is God's gift to humanity'.[18] The meaning is unambiguous: America and American military power are the servants of God's purposes in history not just for America but for the world.

For John Page, the angel that rode in the whirlwind of the American Revolution and directed the storm indicated that the hand of God was on the side of the underdog, the small emergent communities of the new America in their long struggle to overthrow imperial power. But for Bush, God is now on the side not of the weak but of the strong. The storm is not visited on America so much as of America's own making. Whereas for Page God is the author and director of human history, and in particular of America's story, for Bush America is the author of her own story, and God's agent in redeeming human history.

At first sight, the rhetoric of Bush and his speech-writers seems out of tune with the First Amendment which separated Church and State in the American Constitution. But in the minds of those who framed it the First Amendment was not at odds with their belief that the destiny of America was caught up in the larger sacred narrative of the divine plan for humanity revealed in the Bible. Thomas Jefferson viewed the birth of the American Republic as proof of divine providence rather than human power. He even wanted the seal of the new nation to depict the children of Israel being led in the day by the cloud and at night by the pillar of fire. President George Washington in his first inaugural speech spoke of the 'sacred fire of liberty' with which the American people had been entrusted.[19]

The sacred narrative of America's origins is nowhere more clearly revealed than in the hallowing of America's wars – with native Americans, Canadians, Indians, Spanish, Mexicans, with the British, the American Civil War, in the twentieth century with the Nazis, the Communists, and now the Muslims. This hallowing reflects the apocalyptic and millenarian beliefs of the Puritans who first migrated to America and it has become a dominant feature of the modern American evangelical and fundamentalist imaginary. This cast of mind can be traced even further back: Christopher Columbus on 'finding' America after an exceptionally long and arduous ocean voyage wrote 'God made me the messenger of the new heaven and the new earth of which he spoke in the Apocalypse of St. John ... and he showed me the spot where to find it'.[20] The very name 'the New World', which was adopted to describe the American territories, carries this sense that America was the 'new heaven and new earth' of which the Book of Revelation, the last book of the Bible, speaks. Thus even the agnostic Tom Paine, a central figure in the framing of the American constitution, announced that 'we have it in our power to begin the world over again. A situation, similar to present, hath not happened since the days of Noah until now. The birth-day of a new world is at hand'.[21]

Bush uses this same apocalyptic language to advance an imperial vision of American power and in so doing he taps into a core feature of American evangelicalism. Around 40 per cent of Americans describe themselves as evangelical Christians, and opinion polls regularly indicate that a quarter of all Americans believe that they are living in the end times.[22] And even beyond Christian circles, apocalyptic plots – alien invasions, asteroids that threaten to destroy the earth, skyscrapers razed by fire, cities over-run with vast spiders, people scratching out a living in a post-nuclear war world – are the stuff of many American movies and novels.

Why are Americans so drawn to the apocalyptic? There are a number of possible answers to this question. One is that the American Revolution and the terrible Civil War that followed represented a unique combination of apocalyptic violence and religious fervour. Ministers in the Civil War believed that its extreme violence presaged the end of the world, and as the blood of thousands stained the land, soldiers sang the apocalyptic anthem 'mine eyes have seen the glory of the coming of the Lord' who was 'trampling out the vintage where the grapes of wrath are stored' with its implicit sacrificial theme.[23] Another answer may be found in the terrible economic depressions of the 1870s and 1930s, as America embraced the new corporate capitalism that set industry and technology against the health of the land and the welfare of workers and local communities, and whose effects were so powerfully memorialised in Steinbeck's novel *The Grapes of Wrath*. Then there was the fear of nuclear annihilation after the Soviets had successfully followed America in making and testing the atom bomb, an event that planted fear into every American and which saw the emergence of a new genre of apocalyptic movies about alien invasions, body-snatchers and other terrors. For decades afterwards, every neighbourhood in America had its own nuclear fall-out shelter and school children were drilled in what to do in case of attack. The nuclear mushroom cloud is often compared by millennialists with the battle of Armageddon, spoken of in the Book of Revelation, in which the fire and heat is so intense as to melt the crust of the earth. American Apocalyptic lives off fear: fear of the outsider, fear of the slave who became a citizen, fear of communists, fear of corporations and the military, fear of aliens, fear of criminals, fear of the federal government. As Michael Moore showed in his Oscar-winning documentary movie *Bowling for Columbine*, American cable news and TV shows provide viewers with a daily fix of fear with their constant footage of criminal acts, police shoot-outs, police car chases, the war on drugs, the war in Israel, and now the 'war on terror'.

Ironically and tragically for America, apocalyptic violence of a sort was visited on the American mainland on September 11, 2001. Its agents were also apocalyptic believers. Like American millennialists, Osama bin Laden and his followers believe that history will end in violence and that only through violent wars will the new history that is foreordained come about, which is to say when the Grand Caliphate will emerge as the united global government of all the Muslims on the earth. Bin Laden and his followers want to shape a new history, to set the world on a new path, and they are willing to sacrifice their own lives for this cause by generating acts of terrifying violence. Nothing could be more terrifying for most Americans than to see their financial and military headquarters literally melting down before their eyes in the face of this Arab onslaught. It was as if all those apocalyptic movies from the 1990s, which had painted the Muslim as the new enemy after the demise of communism, had come true.[24]

Bush seemed to anticipate the crisis which was to come when he suggested in his Inaugural Address that America stood at a crossroads of history. He said that he had been privileged to have been chosen by God to direct America's military forces to be the divinely ordained instrument that would bring liberty and democracy to the nations of the world, and to struggle against America's enemies – especially those who possessed 'weapons of mass destruction' – in advancing these values and practices.[25] After the 'day of terror' Bush announced a 'crusade' against the wicked men who had organised the attacks, and a military campaign – Operation Infinite Justice – to seek them out and destroy them, albeit resiling from such overtly religious language after it was pointed out it offended Muslims. Like so many other apocalyptics, including Osama bin Laden, Bush believes that he and those who fight with him are servants of the good and have history on their side, while those they fight with are clearly evil and 'will be defeated' – a refrain he often repeats.

Bush's 'neoconservative' supporters espouse other elements of the millennialist credo, and in particular the centrality of Israel to 'end time' history. While the attack on Afghanistan was portrayed by many as an act of self-defence given that Al-Qaeda had its headquarters there, the attack on Iraq was clearly not, and was driven by an entirely different purpose, which clearly included the desire to reconfigure the Middle East to make it safe for what America regards as the only functioning democracy in the region, the nation of Israel. And just one year after the American 'victory' in Iraq, Bush stood with Ariel Sharon in the White House's Rose Garden in April 2004 and declared his approval of Sharon's plan to consolidate Israel's illegal occupation and settlement of more than 40 per cent of the West Bank of Palestine. The Bush administration has also adopted many other core elements of the conservative Christian right's economic and political agenda. It has rolled back Federal government spending on education and welfare and transferred billions of dollars to faith-based social service initiatives; it has massively enhanced the military budget while cutting corporation and income tax for the wealthy; it has emasculated environmental, financial, labour and market regulatory bodies and rewritten federal laws protecting wild land, coastlines and fragile ecosystems from oil-drilling and commercial logging. The administration has also reneged on American commitments to international environmental and justice treaties, refusing to recognise the authority of the World Court or to ratify the UN Convention on the Rights of the Child, rejecting the Kyoto Protocol on Climate Change, and repudiating the authority of the UN and of the Geneva Conventions on the conduct of war.

The Bush administration's policies combine a commitment to untrammelled capitalism, and hence a corporately restrained democracy, with a willingness to spend inordinate amounts of money on American corporations producing military technology. At the same time these policies are represented as America's sacred mission to lead the world to its destined future of democracy and freedom. While Bush is clearly driven by a faith in unbridled capitalism that verges on religious fervour, these policies are not just the product of modern ideology.[26] There is a deep millennial spirit here, which goes right back to the emergent belief of Americans that they were a 'redeemer nation' destined to lead the world to the end of history.

It is the burden of this book to show that this millennial spirit rests upon a tragic deformation of true Christianity. The faith of the first Christians was that the apocalypse had already taken place in the events of the life, death and resurrection of Jesus Christ. For the first Christians the apocalypse was manifest in the enthronement of Christ on the right-hand of God at the ascension, and in the alternative ethics and politics displayed in the communities that worshipped him, and which represented, as Christ himself did, such a threat to Roman imperial power. The first Christian communities were places of counter-cultural egalitarianism, economic sharing and practical care for the orphan, the poor, the sick and the widow. Christianity was however corrupted by its own success. With the conversion of the Emperor Constantine in the fourth century of the Christian era Christianity was turned from its non-violent and anti-imperial origins into an imperial cult.

Like so many of the emperors and monarchs of what came to be known as Christendom, Bush and his speech-writers use a distortion of Christian apocalyptic, combined with American civil religion, to legitimate and sacralise imperial violence. They use the language of apocalypse not to proclaim with St John the Divine that they see the devil falling from the sky after being defeated by the angels, but rather to say that America's enemies will see America's weapons falling from their skies. Bush may speak in the tradition of the American dream, he may speak for the religion of the American flag in his confidence that violent power can achieve relatively good ends, but he cannot be said faithfully to represent the politics of Jesus.

My argument in what follows is not that politics and religion are best kept apart. On the contrary, my intention is to aid the recovery of a spiritual reading of geopolitics in our time. Political economists who describe modern government in terms of rational constitutions, social contracts, and the 'laws' of supply and demand disable a proper understanding of the apocalyptic spirit that drives the politics of American empire, the civil religion that sacralises it, and the idolatrous rituals of consumerism which it sustains. I will demonstrate that the current Bush administration is not some wild aberration from the normal course of American history, or even from the rhetoric of other recent Presidents, but instead has deep roots in the false religion of American millennial apocalyptic. And I will argue that orthodox Christianity, including some of the radical forms it has taken in North America, represents a genuine ethical and spiritual alternative to the apocalyptic violence of extreme corporate capitalism and militarist imperialism, and provides important resources for challenging and resisting them in the public square.

The urgency of Christian resistance to American empire is heightened by the knowledge that both George W. Bush and Tony Blair claim to have prosecuted their illegal war in Iraq, and the larger war on terror, as a consequence, at least in part, of their Christian desire to 'do the right thing' – even when it is not the democratic or the popular thing. That Christian ethics can be put to such use is perhaps the greatest indictment of Christianity for many secular humanists in the first decade of the third millennium. It is no part of our endeavour to deny that Christianity since Constantine has sacralised many other imperial wars. But precisely when Christians have lived up to their calling to form communities of justice and of peace that are radically at odds with empire they have also provided the impulses which prepared America, and other societies, for the practices of democracy, economic justice, public education and health care, and the discourses of civil and human rights, economic justice, gender equality, wealth redistribution and ecological conservation. This book is written in the belief that were more Christians in America, Britain and beyond to recover the radical Christianity of the founder, then the abuse of religion by political leaders and by terrorists to sacralise their wars, and their apocalyptic divisions of humanity into the wicked and the righteous, would be undermined.

1 – American Apocalypse

The Puritans who fled persecution in England to settle the 'wilderness' of America believed that they were enacting the final era of human history, and they justified this belief by extensive references to scripture.[1] America was the new Canaan, and on this land would emerge the fabled millennium of peace foretold in the Book of Revelation. Cotton Mather, the Puritan divine and Harvard luminary, wrote a Virgilian-style epic poem of New England which he entitled *Magnalia Christi Americana* (Miracles of Christ in America), in which he described the story of America as the gradual ascent of the colony from the settling of virgin territory to the establishment of a righteous Kingdom of Christian communities which would end in a final conflict with the Antichrist. The millennial conclusion of this sacred history would 'outshine the Augustan *Pax Romana*'.[2] Mather likened the journey from Europe to the flight of Israel from slavery in Egypt, the journey across the Atlantic to the Israelites' years in the wilderness, while the progressive settling of the New World represented the overturning of Satan's rule on a fallen earth in which a wilderness becomes the new Promised Land, the 'Garden of God'. In Mather's account history, geography, time itself are remade and hallowed as New Englanders march westwards through the New World.

The New England divine Jonathan Edwards was also a millennialist. His inspirational preaching helped to provoke the New England revivals of the 1730s and 1740s, in which colonists turned back to the church in droves. Edwards, like Mather, believed that the colonists were living in the end times, and he saw the revivals as evidence of the end time:

> Tis not unlikely that this work of God's Spirit, that is so extra-ordinary and wonderful, is the dawning, or at least a prelude, of that glorious work of God, so often foretold in Scripture … And there are many things that make it probable that this work will begin in America.[3]

Edwards dated the Millennium around the year 2000 and believed that before it came America would have to do battle with Satan's Kingdoms, the Papacy and the Turkish Ottoman Empire. The new era would also be ushered in by the preaching of the Gospel in every nation on earth and by the conversion of the Jews.

These early American settlers and divines were *post*millennialists, which is to say that they believed that in building a godly common-wealth in the New World they were ushering in the millennial rule of the saints on earth *after* which they believed Christ would return as judge of the earth. The term postmillennialism is used to distin-guish this older variety of millennial belief from *pre*millenialism which now predominates in American apocalyptic religion, and which I examine in the next chapter. Premillennialists believe that the last judgement will happen *before* the millennial rule of the saints. Both varieties of New World millennialism involve the claim that Americans are in some exceptional sense in charge of human history, that their story represents the fulfilment of Biblical passages about the end of history, the last judgement and the final revelation – the word apocalypse means revelation or unveiling – of the millennial rule of the saints in which human history is finally redeemed. Americans in this millennial reading of history came to see America as the 'redeemer nation', the first nation fully to realise the true salvific intent of human history.[4]

For Jonathan Edwards this meant that the nation as a whole was the true church, 'a type of New Jerusalem' in which the spiritual community was carrying forward the work of redemption. As the American historian Sacvan Bercovitch suggests, this adaptation of Puritanism to a larger vision of American theocracy helped pave the way for the Revolution itself, in which Americans finally asserted their identity as the true 'chosen people' against the English usurpers of this Biblical calling. It also laid the foundation for American enlightenment progressivism in which the earthly paradise of America could be secularised into a modernist utopia, a this-worldly Kingdom of God.[5]

If America was the true home of the saints of God, then in its military and commercial struggles with the old empires of Europe, and its conquest of native barbarians, it was realising a divine destiny 'to give law to the rest of the world'.[6] The events of America's origins – the harrowing years of the first pilgrims, the gradual settling and taming of the 'wilderness', the wars with France, Britain and Spain, the Native American wars – were events of the new millennium such that America's history became quite literally the apocalyptic history of the New Jerusalem.[7] Dark clouds, battles, internal divisions, set-backs, were all inevitable in this great progression towards the final appearance of Christ's kingdom. It was such times of testing, such battles with the enemies of God's people, that indicated the nearness of 'heaven on earth'. From such struggles America would emerge as the kingdom of God on earth, and would become the 'city set on a hill', a sacred nation to which all nations and peoples would be drawn. The empire of France, and the Indians who fought with the French against the Yankee, would fall in a final great struggle between the Lamb and the Beast that would prefigure the battle of Armageddon. This spiritualised rhetoric of war first appeared in the context of the American Revolution so that the struggle for nationhood became in the words of John Quincy Adams 'the fulfilment of the prophecies, announced directly from Heaven at the birth of the Savior and predicted by the greatest Hebrew prophets six hundred years before'.[8]

This millennial cast of mind is deeply influential in the formation of the American conception of liberty, and of American liberalism, which is very different to what Europeans call liberalism, and much more like what is now called economic neoliberalism.[9] American liberalism traditionally named the belief that individuals should be free to determine their own destinies, free from an interfering state and free from the monarchs, aristocrats, traditions and customs that ordered life in Europe. It is archetypally encapsulated in the core values of the American Declaration of Independence – liberty, egalitarianism, individualism, populism, and laissez-faire.[10] American liberalism involves a progressive and future-oriented cast of mind that depicts the American story as that of a liberated people who planted their new society on a 'virgin' land. It is this historicist and progressive liberalism which is the source of the pragmatic confidence with which Americans seek to shape their destiny and face their perceived enemies. They came to see America as the first true exception in the quest of humanity for the good society, the first truly free and democratic nation, the first non-feudal, non-aristocratic, anti-monarchistic society, in which the rights and liberties of individuals took precedence over servitude to any ideology or hierarchy, prelate or priest.

The postmillennial cast of mind gave to American culture a confidence in the possibility of change and a dynamism which is often absent in Europe and which to an outsider is one of the most attractive features of America. It also fostered the belief that America would not only become a nation of liberty, but that she would use her growing wealth and prestige in the world to advance the Christian cause across the globe. The influence of Christian faith and values would produce a period of spiritual and material prosperity and of progress towards a peaceful world. This postmillennial optimism in the possibility of human progress provided American liberalism with the confidence that its core values of freedom, individualism and entrepreneurialism would over time result in a better world for all. The Kingdom of God in postmillennial perspective truly would be built in America, and even beyond America, through the cultural and economic dynamism of Americans, their corporations, their military and their values.

Puritan Individualism and the Birth of Democracy

Alongside millennialism, the other key Puritan contribution to the American liberalism that has shaped the destiny of America is Protestant individualism. Belief in the imminence of the coming judgement of the world involves the idea that each individual will stand before God to answer for her own life, and that there will be a division of humanity into the saved and the damned. This belief fosters a narrative of the uniqueness of each individual's personal destiny and is linked with the Protestant and particularly Lutheran idea of the 'priesthood of all believers'. In Puritan tradition this conception of the church's polity produced an understanding of the unique identity and worth of every individual as members of the elect of God.

The Puritan account of the equal standing of each individual as called by God produced the unique emphasis on the congregation as the basic unit of the church's social life in Puritan society, and more especially in the New World, where Puritan religion was freed from European political and religious arrangements. David Lindsay argues that this congregational and egalitarian culture provided the seedbed of American democratic practice, and that the fellowship and governance of Christian society through the congregation as a public open meeting was the form in which American democracy first appeared.[11] As Jeffrey Stout points out a key element in this culture of the open meeting was the radical Protestant belief in prophetic utterance. Everyone has a right to speak, for what they say may be inspired by God: only when it is uttered can the community decide whether it is or not.[12] Thus Quakers believe that because there is 'that of God' in everyone, everyone has a right to be heard in public worship provided what they have to say is orderly and peaceable. The Quaker meeting is therefore a key precursor of American democratic practice including freedom of speech.

It is impossible to underestimate the significance of the local religious roots of democratic culture in America and the contrast with the more centralised and humanist forms of democratic governance that emerged in much of Europe. It is a major factor in the explanation of the deeply democratic nature of America, which, despite the rise of new kinds of corporatism in the twentieth century, and especially multinational business corporations and the military industrial complex, remains much in evidence. While popular participation in Congressional and Presidential elections has declined such that Bush in 2000 received the votes of only one-quarter of the potential electorate, nonetheless levels of participation in political campaigning, and the sheer number of elections remain much higher in the United States than in Europe. Similarly, public debate in America remains remarkably vibrant despite corporate control of the mainstream media. National Public Radio and the plethora of radical magazines and websites provide a far richer range of dissenting voices in America than may be encountered in Britain. It must be admitted though that since September 11, 2001 attempts to suppress dissent and freedom of speech have been imposed by the Washington establishment, which indicate the anti-democratic tendencies set in motion by the Patriot Act, the 'war on terror' and the project of 'homeland security'.

The association of the American democratic ideal with the local congregation indicates the deep connections between the voluntarist character of American religion and the voluntarism of American society. The American story is of pilgrims and citizens actively choosing to shape their own destiny, and choosing their religion. The Constitution firmly states that 'no religious test will ever be required' of American citizens (Art. 6. k Sec. 3.). This is why it is unlawful for state schools to hold formal prayers or religious instruction. Voluntariness, personal choice, is at the heart of what it is to be American, and what it is to be religious in America. This principle is what is defended in the First Amendment when it states that 'Congress shall make no law respecting an establishment of religion'. Freedom *of* religion, not *from* religion, is what it seems to safeguard.[13]

Rodney Stark suggests that the anti-centrist and voluntarist character of America has produced one of the few advanced industrial societies in which religion, far from declining, has continued to flourish: religion in America thrives because it is diverse and competitive.[14] Whereas in Europe the association between Church and State produced monopolistic state churches where clergy were virtual civil servants, in America the clear separation between Church and State allowed for a vast range of denominations and sects to thrive, whose multiplicity is the strength of religious association in America. This great array of different kinds of Christianity, and more recently religions of all hues, produces a thriving religious 'market' in which religious aspirants can find their myriad desires and needs met. Consequently the majority of American Christians belong not to historic world Christian communions such as the Roman Catholic or Lutheran churches but to small sectarian groups, from Appalachian snake-handlers to Minnesotan Mennonites.

This plethora of choice in the religious market-place means that American religious organisations are more sensitive to cultural change than their more monopolistic European counterparts and they cannot afford the luxury of hanging on to traditions that their 'customers' find outmoded or peculiar. Cultural and organisational flexibility are of course two of the key determinants of the thriving business enterprise and it is this capacity of American religious organisations to be responsive to the needs of religious 'consumers' that has made of American religion a uniquely successful Western phenomenon. But this success is not without ambiguity. It is the very adaptability of American religion to the market-place of American consumer capitalism, and to the individualistic values and behaviours this market-place fosters, that has enabled the emergence of the misalliance of conservative Christianity with the neo-imperial political ideology that now dominates the political economy – and foreign policy – of the United States. It also explains the alliance of market fundamentalism with religious fundamentalism on the religious and Republican right, which has found its most potent advocates in Presidents Ronald Reagan and George W. Bush.

American cultural Christianity lacks adequate resources for the critique of American capitalism, consumerism and imperialism precisely because of its voluntarist character. As Stanley Hauerwas suggests, despite the claim that the separation of Church and State guarantees freedom of religion, in reality the churches, and religion in general, have become captive to the American way of life. Americans have effectively refounded Christendom in the New World.[15] Consequently the religion of the New World is not so much the anti-imperial Christianity of the founder, Jesus Christ, as it is the civil religion of America. Its core values are more American than New Testament, and include the curious combination of individual liberty and patriotism that requires individuals regularly to commit themselves and their children, and the lion's share of the nation's public budget and hence their tax payments, to war and preparations for war. This is why it was not hard for Bush to enlist the majority of American Christians in his neo-imperial crusade.

Manifest Destiny and American Expansionism

American historians have conventionally argued that America is not an imperial nation, and that the engagements of the United States in foreign wars have been exceptions to the general preference for Americans for peace within their borders and distance from the conflicts of the rest of the world. The United States is in this narrative described as a 'reluctant superpower', as only engaging in military activity abroad when called upon so to do, or when American interests are seen to be significantly at risk.[16] However, the long history of American interventions on foreign soil indicates that this idea of an isolationist and anti-imperial America is a chimera. Former American Army General Andrew Bacevich in his *American Empire* debunks the myth of an isolationist America and suggests that the American Republic has always been imperial in its ambitions and aims.[17] Michael Ignatieff suggests that the time has now come for Americans to own the 'burden' of empire and the implicit responsibilities to civilise and police the world that such a burden implies. For Ignatieff, American history is nothing if not a history of an empire in the making:

> From the very beginning, the American republic has never shrunk from foreign wars. A recent Congressional study shows that there has scarcely been a year since its founding that American soldiers haven't been overseas 'from the halls of Montezuma to the shores of Tripoli,' chasing pirates, punishing bandits, pulling American citizens out of harm's way, intervening in civil wars, stopping massacres, overturning regimes deemed (fairly or not) unfriendly and exporting democracy. American foreign policy largely consists of doctrines about when and where to intervene in other people's countries.[18]

The seeds of American Empire were already contained in the post-millennial vision of America as the Promised Land, and its people as the new chosen race. Americans in the 1840s coined the term 'manifest destiny' to describe their sense of a divine purpose being worked out in American history, and in the extension of the Promised Land from the East and mid-West to the Spanish-ruled

territories of California, Northern Mexico and Texas. In the utopi-
anism of the mid-nineteenth century, America was a sacred space
in which the people were being guided by providence to become a
'new nation of liberty' that would exhibit for the first time in human
history 'a new world order, a great "experiment" for the benefit
of humankind as a whole'.[19] This vision recalled the first settler
traditions, which saw America as 'asylum of the oppressed' and as
the 'guardian of liberty', core elements in the American imaginary
from John Adams to Woodrow Wilson.[20] Imperial expansion was
lent sacred legitimacy by the idea that 'God's American Israel' was
destined to rise in honour among the nations of the earth; these
imperial adventures were then simply the fulfilment of the divine
plan.[21]

The vision of America as the new Israel implied a redemptive
purpose in God's hand on American history not just to confer liberty
on Americans but literally to redeem the world from tyranny and to
reconcile humanity with God. And this destiny then justified the
expansion of American supremacy. As Boston Unitarian preacher
William Ellery Channing put it in 1837:

> The more civilized must always exert a great power over the
> less civilized communities in their neighborhood. But it may
> and should be a power to enlighten and improve ... We are
> *destined* (that is the word) to overspread North America; and
> intoxicated with the idea, it matters little to us how we
> accomplish our fate.[22]

Drunk with destiny, America need not scruple at the violence it
deploys to subdue and civilise the neighbourhood.

Democracy in America also required territorial expansion if the
continuing stream of European migrants were to continue to find
smallholdings on which to make a living. The large quantity of land
at the disposal of the colonists enabled farm-workers, smallholders
and new immigrants to move Southwards and Westwards in search
of their own piece of the American dream. The Westward migration
was memorialised into a sacred journey in the Great Trek of Mormon
mythology. Mormonism was the archetypal American religion
because it narrated the migrant conquest of the 'heathen' land of

America in sacred and apocalyptic terms as the means by which God intended to refound a righteous and prosperous nation of saints in the latter days. When land in the West finally ran out American constitutionality was faced with the same dilemma that European empires also faced. The unique conceptualisation of the American constitution around the 'empty' space of the frontiers of the New World – setting aside as it did the fact that these spaces were already inhabited by native peoples – sustained what became in the later nineteenth century an extra-territorial drive towards an American empire.[23]

As America began to ape European empires in its mercantilist and territorial expansion it also found itself in conflict with them in the emergent global economy of the mid-nineteenth century. Rising global production led to falling prices, which brought on a global economic depression from the 1870s. A core feature of the American response was the emergence of the joint stockholding corporation, which from its inception represented a direct attack on the principles of local democracy and voluntariness. As corporations rose in power and acquired the legal capacity to act independently, and increasingly against the interests of the democratic communities which at first owned and regulated them, they became involved in attempts to control markets and fix prices both between and beyond America's shores.[24] Some corporations even founded company towns in which residents not only worked for the company, but were forced to spend all their wages in company-owned businesses and live in company housing.

The rise of the American corporation was a major factor in fuelling an imperial and mercantilist quest for resources from overseas to compensate for the democratic failure to restrain the excesses of the emergent corporate economy in the factories and slums of the new industrial cities. There followed the development of a navy to match the imperial navies of the European imperial powers and in 1898 the United States began its extra-territorial drive by annexing Hawaii, a domain already dominated by American-owned sugar plantations. In the Spanish–American war that followed the United States subsequently seized the territories of Cuba, Puerto Rico, Guam, Wake Island, and Manila in the Philippines.[25] The war ended with the American annexation of the Philippines in 1902.

American divines saw these events as a clear extension of the civilising destiny God had already prepared for America:

> God did not make the American people the mightiest human force of all time simply to feed and die. He did not give our race the brain of organization and heart of domination to no purpose and no end. No! He has given us a task equal to our talents ... He has made us the lords of civilization that we may administer civilization.[26]

Confident belief in the political and spiritual superiority of American civilisation was combined with a mercantilist desire for imperial expansion to sustain America's rapid economic and technological advances. Hence the United States began its now common imperial intervention in foreign nations beyond the Pacific region when, in 1903, it sent marines to Beijing to quell the Boxer Rebellion, which threatened US trade and economic interests in China, and when it dispatched 12,000 troops to Russia to help the anti-Bolsheviks in the Russian Civil War in 1918.[27] Aside from the territories grabbed in the context of the Spanish American War, America did not though proceed to grow an empire by further territorial expansion. Instead it used the projection of American military and economic power over other nations to establish American hegemonic dominance over territories beyond its borders. It was not that America lacked imperial ambition. On the contrary, as Ignatieff argues,

> It is the only nation that polices the world through five global military commands; maintains more than a million men and women at arms on four continents; deploys carrier battle groups on watch in every ocean; guarantees the survival of countries from Israel to South Korea; drives the wheels of global trade and commerce; and fills the hearts and minds of an entire planet with its dreams and desires.[28]

The United States *is* an empire, but its governing class found a new and more economical way to achieve their imperial ambitions than the European empires. Its leaders formed a post-territorial empire, an 'empire-lite',[29] using a worldwide network of lightly manned military bases and a sophisticated set of managerial and political processes through which local clients of the United States govern their countries in such a way as to favour US corporate and strategic interests. These local clients who rule Mexico or Guatemala, Venezuela or Columbia are often descended from the original conquistadors and have been in many cases systematically corrupted by their colonial ties. Spanish and American imperialists are no different here; they have traditionally preferred local leaders who are biddable, who will accept bribes and act corruptly against the interests of their own people and in the interests of the colonisers.

The Monroe Doctrine was the name given to US foreign policy in the Americas, after President James Monroe, who first enunciated it in 1822. The doctrine expressed the claim of right of the United States to dominance without interference from the old world of Europe in the New World of the Western hemisphere – the Americas and the Pacific.[30] It was in pursuance of this doctrine that the United States in the nineteenth century annexed first Mexico and Texas, then Puerto Rico and Cuba, and later Panama, and fought wars in Nicaragua, giving to the American Republic an imperial domain analogous to those of Britain or Holland, Spain or Portugal. But the Munroe Doctrine involved the claim that American empire was more 'righteous' than the monarchistic European empires with which it competed. Its advocates claimed that American expansion involved the spread of liberty, which the federal Constitution of the Union had enshrined in the doctrine of the separation of powers. The extension of the federal principle was supposed to ensure the first truly righteous empire in human history. Behind pan-Americanism lay the universal ideals of liberty and restrained government, the means by which America would redeem the Americas and even human history.

From Redeemer Nation to Cold War Empire

The idea of America as the 'redeemer nation' imposing peace and liberty on a recalcitrant world is most associated with the Presidency of Woodrow Wilson. When Wilson took America into the First World War in 1917 he declared the war a millennial battle for democracy:

The world must be made safe for democracy. Its peace must
be planted upon the tested foundations of political liberty.
We have no selfish ends to serve. We desire no conquest, no
domination. We seek no indemnities for ourselves, no material
compensation for the sacrifices we freely make. We are but one
of the champions of the rights of mankind.[31]

Clergy and hymn writers took up Wilson's enthusiasm in a renewed
sacralisation of American foreign policy. The United States Army
was 'the American Church in France' according to one Episcopal
minister, while a hymn writer pronounced the American republic
engaged in a 'fight for worldwide freedom' in which 'God is marching on'.[32]

After the war Wilson used apocalyptic language to describe
America's leadership of the League of Nations, which he declared
'had come about by no plan of our conceiving, but by the hand of
God who led us into this way'.[33] After the 'Armageddon' of the Great
War, America was, according to Wilson, a 'great nation, marching at
the fore of a great procession' whose goal was 'those heights upon
which there rests nothing but the pure light of the justice of God'. On
America God had conferred

... a liberating power, a power to show the world that when
America was born it was indeed a finger pointed toward those
lands into which men could deploy some of these days and live
in happy freedom, look each other in the eyes as equals, see that
no man was put upon, that no people were forced to accept
authority which was not of their own choice, and that out of
the general generous impulse of the human genius and the
human spirit we were lifted along the levels of civilization to
days when there should be wars no more, but men should
govern themselves in peace and amity and quiet.[34]

The end in view was the end of all wars and ultimately 'the liberation and salvation of the world'.

During the years of the Great Depression, America entered a
period of relative international isolation, although it continued its
occupation of those territories in the Pacific, Caribbean, Central and

Latin America that it had earlier annexed. It was an attack on one such territory, Pearl Harbor in Hawaii, that would draw America back into world events in the form of the Second World War. By the end of the struggle with the Japanese and with Nazism, America had organised its military forces on a global scale which provided a new template for American foreign policy in the post-war era. America's leaders adopted the mantle of 'leader of the free world' in a new global war, this time against the Soviets, who were said to be pursuing a plan for world conquest which only America had the will and the resources to contain.[35]

The epochal event that galvanised the American people behind the Cold War was the first Soviet test of a nuclear weapon in 1949. This event set off an era of paranoia in America that Mike Davis suggests provides the most significant precedent for American reactions to September 11, 2001:

> Truman's National Security Council reacted quickly with 'NSC-68', a blank cheque to create what President Eisenhower would later describe as the 'military industrial complex'. Simultaneously Senator Joseph McCarthy and FBI Director J. Edgar Hoover used the public's fears to initiate a merciless pursuit of an 'enemy within'.[36]

For Truman there were only two sides in the Cold War, just as George W. Bush announced there were only two sides in the 'war on terror': those who were with the United States, and those who were against it. Anathematisation of the enemy provides the excuse for an emergency that requires suppression of dissent at home and covert wars to contain the evil abroad, all in the name of the survival of the American people. But this response is ultimately corrosive of democracy and of liberty, the very practices and values whose survival is said to be threatened by the enemy.[37]

The Central Intelligence Agency and the Washington elites saw every threat to American economic and political interests as evidence of communist infiltration. The paranoia that fuelled the notorious public arraignments of individuals accused by Senator McCarthy of 'un-American activities' paralleled the insidious effects of the anti-communist drive on American foreign policy. In these ways the

United States began to mirror the very expansionist imperialism, and the associated suppression of the liberties of other nations and of some of its own dissenting citizens, that it accused the Soviets of perpetrating. The Cold War saw a dramatic expansion in American military interventions and American economic and political power across Central and Latin America, the Middle East, Southeast Asia and parts of Africa. And so American foreign policy was also turned into an instrument of totalitarian subjugation which the Soviets had themselves adopted. But so long as the American elites could convince themselves, in the spirit of Wilsonian postmillennialism, that theirs was a righteous empire, that their cause was just, then all the killing and brutality, the replacement of legitimate and often democratic government with 'friendly' dictators could seem justified, as means to a greater good.

The people of Guatemala were the first victims of this new interventionist and expansionist foreign policy. In 1944 they had elected a government that for ten years pursued a social democratic programme that saw the provision of universal schooling and health clinics, and widespread land reform.[38] But in 1954 landowners and foreign companies – and especially the American United Fruit Company – protested that their interests were threatened and the Central Intelligence Agency organised a bloody civil war. The military junta installed by the CIA killed more than one million people in the following 30 years. Guatemalans went from being among the best educated and most democratic of Central Americans to being among the poorest and most repressed not just in the region, but the world.[39]

After Guatemala, Chile, Brazil, Uraguay, Paraguay and Argentina all saw elected governments overthrown by rightist militias supported by the United States. The Chilean President, Salvador Allende, had been elected in 1970 but his socialist politics were seen as inimical to US business and strategic interests. Henry Kissinger adopted a range of strategies to 'limit his ability to implement policies contrary to US interests', commencing with a failed coup in 1970.[40] On 11 September 1973 US intelligence and military forces, together with extremist elements in Chile organised what a naval attaché described as 'our D-Day' and a 'perfect coup', in which Allende was assassinated and replaced by General Pinochet.[41] There followed the most violent period in the history of modern Chile in which thousands were slaughtered by Pinochet, while tens of thousands more were imprisoned, tortured, forced into exile or else 'disappeared', actions strongly supported by Kissinger and the Nixon administration.[42]

US Cold War intervention was not of course limited to the Americas. US influence in the Middle East had been minimal until the end of the Second World War, when it began to take up the imperial role of Britain, whose capacity to run an empire after a war that left the country in deep penury was at an end in 1945. US interests in the Middle East were in part explicable under the Cold War doctrine. But there are two vital factors driving US policy in this region that have nothing to do with Communism or the Soviet Union, or at least not ostensibly: one is the US commitment to a Jewish homeland, which has deep roots in US Christian millennialist readings of the end of history; the other relates to the United States' gargantuan appetite for oil. It was this second factor that drew the United States into organising a coup that overthrew a democratically elected government in Iran in 1953, and which has involved the installation or support of other dictators and totalitariain regimes in the Middle East, including most notoriously the extreme Islamist regime of Saudi Arabia.

The occasion for the American action in Iran was that the democratically elected government of Prime Minister Mohammad Mussadiq was seen as a threat to British and American interests because it challenged the right of the Anglo-Iranian Oil Company – later renamed British Petroleum – to extract oil from Iran while only paying ten per cent of the proceeds to the government of Iran.[43] When Musaddiq nationalised Iran's oil fields and refineries, the British under Winston Churchill decided to attempt to replace him with the then exiled Shah of Iran. Fearing that the British were organising a coup – which they were – the Iranians closed their Tehran embassy and so the British turned to the CIA to do the business, which they duly did in June 1953.[44] In an agreement with the newly installed dictatorship a year later, the British and Americans reasserted foreign control of Iran's oil production, agreeing to split an 80 per cent stake, leaving 20 per cent for the Iranians.

The Shah's repressive rule deployed torture on a vast scale, and capital punishment was so frequent that the Shah was the biggest judicial killer in the world in the 1970s. The secret police (SAVAK) responsible for many of these crimes were funded and trained by Americans, with the help of the Israeli secret service, Mossad. The training included torture techniques. By the late 1970s the country was in a state of civil war and the Shah went into exile just a few days before the triumphant return of Ayatollah Khomeini from exile.[45] Thus began the first Shiite theocracy in modern times and an inspiration to Islamists across the world who sought the overthrow of Western-influenced Muslim rulers. The invasion of the American Embassy in Tehran, and the kidnapping of its occupants for more than a year, saw relations between the United States and the new Iran take a dramatic down-turn from which they have never recovered.

In retaliation for the anti-American stance of Revolutionary Iran, the United States lent money and weaponry – including chemical weapons such as anthrax and chemical warfare production facilities – on a vast scale to the dictatorial Saddam Hussein in support of an invasion of Iran, which launched the Iran–Iraq war of the mid-1980s.[46] Hussein was supported, like the Shah before him, because he was seen as 'America's man', a pro-Western dictator who would ensure a continuing flow of oil to America. He was ideologically both anti-communist and anti-Islamist and so suited American designs for the Middle East very well. Hussein was also a Sunni and prepared to use all means to suppress the Shiite majority in Iraq, and at the same time to subdue the Kurds in the North who were seen as a threat to Turkey, another key US ally in the region. It was because of the extent of US support for Hussein's atrocities in the region – including his mass-gassing of Iraqi Kurds at Halabja in 1988, an atrocity the US State Department agreed to blame on the Iranians[47] – that Hussein felt confident in his attempt to annex the oil fields of Kuwait which had been sequestered for the use of British Petroleum when the British conferred independence on Iraq in the 1920s. The subsequent war with Iraq launched by President George Bush Senior from newly established military bases in Saudi Arabia was pivotal in the emergence of Al-Qaeda, and more especially in the turning of Osama bin Laden into an anti-American Saudi dissident.

From Cold War to Holy War

More than a decade before Iraq's invasion of Kuwait, in 1979, the CIA under the administration of President Jimmy Carter sought to inveigle Russia into an unwinnable and draining war in Afghanistan. The strategy was to fund and arm Islamic extremists from Pakistan, Saudi Arabia and elsewhere to fight for a radical Islamic government in lawless Afghanistan. According to Carter's National Security Advisor Zbignew Brezinski the intention, which was highly successful, was to provoke a Soviet invasion that would issue in a war so costly in Russian lives and military expenditure as to threaten the very existence of the Soviet Union.[48]

The CIA viewed resurgent Islamists in Central Asia as key allies in the Cold War both with the Soviet Union and with Communist China. They poured billions of dollars in aid and military equipment into the mujahideen resistance funnelled through the Pakistan Inter Services Intelligence.[49] The result was that militant Islamists from over 20 Muslim countries were drawn into Islamist training camps on the Pakistan–Afghanistan border. As Ahmed Rashid observes:

> With the active encouragement of the CIA and Pakistan's ISI [Inter Services Intelligence], who wanted to turn the Afghan jihad into a global war waged by all Muslim states against the Soviet Union, some 35,000 Muslim radicals from 40 Islamic countries joined Afghanistan's fight between 1982 and 1992. Tens of thousands more came to study in Pakistani madrasahs. Eventually more than 100,000 foreign Muslim radicals were directly influenced by the Afghan jihad.[50]

These radical Islamists included Osama bin Laden and others like him, reflecting the joint sponsorship of this Islamist war by Saudi Arabia as well as Pakistan and the United States. In Saudi-funded *madrassas* in Pakistan and Afghanistan, the mujahideen acquired a picture of an idealised Muslim society, supposedly based on the Prophet Mohammed's Medina more than 1,400 years previously, which, as the Taliban, they would later attempt to reconstruct in Afghanistan. And in CIA-funded camps in Afghanistan the mujahideen acquired training in guerrilla warfare and terror techniques which not only aided them in ousting the Soviets but which after the war were put to use in a devastating civil war in Afghanistan, and later in terrorist attacks on America.

For the United States the war against the Soviets was a righteous crusade against communism. For Islamists the war against the Soviet invaders was a jihad, and ironically the CIA favoured the jihadis for the passionate dedication and suicidal courage which made them likely winners in the war. As John Esposito puts it, 'for America this was a "good jihad"', in which the US government 'was able to cheer and support Afghanistan's holy warriors, providing considerable funding as well as CIA advisers'.[51]

It is a strange irony that the establishment of this Saudi-influenced medieval ideal of an Islamic society in post-Soviet Afghanistan was undertaken with the support of the United States. Through Pakistan's ISI, the CIA helped build Al-Qaeda's training camps and heavily defended Tora Borra Cave Complex in the mountains between Afghanistan and Pakistan, and funded the communications and weapons technology that they deployed there. These advanced technologies of warfare certainly helped the mujahideen to succeed in ousting the Soviets. They also enhanced the already viciously violent tendencies of Saudi, Yemeni, Egyptian and other jihadis who were drawn into Afghanistan. With the ousting of the Soviets the mujahideen were caught up in a vicious civil war in Afghanistan which ended with the installation of the extremist Islamist regime of the Taliban over a ruined country. But their effectiveness in ousting the Soviets was not matched by their achievements in government. They failed to establish a parliament or any method of administering the country as a whole and they had no plan for the revival of agriculture, although they were successful in suppressing opium production. The Taliban believed that instead of an organised state or civil service 'Islam will take care of every-one'.[52]

Alongside the United States and Pakistan, Saudi Arabia was the other principal sponsor of the mujahideen and the Taliban. The Saudi state was founded in the eighteenth century by Muhammad al-Sa-'ud, the tribal chief who gave his name to the house of Saud, together with an Islamic reformer named Ibn 'Abd al-Wahhab who gave his name to the religious movement of Wahhabism, which has dominated Saudi Arabia ever since.[53] Wahhabi Islam is the most puritanical and militantly apocalyptic of all modern forms of Islam and under its influence Saudi Arabia has become one of the most tyrannical and oppressive states in not only the Middle East but the world. Throughout the Muslim world, Wahhabism has funded thousands of Mosques, Mullahs and Maddrasas that spread vicious extremism and supplant benign and tolerant forms of Islam. And as Rashid observes, 'the Saudi export of Wahabbism has now boomeranged back home and is increasingly undermining the authority of the Royal Family. Osama bin Laden's critique of the corruption and mismanagement of the regime is not falling upon deaf ears amongst the Saudi population'.[54] This internal alienation between royal autocrats and Islamists was a key element in the prehistory of Saudi involvement in the attack on America. The other key element was a growing alienation between bin Laden and his former Saudi and American backers.

After the eviction of the Soviets from Afghanistan, bin Laden returned to a hero's welcome in Saudi Arabia. But he found on his return home an increasingly corrupt ruling elite living in unparalleled splendour, while the majority of Saudi people lived in relative poverty. Unemployment and urban poverty were widespread in Saudi Arabia in the 1990s and bin Laden gathered around him a following of young middle-class Saudis who were radicalised by the growing inequality and social unrest in their country. The event that triggered bin Laden's decision to commence a holy war against the House of Saud and its US backers was Saddam Hussein's invasion of Kuwait. Bin Laden suggested to King Fahd that he would reassemble an army of mujahideen to evict the Iraqis from Kuwait, but the Saudis accepted an American offer and allowed US forces to construct military bases to the South of the Saudi Peninsula from which to prosecute the Gulf War.[55] For bin Laden and his followers, these military bases represented an alien occupation of the Muslim holy land, which was deeply humiliating and a blasphemy against the Prophet Muhammad.[56] He left Saudi Arabia, first for the Sudan, and then back to Afghanistan where in 1996 he took up with the Taliban high command and made a formal 'Declaration of Jihad' against America. His aims were to remove US troops from the Holy Land of the Prophet, and to bring down the corrupt House of Saud and other corrupt US-supported Middle Eastern governments.[57] In 2002 in his 'Letter to the American People' bin Laden moved the occupation of Palestine by Jews from the United States and Europe to centre stage in his declared war aims. In answer to the question 'why are we fighting you?' he responds 'because you attacked us and continue to attack us' and he describes at length the extent of US support for the attacks of Ariel Sharon's government and army against Palestinians.[58]

As the principal economic and military backer of Israel, bin Laden holds America responsible for the oppression of Palestinians, and there is some truth in this position. One-sixth of America's foreign aid budget is devoted to Israel, although Israel is the sixteenth wealthiest nation-state on earth. In addition to massive foreign aid, Israel receives 1.8 billion dollars annually from the United States in military aid.[59] Another third of America's overseas aid budget goes to the neighbours of Israel – principally Egypt and Jordan – so as to give America leverage over them and prevent them from hostile acts against Israel. As Robert Fisk notes, this American largesse buys Egyptians a government whose Prime Minister claims to have been elected by 98 per cent of the electorate, while his opponents languish in jail or are otherwise disqualified from taking part in the 'democratic' process.[60] Bin Laden consequently portrays attacks on Americans by Al-Qaeda as acts of defence:

> The mission is to spread the word of God, not to indulge in massacring people. We ourselves are the target of killings, destruction, atrocities. We are only defending ourselves. This is defensive jihad. We want to defend our people and our land. That is why we say, if we don't get security, the Americans, too, won't get security. This is the simple formula even an American child can understand. Live and let live.

For bin Laden, Muslims are not the aggressors but the Americans, for it is they 'who rob us of our wealth and of our resources and of our oil' and who attack the Islamic religion.[61]

Bin Laden portrays himself as a lone charismatic figure fighting against the might of America and its allies for a new Islamic order, and many Muslim boys wear his image on their T-shirts. But without American support for the house of Saud, and without American and Saudi backing for the establishment of Al-Qaeda and its bases in Afghanistan, bin Laden and his network of extremists would never have had the resources to attack America, and there would be no worldwide Al-Qaeda network. The CIA have long had a word for this kind of unintended consequence of their covert operations – 'Blowback'.[62] The CIA's methods involve them in frequent alliances with corrupt and vicious men who are not to be trusted, and this is one of the classic features of imperialism. Just like the Roman Empire, the American Empire needs local client allies, collaborators, and it needs them to be corruptible and to act against their own people. It is precisely for this reason that America both in its covert and in its overt imperial wars finds itself backing those whom insiders in its imperial terrains know to be the wrong people. This was not though the Bush administration's account of the origins of Al-Qaeda.[63]

Modern Apocalyptic Politics

Islamism is of course not American in origin. But it shares with America more than just a financial sponsor. In the same way as the secular and religious right in America, Islamists see themselves as engaged in an apocalyptic global struggle over the outcome of modern history. It was in 1989 that Francis Fukuyama published an influential essay with the apocalyptic title 'The End of History', in which he claimed that with the end of the Cold War the ideological struggle over the meaning of modernity was over because the free market had triumphed over state socialism.[64] American free market capitalism in this view was the final form of political economy to appear in the evolution of human history. Just like the postmillennial Puritans, Fukuyama argues that America is history's goal. Fukuyama's view is now widely shared among politicians of all stripes in America, including those on the religious right who have argued for the sacred legitimacy of an American foreign policy which is strongly anti-communist, pro-Israel, pro-capitalist, and pro-American global supremacy. Evangelical TV and radio evangelist Gary Bauer argues that the global spread of American capitalism and

American religion is indicative of the approach of the end of history and of the mandate of Christ to evangelize all nations before the end of time. For Bauer and others like him, 'globalisation is a fulfillment of dire Biblical prophecies foreshadowing the return of Christ and the onset of Armageddon'.[65] This puts a significant new twist on Fukuyama's declaration of the end of history. Whereas Fukuyama's apocalyptic is a version of Enlightenment progressivism, and involves the claim that history has evolved to its final ideological form, the Christian right believe that the end of the Cold War literally brings near the end of the world.

The religious advocacy of American global supremacy, the reading of the spread of American capitalism as a form of evangelism that presages the end of history, is remarkably reminiscent of the radical Islamist doctrines that inspired the Islamist founders of Al-Qaeda. As John Gray argues, modern Islamists share with neoliberal capitalists and the American Christian right the view that they are in charge of history, that their ideology and their political practices will eventually determine history's outcome and that the end of history cannot come until they have triumphed.[66] They share with neoliberal capitalists also the desire to wipe out divergent forms of civilisation, politics and values. They believe that humanity is destined towards one set of universal beliefs and practices and that they represent the revolutionary vanguard who are divinely charged to bring the rest of humanity into line with the future they uniquely have perceived.

Islamism originated in Islamic anti-colonial and nationalist movements such as the Egyptian Muslim Brotherhood and the South Asian Jamaat al Islami. These groups were united in their suspicion of Muslim rulers and teachers who had compromised Islamic teaching through cultural, economic and political accords or exchanges with colonial and post-colonial Western powers. Muslim intellectuals in the mid-twentieth century also began to realise that imitating the West did not lead to prosperity, but rather brought about a situation of under-development and subjugation to the West, even in supposedly post-imperial contexts.[67] Their response was to return to their own tradition as source of a new identity, and as the locus for a new moral, political and spiritual 'jihad' against the world dominance of Western culture and capitalism, or 'Westoxification' as an Iranian intellectual put it.[68] Islamic reformers sought to reorder

Muslim moral and religious practices, and the organisation of the Muslim state and economy, along what they claimed were traditional Islamic lines, and in contradistinction to Western colonial and post-colonial influences.

The new Islamist teaching is however by no means simply traditional Islam reborn, but rather an attempt to harness traditional Islam to a revolutionary movement that owes more to Marx than it does to Muhammad.[69] Islamic intellectuals, many of them educated by Reformist Islamic schools in Egypt or by teachers taught in these schools, reinvent Islamic tradition so as to secure it from colonial and postcolonial annexation and circumscription. They reject the colonial distinction between a secular public sphere regulated by European-derived economic and legal practices, and the personal sphere of dress, sexual relations, dietary and ritual practices.[70] This is why it is around dress codes and separation of the sexes that reformist Islam first comes into conflict with mainstream Islamic practice, or, in the case of Muslim minorities such as those of France or Spain, with the civil authorities. These early symbolic skirmishes are the first frontier of a larger programme of reform, which in countries such as Saudi Arabia, Iran, Pakistan, Nigeria and the Sudan, and in two regional states in Malaysia, has developed into a systematic project to submit the whole society, including non-Muslims, to Islamic Shari'a law.

Many of those attracted to radical Islamism are rural migrants newly arrived in industrial cities, ejected from their traditional villages by the economic and technical forces of modernity from which Islamic governments have failed, or been unable, to protect them. The experiences of poverty and social dependence among these new city dwellers opens them to forms of religiosity that militantly challenge the assumed relationship between social progress and the modernisation and Westernisation of their societies.[71] Other radical Islamists are returnees from study in the West, where they have been radicalised by their experiences. In student hostels they often come under the influence of radical Islamists who use new students' sense of alienation in the midst of different cultural and particularly sexual mores, and the fact that they are far from moderate influences at home, to convert them to the radical Islamist struggle with the West and with compromised Muslim rulers.

The concept of *jihad* is central to the militant Islamist cause. *Jihad* means, literally, 'struggle', but traditionally it does not indicate the need for violence. On the contrary, it refers to the moral and spiritual struggle of the Muslim with temptation and all that threatens a pure and holy life. But as adapted by the Egyptian Sunni Muslim leader Sayyid Qutb, *jihad* indicates the militant struggle within Islam for the truly Islamic way of life and hence the struggle against the West and its allies among Muslim rulers. Qutb studied in America and was disgusted by what he saw as its spiritual vacuity and sexual licence. He returned to Egypt where he wrote his widely read *Milestones* in prison under Nasser. He wrote that Muslim rulers and their citizens had compromised with the immoral West and were therefore *Jahiliyya*, which means living in 'a state of ignorance of the guidance of God'. Enlightened Islamists have a duty to struggle against these ignorant Muslims – often insultingly called 'Kafir' (which means infidel) by Islamists – to re-establish Islam as a total way of life.

Qutb was influenced by the Indian Muslim intellectual Maulana Maududi, who founded the South Asian Islamist network Jamaat-i-Islami, and whose leader in Indonesia was accused of organising the 2002 Bali bombing. Maududi is a towering influence in modern Islamism, for it was he who first articulated the modern use of *jihad* to indicate militant struggle with colonial powers and their Muslim collaborators. Maududi developed an account of Islam as a total way of life in contradistinction to the colonial subjugation of Muslims to foreign legal, political, economic and religious concepts and practices. From his pen flowed articulations of Islamic economics, Islamic politics and an Islamic constitution, which together were intended to enable Muslims to live a life in complete subjection to the revealed law of the Qur'an and the teachings of the Prophet.

For Qutb the struggle for this way of life involved the 'universal proclamation of the freedom of man from servitude to other men, the establishment of God and His Lordship throughout the world, the end of man's arrogance and selfishness, and the implementation of the rule of the Divine Sharia'ah in human affairs'.[72] Qutb's apocalyptic language and aggressive rhetoric indicate that he envisaged the struggle would involve violence against the enemies of Islam, including corrupt Muslim states: it is the responsibility of the reformist Muslim to 'liquidate' such states completely, with the intention that the new purified Islam can claim 'the whole earth' for 'it wants and requires the entire inhabited world'.[73] Qutb sees this war for a new global Islam as an Islamic *jihad* whose true meaning is not so much a defensive movement as a struggle for the sovereignty of Allah in 'a movement to wipe out tyranny, and to introduce true freedom to mankind, using whatever resources are practically available'.[74]

The rhetoric of bin Laden carries strong echoes of this Islamist philosophy of global conquest. However, the claim of bin Laden and of Qutb before him to be traditional Muslims is deeply suspect. When they propose, or initiate in bin Laden's case, violent revolutionary struggle against Muslim and Western governments they reveal not so much a reading of the Qur'an as the influence of Bolshevism and Marxism. As Gray proposes, while claiming to be anti-Western they share with their Western adversaries the modern belief that 'the world can be reshaped by an act of will'.[75]

There are also important parallels between the Islamist project to remake the world and the neoliberal capitalist project of global deregulation and 'free' trade and its advocacy by the 'neoconservative' cabal who now run American foreign policy and who under Bush have taken it in such an explicitly apocalyptic direction. Like bin Laden, the goal of Bush, Cheney, Rumsfeld and Wolfowitz is universal global conquest, world domination. They too would put down every enemy of America, every opponent of 'free' trade, democracy and liberty in whatever quarter of the world they may be found and by whatever means may be appropriate. Bush believes as passionately as Qutb or bin Laden, as William Channing or Woodrow Wilson, as Jerry Falwell or Ronald Reagan, that America's cause is just and true because America is the truest exemplar on earth of the sacred values of freedom and democracy. As Stanley Hauerwas suggests, what is dangerous about such values is precisely the belief that they are universal, that all reasonable people ought to believe them and that therefore those who oppose them are unreasonable, even deranged.[76] It therefore seems eminently reasonable to go to war to impose the values of freedom and democracy. In other words, the mutation of the American dream into a global war with those who are said to oppose America's interests and its values is a consequence of Enlightenment rationalism. The universal story of an enlightened humanity progressing toward peace legitimates a perpetual war to bring it about.

However, it is not in the name of reason, but of an apocalyptic faith that Bush and bin Laden seek to take charge of the destiny of the world. Bush and bin Laden are hardly representatives of the Enlightenment. Their frequent appeal to a sacred charge, a divine destiny, their messianic belief that they are uniquely chosen to defend their people from attack, bespeaks of a pre-enlightenment and religious particularism. The problem is not that they are reasonable but quite the opposite: neither sees conversation, dialogue, rational discussion as adequate to the task at hand – enemies are evil, they only respond to force and violence. You do not reason with terrorists – or Americans if you are bin Laden – you just try to kill them. It is precisely the apocalyptic beliefs of both Bush and bin Laden that their view of the world is the only possible view, the only reasonable view available, that makes them both so deeply dangerous to the peace of the world.

At the height of the Cold War the foremost American theologian of the twentieth century, Reinhold Niebuhr, offered a theological benison on America's struggle with the Soviets. In his *The Irony of American History* Niebuhr expressed the view, now common among the intellectual and political acolytes of the Bush administration, that American political arrangements, the American way of life, are the most desirable, even the only kinds of social arrangements that all reasonable people do, or in any case ought to, aspire to. Niebuhr had come to believe, despite his own earlier warnings about the dangers of democracy being overtaken by sectional interest,[77] that American civilisation was divinely charged in its struggle with communism to shape human history towards its destiny. Despite his earlier criticism of the social gospel, the paranoia of the Cold War meant that Niebuhr finally reverted to the classical American postmillennial belief that the Kingdom of God had truly arrived in the history of America as the first truly democratic nation.

The postmillennial account of American superiority finds equally articulate advocacy amongst the contemporary intellectual East Coast elite, though now it is put in less theological and more classical prose. In his influential *Paradise and Power*, Robert Kagan constructs a narrative of American ideological and military power and correlatively of European weakness that is deeply reminiscent of Niebuhr, as well as the rhetoric of Bush and his speech writers.[78] Kagan traces the belief in the 'transcendent importance of the American experiment' right back to the founding fathers, for Americans 'have always been internationalists' but not on the basis of international institutions but rather of their own principles:

> That is why it was always so easy for so many Americans to believe, as so many still believe today, that by advancing their own interests they advance the interests of humanity. As Benjamin Franklin put it America's cause 'is the cause of all mankind'.[79]

Niebuhr anticipates Kagan in a remarkable number of ways, including the claims that Americans are interested in winning wars while Europeans are interested in avoiding them; that America is strong both technically and militarily and Europe is weak; that America is therefore uniquely fitted and destined to be the upholder of right and good on the world stage; that America in the pursuit of the 'universal good' is thwarted as much by her friends as her foes, and hence that America is justified in acting unilaterally in defence of freedom.[80] Underlying both Kagan and Bush's positions is the neoliberal economic assumption that individuals serve collective welfare best when they act in their own interests.[81] This prioritisation of the economic over the moral sustains the larger political claim that America serves humanity best when she acts likewise in her own interests.

This neoliberal and imperialist conception of political economy is as apocalyptic as more openly religious forms of millennialism precisely because it sets up an ideology of human redemption which its advocates believe they are charged to follow regardless of the destruction and violence it may entail.[82] And so, despite the claims of Kagan and others to be the conservative heirs of the American Republican tradition with its Enlightenment roots, there is nothing truly conservative or traditional about the version of neoliberal political economy that American Presidents from Reagan to Bush have pursued over the last 30 years. Far from conserving traditions or communities or the natural environment, the mindless pursuit of

economic dogma has wreaked terrible destruction on human and
ecological communities. The advocates of this dogma believe in their
cause whatever the countervailing evidence. Indeed, the more
opposition they encounter, the more violence and destruction their
pursuit of their sacred charge seems to require, the more this simply
confirms the apocalyptic in their chosen path. For redemption
necessitates violent struggle and sacrifice.

Norman Cohn traces modern Western apocalyptic politics back
through history to medieval millenarians who protested at the
corruption of the late medieval papacy; they promised to redeem
the world from corruption and evil through violent revolt against the
established order.[83] Apocalyptic of this kind was and is a powerful
perversion of New Testament eschatology. Although Jesus attracted
Zealot revolutionaries as his followers, he nonetheless resisted
those who advocated violent insurrection against the unjust rule of
imperial Rome. Jesus certainly did predict violent events that would
presage the second coming of the 'son of Man'. But the disciples
themselves are warned not to try to take control of these events. They
were not to follow those who would come after him and claim to
have rediscovered the messiah, or to have identified the precise time
of the end of history, for 'about the day or the hour no one knows'
(Mark 13. 32). Above all they were not to use violence to try to
control history or to bring about its end.

American postmillennial apocalyptic involves the claim that the
American Republic, and in particular the free market combined with
a form of marketised democracy, is the first appearance in history of
a redeemed human society, a true godly Kingdom. But true Christian
apocalyptic, the Christian belief that Christ has come, that the Spirit
of Christ is present in the Church, and that Christ will come again,
points Christians precisely to the temporary and imperfect nature
of all their efforts to establish the reign of God on earth. Christian
eschatology indicates that the end of history is already known by
Christians who truly discern the death and resurrection of Christ; for
these events are the apocalypse through which God has already
redeemed the world from evil, and inaugurated the Church to
witness to the rule of Christ above all other authority or power. But
this witness is always provisional because Christians also await the
Second Coming; they live 'between the times' of Christ's Ascension

to the right hand of God whence he reigns as the Lord of history and his promised Second Coming before the Last Judgement. For now though, the reality of Christ's Lordship is only visible to those with the eyes of faith. But its political import for those of the faith is clear. After the Resurrection and Ascension no nation, no polity, any longer has the right to rule; all government is henceforth provisional and limited: the core apocalyptic claim of Christians is that Christ is the only true ruler. And this recognition relativises all other claims to authority, power and redemption and unveils their claims to final authority or universal supremacy as false and ungodly.[84]

This does not mean that the Church is called to rule in place of the nations as Christian Popes and Emperors erroneously came to believe. Nor does it mean that a nation that claims to be Christian, as the Puritans imagined their American colony to be, is the Kingdom of God on earth and hence has the right to extend its rule over other peoples. On the contrary, the recognition that Christians live between the times prevents them from complacently identifying their own communities as the perfected realisation of the Kingdom. For the Kingdom, while breaking into history decisively in the coming of Christ, is at the same time still to come in all its fullness. The first Christians knew that their own communities and political arrangements were provisional and that on earth they had 'no continuing city'. This recognition sets Christian apocalyptic apart from the judgemental violence that characterises modern apocalyptic politics. The Christian who discerns the true meaning of apocalypse has no right and no cause to use violence in defence of Christian values, or of a Christian city, for she still looks for a city that is to come.

2 – The Fading of the Dream

The postmillennialist belief that America is close to realising the Kingdom of God on earth is no longer the dominant strain in American apocalyptic, despite the vestiges of this tradition in Wilsonian political rhetoric and neoliberal economic dogma. Ever since the Civil War, American evangelical Protestantism has been overtaken by a newer apocalyptic faith, that of premillennialism, sometimes also known as dispensationalism. This version of apocalyptic religion has a much darker perspective on the history of America, and of the planet. Premillennialists believe they are living in the end time, and it is an era of growing lawlessness and dreadful wars which threaten to extinguish human life on earth. Only after these events will Christ return to inaugurate a literal 'thousand year reign of peace', which millennialists believe is predicted by the Book of Revelation. Premillennialists also believe that true believers will be 'raptured' or plucked off the planet by God before the Great Tribulation, so that only those 'left behind' will have to face the terrors of the end time.

The widespread adoption of premillennialism in twentieth-century America was driven forward by the fading of the dream of the founders of a liberal commonwealth of self-governing communities. The dream faded in the appalling devastation of the Civil War, and the subsequent rise of the new megaliths, the joint stock-holding corporation and an increasingly powerful federal government,[1] which bestride American history from the mid-nineteenth century.

The Market Republic

Americans participate in more local and regional democratic elections than any other people in the world except the Swiss. They elect mayors, state prosecutors, state governors, representatives to state governments and to the two houses of Congress, and the President. This range of local, regional and national democratic activity is matched by an extraordinary multiplicity of religious organisations and local associations in small towns, suburban communities and city neighbourhoods. To the extent that this thriving local democratic and voluntarist culture still exists, it displays the original American ideal of the small open meeting as the place where local communities may best govern their affairs. But the existence of this culture, and the 'habits of the heart' that sustain it, are increasingly threatened.[2] Since the industrial revolution more centrist and corporatist tendencies have overtaken this early democratic vision.

The early American ideal of government rested on the assumption that little government was actually needed because individuals and local communities were, through the influence of the churches, mostly virtuous, self-reliant and self-governing.[3] But the emergence of an industrial economy and of mercantile capitalism produced a new collective mode of social life, and of governance, which meant that modern humans in general, and modern Americans in particular, found themselves caught up in an economic market that made of them one society. The existence of this new collective economic form assisted and enabled the emergence of a more powerful nation-state whose ruling elites were closely linked with the key agency of the industrial economy, the joint stock-holding corporation. Initially restrained by the democratic nature of early company law in America, the corporation soon acquired power over the communities that originally owned controlling stock in them. Legal rights were granted to corporations in a series of court judgements in the mid-nineteenth century, which allowed them to ride rough-shod over the wishes of the councils and residents of the towns or cities where their factories or offices were situated.[4]

The growth of the idea of America as a single economic market, and of American corporate capitalism, also has roots in the earliest settler traditions. Alongside the Puritan political and religious tradition of the self-reliant individual, and of the congregation as a democratic and self-governing assembly, was the tradition of capitalist mercantilism, whose first form in the Americas was the plantation economy of the Virginian settlers with their aristocratic conception of society. Virginia, unlike New England, was from its inception a highly stratified society in which the propertied landowners were few, while poor whites – and enslaved blacks – were the large majority.

As David Fischer has shown, the contrast between the structures of colonial Virginia and New England reflects the differing origins of the settlers in these areas.[5] The Puritans who first settled in what is now New England mostly emanated from the dissenting traditions of the North and West of England, and were democratic and egalitarian in orientation. But many Virginians were aristocratic royalists who created a deeply hierarchical society, modelled on the English establishment and at whose pinnacle were the landowning class from among whom the emergent republic would choose its first presidents, including Washington and Jefferson. In Virginia, in contrast to New England, political participation was limited to those with land and property, which is just the way it was in the South of England where most Virginians originated. Freedom for the Virginian meant the power to rule, just as it had for the English aristocracy. The Virginian political ideal was what Fischer calls 'hegemonic liberty'.[6] Its social corollary was slavery, the natural condition into which even an Englishman might fall through ill luck or extreme indebtedness, a belief that was underwritten by the teachings of the English philosopher John Locke, who argued that every natural resource, including a man's body, was rightly and properly subject to the law of private property. Just as bad fortune could result in a person losing their farm, so it might also have the consequence of their losing their freedom. The outcome of the Civil War between North and South was of course the eventual abolition of slavery. But the deep social stratification of Southern society along racial and economic lines was not eradicated by the war, and indeed remains to this day.

The American Republican tradition is an amalgam of propertied aristocratic and Puritan egalitarian tendencies, and the Declaration of Independence and the American Constitution should be read as an attempt to marry these competing traditions. In essence the outcome was a Constitution that affirmed the right of political liberty, but this right remained inextricably tied to the ownership of property. The Founding Fathers did not establish a libertarian Republic in which slaves or indentured servants might rise up against their masters and claim their freedoms. On the contrary, as Richard Hofstadter argues, the constitution, despite its egalitarian preamble, guaranteed freedoms of more relevance to the propertied than the poor, including 'freedom from fiscal uncertainty and irregularities in the currency, from trade wars among the states, from economic discrimination by more powerful foreign governments, from attacks on the creditor class or on property, from popular insurrection'.[7] Freedom was essentially conceived as the freedom to own and enjoy the fruits of property. Influence on government in the political process was not according to a universal democratic franchise but according to the quantity of property a person or group of persons possessed. George Washington and Thomas Jefferson, at odds in some matters, were united in their fear of the landless and unpropertied masses. Consequently the inauguration of balanced constitutional government ultimately offered no relief from the conflict between the property-poor and the wealthy, which still characterises the core problem of modern American politics to this day.

The New Theology of Private Property

What of the philosophical and religious roots of this propertied and corporate Republicanism? Are these as significant as Puritanism in the formation of the American sacred story? The evidence is that they are. The English traveller and philosopher abroad, John Locke, provided the paradigmatic account of the nature of property and freedom on which America has relied ever since. Locke travelled widely in America and spent much time observing the growing struggle between English settlers and Native Americans over the formers' appropriation of Indian land. Consequently Locke devoted much of his writing on government and politics to the defence of colonial policy regarding land, and in particular the colonial law under which the Crown claimed ownership of colonised land, and conferred its title on settlers. While Locke held that the Indian had a right to venison and to the uncultivated fruits of the land, he argued that the soil itself, the very land, belonged not to Indians, who because they were uncivilised and lacking in industry had failed to cultivate it, but to those who through their labour had tilled and enclosed a portion of the land for agricultural production. Locke's justification for this view was theological. He argued that although God had given 'the world in common to all Mankind', God also commanded man to work the land and it was only those who 'in Obedience to this Command of God, subdued, tilled and sowed any part of it' who had a right therefore to annex it to their own persons as their own property, and to hold title upon it.[8] It had never been the divine intention that the land should remain in common and therefore uncultivated. In this way Locke took the biblical injunction in Genesis 1. 28 to 'subdue the earth' as the basis for the colonial claim to dominion over the particular portion of the earth that is America, and the supplanting thereby of the native inhabitants' claim to this same portion. The Englishman acquires title over his land by cultivating it and then by enclosing it in fences, because such cultivation and enclosure adds value to land, and makes of what Locke called 'waste land' a productive resource for the colonial economy. Land held in common, as by the native Americans, is unproductive valueless land and cannot rightly be said to belong to anyone. Indians may have enjoyed a wealth of land but lacking civilisation and education they failed to use it rationally and so consequently had not improved it. The English by their industrious- ness were therefore the rightful owners of the land according to divine as well as human law. The English dominated and redeemed the new world by agricultural prowess, whereas the Spanish had only subdued it by violent conquest. In this way Locke gave theological underpinnings to the Puritan idea that they were entering into the millennial inheritance of the children of light, refounding the Kingdom on the virgin soil of America.

Locke also provided the first theological account of the core American beliefs in individual freedom, property-based rights and minimalist government. Government, law and politics were ordained by God for no other purpose than the defence of the individual in the free enjoyment of his own property and the free employment of his own labour to improve it:

> To understand political power right, and derive it from its original, we must consider, what state all men are naturally in, and that is, a state of perfect freedom to order their actions, and dispose of their possessions and persons, as they think fit, within the bounds of the law of nature, without asking leave, or depending upon the will of any other man.[9]

The essence of the political task is not to work for the good of all, as the Anglican divine and political theorist Richard Hooker had earlier imagined – and as American Indians also understood and practised in their common land tenure customs – but to protect and promote the enjoyment of private property by individuals and to prevent those who would interfere with this enjoyment:

> The state of nature has a law of nature to govern it, which obliges every one: and reason, which is that law, teaches all mankind, who will but consult it, that being all equal and independent, no one ought to harm another in his life, health, liberty, or possessions.[10]

Locke observed that it was Indians who were likely to threaten the Englishman in the enjoyment of his industry and his title. Consequently it was to defend the Englishman in his property against those who might take it from him that government in America was primarily needed.[11]

In both his account of property and of politics, Locke stands in marked contrast to the orthodox Christian tradition, which had adopted the ancient Israelite view that the enjoyment of land or property by its owner was conditional on respecting obligations and duties to God which included moral laws designed to limit debt slavery and inequality among the people of God. For Thomas Aquinas, theft of private property from the rich by the poor when otherwise they would go hungry did not constitute an infringement of the commandment 'thou shalt not steal'.[12] But American colonists who resisted the controlling hand of the Church over worship and doctrine also rejected religious restraints on property and wealth. Locke may have worried about the moral consequences of avarice and acquisitiveness but his essentially post-Christian narrative of a propertied polity was crucial to the emerging political order in America.[13]

Locke's argument that God gives the fruits of the earth not to all men equally but to the industrious and the enterprising above the lazy and indolent was the inspiration not only for wars against the Indian, but for revolutionary war against the British crown, which used privilege rather than industry to benefit from the work of (colonial) others. And once having rejected the tutelage of the Church and the governance of European monarchs who looked to the Church for legitimacy, the settlers were not anxious, after the Revolution, to reinstitute strong government. Their interest was primarily in a government to defend them from the Indians and to enable them to enjoy the fruits of their own labours.

The American Revolution was an attempt to dissociate the New World from the Old and to assert a novel form of political sovereignty that did not claim the kind of transcendent absolutism that characterised the birth of the European nation-state. It was after all because of persecution from the new rulers of Europe that the Puritans and other dissenters had taken to the seas to found a new society across the Atlantic. Millions of those who lost their livelihood in the vast land-grab of the newly powerful aristocracy followed them. The American Revolution was not fought about theological matters and nor was it a war whose intent was to bring freedom or democracy to native Americans, or to the myriad indentured servants and slaves of Bostonian gentlefolk and aristocratic Southern plantation owners such as George Washington. No, the war was fought about taxes; in particular those imposed by Britain on imports to the colony of products such as the tea that ended up at the bottom of Boston harbour in the opening protest of the Revolution. These taxes paid for the colonial armies that Britain kept in the American colonies to defend the colonials from the French and the Spanish. But plantation-owners and urbanites alike were furious at having to pay tax on their imported European luxuries – tea, printed cloth and so on – while American exports of tobacco and cotton were sold as raw materials at little over production cost back to Europe.

The emergent federal state of post-Revolutionary America represented the first attempt by Europeans – who would come to see themselves after the war with Britain for the first time as 'Americans' – to formulate a post-monarchical mode of political sovereignty. It was to the Lockean model of the affirmation of property rights that the framers of the federal constitution looked for the affirmation of state sovereignty and the legitimacy of its use of violence. The American Republic was essentially a property-owning republic, in which humanity's subduing of nature provided the core justification for the autonomy of the property-owner.

Property alone could not of course provide the basis for a virtuous and ordered society of the kind imagined by the founding fathers. What was equally needed was some account of how the colonists would commit to a shared project, to the creation of a virtuous and ordered society of the kind that Jonathan Edwards and other post-millennialists had imagined. As we have seen, postmillennialism put Americans in charge of a sacred history whose end would be the 1,000-year reign of peace and the return of Christ. But Deist Republicans such as Madison and Jefferson rejected the idea of the redemption of human society from original sin through a divine redeemer figure, Jesus Christ. They conceived of the Republic as a polity of liberty and reason constituted of virtuous and reasonable people who have been brought to this condition through appropriate education and nurture. What stood in the way of the achievement of the free Republic was not original sin but the tyranny of over-weaning state power whether in monarchic or bureaucratic mode, and persecution from outside powers or empires.[14] It was around such ideas that Christian Puritanism and Enlightenment Republicanism found common cause in the American Revolution and in the construction of an American Republican tradition. Both traditions promoted a view of individual human autonomy in achieving a better America, both aspired to found a utopian society in the New World, and both shared a belief in the inevitability of deep opposition, and hence of conflict and struggle, in achieving this utopian project.

The Religion of America

The alliance between propertied Republicanism and Christian Puritanism in the eighteenth century resulted in what Mark Noll calls an 'American synthesis' of 'evangelical Protestant religion, republican political ideology, and commonsense moral reasoning'.[15] After the Civil War, evangelical pietists sought a new model of society to replace the traditional Puritan conception of a covenantal and separated church and they found it in the nationalistic enterprise of a 'civil millennialism' or a 'Christian republicanism'.[16] Vice and virtue were to be the touchstones of this religious republicanism, and evangelicalism became the dominant national religion of the emergent republic. This partnership involved a religious embrace of the doctrine of liberty, of America as the 'land of the free', which celebrated possibility and potency in politics and economics, science and religion.

American republicanism was constituted at its core of two ideas: resistance to the abuse of political power and a 'nearly messianic belief in the benefits of liberty'.[17] Linked to these was the language of the virtuous ruler and the virtuous citizen; the power of government would be restrained by the checks and balances of the separation of powers of the American constitution, and by the virtue of its governors. Similarly, the polity could only produce human flourishing when it promoted the freedom of its citizens to enjoy their own property and to live virtuous and happy lives. Here was the place and possibility of the church in the republican project, for citizens would be trained in virtue by their religious communities. As the Congregationalist preacher Ezra Stiles was to affirm at the end of the Revolution, 'true religion' and the 'diffusion of virtue' were necessary for the perfection of the new system of government and for the 'secular happiness of the people'.[18]

Theological critics of republicanism noted that the religion that accompanied it was no longer Christian orthodoxy, for republicanism required a submission of Christianity to a humanistic project of political order, personal liberty, private property and a belief in social and moral progress rather than in divine redemption. The result was a civil religion in which God became a cipher, a distant deity whose purposes come near in the values of the Republic.[19] Although the

Republic could make space for religion, it preferred a religion that did not challenge its founding principles. As Dietrich Bonhoeffer noted during his stay in America in the 1930s, the freedom or possibility that the American Republic gave to religion was to celebrate the American ideal of liberty, and this was a classic form of what he later called 'cheap grace'. But that the world should give the church its freedom was to Bonhoeffer a heresy analogous to the Nazi heresy that required the church to affirm Aryanism and acknowledge the Führer. For Bonhoeffer, the freedom of a church that is capable of resisting tyranny is not given to it by the political power, or 'the world', but is rather a gift of God and a product of the preaching of the Word of God.[20]

Another core element in the alliance of American Protestantism and republicanism was the appeal to reason and experience as the touchstones of commonsense and political and scientific wisdom. Central to the Republican tradition, and the Enlightenment philosophy on which it drew, was the belief that reason and experience, as opposed to tradition, revelation and religion, would guide humanity to a fairer and more peaceful future. Americans in the eighteenth century increasingly adopted a Baconian cast of mind in which judgements of truth were based upon observations of empirical data. The future of humanity was no longer to be determined by reliance on scripture and tradition: deistic republicanism would put experience at the heart of its understanding of the progress of America to become the first society constitutionally committed to the happiness of its citizens. Similarly, progressive republicanism began to challenge belief in a literal millennium.[21]

The German philosopher G. W. F. Hegel read this humanistic turn in American theism as the first full flowering of the religion of the Incarnation. By becoming Incarnate in Christ, God had become subject to time and space, and therefore truly real, instead of an abstract ideal. According to Hegel the Incarnation meant that there is nothing in the universe more divine than humanity and therefore America as the first nation to assert the divinity of the human adventure, and to have no memory or vestige of humanity's primitive past, is the carrier of the spirit of humanity: America was therefore 'the country of the future'.[22] As Richard Rorty argues, Hegel here aptly characterised the progressive and future-oriented cast of mind of American pragmatism, and the belief in the supremacy of human potentiality over any abstract idea or theorem, including God.[23] For pragmatists such as John Dewey, America was great because she had put aside in her founding principles, and in her modes of governance, any claim or desire to fashion life on earth after absolute and heavenly Truth. From this freedom from an externally imposed truth arose faith in the uniqueness of American democracy as the only polity that does not 'rest upon the idea that experience must be subjected at some point or other to some form of external control: to some "authority" alleged to exist outside the processes of experience'.[24]

The dream of America in this progressive and pragmatic perspective is the dream of her freedom to create herself, to manifest and shape her own destiny. This destiny took shape in the emergence of a Republican polity whose core task was to allow robust individuals to be in charge and in control of their own lives, and not to be cowed by any institution or tradition or caste or class.[25] This is what many Americans still mean when they speak about 'freedom'.

The Market Revolution and Evangelical Revival

In the nineteenth century there occurred on the Eastern Seaboard – though it would gradually spread West over the agricultural interior – what Charles Sellers identifies as a second revolution, a 'market revolution'. This economic revolution constituted the first establishment on a large terrain of multiple political entities, bound in an emergent federation, of an inter-state market characterised by the classic indicators of capitalist relations: the division of labour, trading for comparative advantage between towns and regions geographically distant that specialised in different products, the rise of a cash crop agrarian economy particularly around the growing of cotton and the development of textile manufacturing. This new political economy of the emergent United States was tremendously productive. For example, the value of cotton exports rose from $23 million to $124 million in just a few decades in the mid-1800s.[26] This emergent economy was assisted by a growing paper economy, a national Bank, bills of exchange and corporate stocks,[27] and it advanced a new kind of political economy at home that increasingly put the interests of corporations and financial institutions above the older small-holder economy on which the majority of settlers had relied.

There was religious resistance to the burgeoning capitalist market in the form primarily of rurally based evangelicalism, which reflected the independent ethic and barter economy of the self-sufficient small-holder farmer. But at the same time, as Sellers and before him Max Weber suggest, American Calvinism provided the 'spiritual medium' of the transformation of America into a capitalist society 'sanctifying worldly work as religious duty and wealth as fruit of grace'.[28] Noll nuances Seller and Weber when he notes an opposition between upper- and middle-class Protestants and lower-class Protestants on the matter of money and the market; the former groups embraced the market relations and paper money whereas the latter distrusted the accumulation of wealth and national economic projects.[29]

Ideological conflict over the nature of American corporatism lay at the heart of the Civil War. Slavery was an institution that was pivotal to the Southern plantation economy, but in the North free movement of labour was essential to the emergence of a vibrant, industrially based American capitalism. This same conflict took on religious dimensions. While the Northern abolitionists viewed the ending of slavery as one of the labours required of the righteous before the millennium would dawn, Southern church people saw the maintenance of slavery and limitations on the power of government as essential to their conception of loyalty to the earlier covenant ideals.[30]

As capitalism was growing apace, and along with it the networks of railroads that enabled regional trade across a large territory, Protestant Christianity was also growing at an unprecedented rate with new adherents joining Protestant churches at twice the rate of population growth.[31] By the late nineteenth century, growing numbers of Protestants had almost universally embraced the new market economy with its corporate actors, which included the national Bank, many smaller regional banks, stock-holding corporations, stock markets, the new retail sectors of American cities and the related development of the mail order company. Indeed many features of evangelical religion were associated with market activity.

Thus evangelical tracts and books were to form the first large-scale market in printed media, anticipating the emergence of consumer culture, while evangelical missionaries and preachers saw the development of a market both within and beyond America as a God-given device for the rapid spread of the Gospel to all regions of America and beyond its shores to the South and across the Pacific.[32]

At the heart of the emergent marriage between Protestant evangelicalism and American capitalism was the centrality of individual choice to evangelical identity.[33] Evangelicalism grew rapidly as the religion of choice in the aftermath of the American Revolution because it was 'better able to meet the needs of rootless egalitarian-minded men and women than were the static churchly institutions based on eighteenth century standards of deference and elite monopolies of orthodoxy'.[34] Evangelical religious experience offered the individual a sense of 'enduring personal stability' and the 'dignity of the self' in the midst of the rapid transformations of the political, industrial and economic revolutions of the eighteenth and nineteenth centuries: individuals so empowered were also empowered socially and politically to affirm the sovereignty of the common people, and to shape the culture in their own interests. Consequently, evangelicals in the nineteenth century wanted both a republic and a market-place unfettered by the traditional hierarchy of church and state. Religious disestablishment in other words had both political and economic consequences, for there was an intrinsic link between the embrace of political disestablishment and freedom in religion and the embrace of the market economy by the new nation. Having rejected hierarchical ecclesiastical regulation of their worship and beliefs and reading of scripture, evangelicals were equally opposed to government regulation of the 'public spaces in which they hoped to promote their religion and they were predis-posed in favor of situations in which individuals could make the choice for God freely'.[35] Analogously, if the Spirit could guide the individual to make the right choice for God, then surely similar processes were at work in the new alchemy of the market economy. Consumer choice thus became an article of evangelical faith.

Evangelicals in late nineteenth-century America responded to the emergence of the modern world – a sovereign nation-state, a science-informed and industrially driven economic market – by abandoning the all-embracing ethic of historic Christianity and replacing it with a form of religion that made fewer claims on the social, focusing instead on the inner life of the religious individual. They made a virtue of necessity and proposed, in the words of the popular American preacher Henry Ward Beecher, that 'while we are taught by the scientists in truths that belong to the sensual nature, while we are taught by the economists of things that belong to the social nature, we need the Christian ministry to teach us those things which are invisible'.[36] A Christian America in the evangelical vision had made a kind of peace between religion and modernity. Piety was the key to evangelical social conscience and economic teaching, and success in business was no obstacle to evangelical piety provided the businessman maintained his honesty and integrity, and used his excess wealth charitably.[37]

However, by the late nineteenth century there were severe strains in this new alliance of evangelicalism and modernity. Modernism in religion issued in the birth of American theological liberalism, whose adherents sought to harmonise the teachings of the Bible, and Christian doctrines, with scientific discovery and teaching. This provoked a reactionary counter-attack by evangelicals who published the famous 'fundamentals' pamphlets, in which they asserted the inerrancy of scripture and the truthfulness of the Biblical account of creation, and of other traditional Christian doctrines. The publishers of these pamphlets had a growing sense that the world of nineteenth-century America was slipping away from the influence of the reformed Christianity that had birthed the new nation through the Pilgrim Fathers and established it as a 'city set on a hill'. This sense of unease with the new modern America grew rapidly in the years before and after the Great War, and shaped a widespread return to millennial fervour during the Great Depression of the 1920s. But instead of postmillennialism, which emphasised the progress of a Christian America towards the earthly and kingly rule of Christ on earth, American evangelicals now turned to the more pessimistic premillennial and dispensationalist doctrines associated with the best-selling Bible edition of Charles Schofield and the teaching of the Pentecostal Edward Irving and the Brethren leader John Nelson Darby.

The Rise of Premillennialism

The English preacher John Darby founded the Plymouth Brethren because he was critical of the corruption of the established religion of the Church of England. His intention was to establish a new church modelled on the principles of New Testament Christianity as he understood them. Many of the Brethren, and ultimately Darby himself, eventually migrated to the United States.[38] According to Darby there are seven dispensations in human history, the first being the paradise of the Garden of Eden, and the last being the 1,000-year reign of the saints referred to in Revelation 20. 1 – 7, which for Darby and his followers lies in the future after the Second Coming of Christ. Premillennialists believe that they live near the close of the sixth dispensation that immediately precedes this 1,000-year reign. On their reading of the Book of Revelation, the time immediately before the promised millennium of peace is a time of 'Great Tribulation', involving an increase in sin and wickedness, and of wars and violence and natural catastrophes, a great falling away from the true faith, and a struggle between the remnant of Christians who remain faithful and the majority who follow the prince of the world and the Antichrist.

According to Darby, the kingdoms of the world cannot be associated with the Kingdom of God; they are as far apart in the divine plan as are Israel and the Christian Church. Israel in the first five dispensations, like the kingdoms of the world, has rejected the lordship of Christ. The sixth dispensation, which stretches from the Ascension of Christ to Christ's Second Coming, belongs to those who recognise Christ as the Messiah and heavenly King; those who live in this new dispensation are no longer citizens of earth but of heaven, for 'the Church is properly heavenly in its calling and relationship with Christ, forming no part of the course of events of the earth'.[39] The world however remains under the control of the 'prince of this world', Satan, but the future belongs to the children of the Kingdom of God. For now the two worlds are in a final battle for souls; the church's divine charge is to save souls, calling men and women to separate themselves from a sinful society and take up their heavenly citizenship in preparation for the return of Christ and the dawn of the seventh dispensation.

Darbyite dispensationalism was taken up with alacrity by American evangelical preachers, who from the Civil War through the Great Depression saw ever more proofs that the millennium of peace was ever further from being realised. Instead of the progressive march of humanity towards the kingdom, which Jonathan Edwards had foreseen, dispensationalists saw a downward spiral of cataclysms that included agricultural catastrophes, political corruption, monopoly capitalism, greedy industrialists, pornography, liberal theology, the growth of corrupting cities, increasing immigration, labour union agitation, the emergence of Communism, the Great War and even the sinking of the Titanic.[40] The influential revivalist preacher Dwight L. Moody summed up the mood of catastrophism:

> I looked on this world as a wrecked vessel. God has given me a life-boat, and said to me, "Moody, save all you can." God will come in judgement and burn up this world, but the children of God don't belong to this world; they are in it, but not of it, like a ship in the water. This world is getting darker and darker; its ruin is coming nearer and nearer. If you have any friends on this wreck unsaved, you had better lose no time in getting them off.[41]

Moody here indicates his own adoption of the dispensationalist account of the 'rapture', when premillennialists believe that the faithful will be taken up from the earth while sinners are left behind to face the tribulation of the end times, and the last battle of Armageddon. The idea of the rapture derives from a reading of 1 Thessalonians 4. 16 – 17, in which St Paul says that 'the dead in Christ shall rise first, and then we which are alive and remain shall be caught up together with them in the clouds, to meet the Lord in the air'.

Premillennialist teaching has clear implications for Christian action in the world. The premillennialist 'scorns all efforts made in the name of religion to correct the ills of society' for 'to inaugurate any programme of social betterment or to set the church as a whole upon an upward course would be to thwart the divine purpose and to delay the advent of Christ'.[42] According to the dispensationalist

preacher and writer Lewis Chafer, social reform was the product
of liberal Christianity and it betrayed the truth of the Gospel of
Jesus Christ:

> Satan, like a fond mother, is bending over those in his arms,
> breathing into their mouths the quieting balm of a 'universal
> fatherhood of God' and a 'universal brotherhood of man'; sug-
> gesting their worthiness before God on the ground of their own
> moral character and physical generation; feeding their tendency
> to imitate the true faith by great humanitarian undertakings
> and schemes for the reformation of individuals and the better-
> ment of the social order.[43]

Instead of trying to improve the darkening world, premillennialists
adopted the project of world evangelisation in response to Christ's
last instruction to the disciples that they should preach the gospel 'in
all the world for a witness unto all nations; and then shall the end
come' (Matthew 24. 14).

Dispensationalists drew on a deep strain of cultural despair that
arose among the millions who having survived the terrible evils of
the Civil War then suffered under the often cruel exigencies of slum
living and wage slavery in the industrial revolution of the nineteenth
century, and under the Great War and Great Depression in the early
twentieth. As Schofield put it in 1918:

> There is a deathless thing in the heart of humanity ... the belief
> that there must yet be for humanity on this earth ... a corporate,
> ordered life, a life not for a few fortunate and powerful ones,
> but a life for all which shall be rich in truth, justice, power and
> love ... The race, after all, is one; and it is a kind of corporate
> logic which keeps the hope of a golden age alive in the univer-
> sal human mind.[44]

The return of Christ and the 1,000-year reign of peace is the only
occasion for Christian hope, but as these events approach the Church
will become apostate and the world will sink ever deeper into a mire
of immorality, unbelief and disorder. Some dispensationalists even
took a perverse pleasure in the terrible turn of world events in the

early twentieth century: 'the darker the night gets, the lighter my heart becomes' intoned Reuben Torrey, of the Los Angeles Bible Institute in 1914.[45]

Dispensational Zionism

While for dispensationalists neither Britain nor America can do anything to ameliorate the ever worsening conditions of the end time for their citizens, they have an important role in bringing the end time nearer in their actions in relation to Palestine and the Jews. A central feature of Darby's dispensational system was the place of the Jews in the divine plan for the end of history: the Jews had rejected Christ and so God had set his originally chosen people aside and the Church supersedes the nation of Israel. But before the Rapture, the Jews play a crucial role in fulfilling biblical end time prophecy by returning to Palestine, resettling the biblical lands, and rebuilding Jerusalem and in particular the Third Temple on the site currently occupied by the Dome of the Rock and the Al-Aqsa Mosque. The new-born Israel is supposed to experience fierce resistance and be subjected to dreadful wars, but the remnant who come through these will ultimately recognise Christ as the true Messiah and so greet him at his Second Coming.

It is around this belief in a divine plan for the resettling of Israel before the end of the present historical era that dispensationalists have come to exert influence on British and American foreign policy, and on events in the Middle East from 1917 until the present day. The British evangelical, the Earl of Shaftesbury, had argued in 1839 that the Jews had to return to Palestine before the Second Coming, and under his influence the British government established a consulate in Jerusalem. The man appointed as consul was a strong evangelical who first promoted the idea of a British protectorate in Palestine to defend the 10,000 Jews already living there, and to give Britain a strategic base at the heart of the Ottoman Empire.[46] Dispensationalists viewed the fall of Jerusalem in 1917, and the collapse of the Ottoman Empire during the First World War, as the golden opportunity for the establishment of a British protectorate in Palestine, which was inaugurated in the Balfour Declaration of 1917.[47] At the same time dispensationalist Christians stepped up missionary effort among Jews in Britain and America.

Christian dispensationalism was a major progenitor of Zionism. The 'love of Zion' movement began in response to a growing wave of anti-Semitism in Russia and Germany in the 1880s and under the influence of the movement 25,000 Jews moved to Palestine as farmers between 1882 and 1903. In 1895 Theodore Herzl published his famous book *Der Judenstaat* (The Jewish State) in which the Zionist cause of a new Jewish homeland was first elaborated. Herzl initially expressed no preference for a particular place. It was the statelessness of Jews that he sought to address, but by the first Zionist Congress in 1897 he had fastened on Palestine as the proper place for the homeland.[48] American Jews were less convinced than their European counterparts that Palestine was to be the new homeland of the Jews as they were still strongly influenced by the idea that America, the New World, was itself the new Zion. However, under the influence of Christian premillennialism they were gradually won over to the Zionist cause. As the prominent American dispensationalist William E. Blackstone argued:

> Why not give Palestine back to them [the Jews] again? According to God's distribution of the nations, it is their home – an inalienable possession from which they were expelled by force ... Let us now restore them to the land of which they were so cruelly despoiled by our Roman ancestors.[49]

Blackstone was later lauded as a 'Father of Zionism' by American Zionists and his place in fostering a political climate in America conducive to the cause of an Israeli State was recognised by Israelis themselves when they named a national forest after him.[50]

The founding of the Jewish State in 1948 was an epochal event for dispensationalists because it seemed to make the return of Christ imminent. The Six Day War of 1967 was equally momentous, because Israel reoccupied the Old City of Jerusalem, and in particular the Temple Mount on which the Third Temple would be built before the end. This event presaged the publication of Hal Lindsey's *The Late Great Planet Earth*, whose popular recasting of dispensationalism around current events in the latter half of the twentieth century – the birth of the Israeli State and of the European Economic Community, the Cold War with Russia, and the establishment of a secular and independent Iraq on the biblical land of Babylon – helped turn dispensationalism from a minority creed of the more conservative evangelical churches and Bible Colleges into a majority faith among millions of American evangelical Christians.

Lindsey adds little to the predictions of dispensationalists who precede him, but he presents their prophecies in a populist form, styling himself the peoples' prophet who offers 'hope for the future' in troubled times when the very future of the planet, and human survival, seem threatened. The Bible for Lindsey is the ultimate store of prophetic wisdom with which to interpret the last days of planet earth which he believes have already begun because the Bible predicts that the end times can definitively be said to begin with 'the Jew returning to the land of Israel after thousands of years of being dispersed. The Jew is the most important sign to this generation'.[51] Lindsey links his interpretation with Puritan American preachers such as Increase Mather, father of Cotton Mather, whose book *The Mystery of Israel's Salvation* predicted the return of the Jews to Palestine hundreds of years before it happened.[52] Writing just after the Israeli occupation of East Jerusalem in 1967, Lindsey suggested that it now only remained for Israel 'to rebuild the ancient temple upon its historic site' for the restoration of Israel in the Bible to come to pass. Lindsey quotes an Israeli historian, Israel Eldad, who when asked how long it would take for the Jews to rebuild the temple after they had 'recaptured' old Jerusalem said that 'from the time that King David first conquered Jerusalem until Solomon built the Temple, just one generation passed. So it will be with us'. Lindsey concludes 'for all those who trust in Jesus Christ, it is a time of electrifying excitement'.[53] It was Ariel Sharon's controversial visit to the Al-Aqsa Mosque on the Temple Mount in 2001, when he seemed to be prospecting the site on which the Temple once stood and might again be rebuilt, which set off the most violent era in Israeli–Palestinian relations in all of the last 50 years. Palestinians are well versed in the long-announced plans of the Zionists as charted by Lindsey and others.

According to Lindsey, and here again he follows in long-established dispensationalist interpretation, it is the prophet Ezekiel who most clearly predicts the end time events. The 'latter years' are the time when Israel will return to the land; this happens after a very long time in which the land of Israel will have been made desolate by war and ecological collapse; the Jews will return 'from many nations' across the earth and experience spiritual regeneration; and finally their return, their resettling of the land and spiritual restoration will provoke great hostility from other nations which will culminate in a great battle, the Battle of Armageddon. Lindsey also tries to find evidence for his prophetic reading of current history in the apocalyptic references of Jesus and Paul, and the Book of Revelation.

Many contemporary scholars understand Jesus' apocalyptic sayings in the Synoptic Gospels of Matthew, Mark and Luke as referring to the Jewish war with Rome in A.D. 70, which included the sacking of Jerusalem and the destruction of the Temple.[54] There in fact seems little doubt, since the Gospels were written after these events, that this is indeed what the Gospel writers are indicating. Christ himself not only predicted that the temple would be destroyed and 'not one stone left upon another', thereby causing enormous offence to the Jewish priestly and political authorities who ruled on behalf of Rome from the Temple, but also predicted that these events would take place within the life time of his followers: 'I tell you this: the present generation will live to see it all' (Mark 13. 30). However, Lindsey, like Darby and Schofield, reads the apocalyptic sayings of the Gospels as referring to events far distant from the time of Christ and the first disciples, events which are said to be happening in the present era, when the 'Jews in Judea' will be forced by conflict to 'flee to the mountains', the precise location of many of the Zionist illegal settlements, and when traditional Sabbath worship will have been restored to Israel by returning Jews. The conflict in Palestine which Jesus predicted is said by dispensationalists to emanate from the 'Northern Kingdom', which Ezekiel, Joel and Daniel are all said to name and which they identify as Russia. On this interpretation, Russia will head up a coalition that includes most of the Arab nations who will make war on Israel, as indeed they had already done in 1967. Egypt as well as Russia are keystones in Lindsey's reading of the biblical predictions concerning the war in Israel. First Russia must be laid waste and destroyed before the end can come and then Egypt, which will have led the opposition to Israel, will be conquered by a fierce foreign king who will rule over them, and who is, for Lindsey, the 'Antichrist'.[55]

Not content with charting the pattern of events in the Middle East, Lindsey wishes to weave many other nations and world political events into his apocalyptic saga. He identifies China, the 'yellow peril', as the great army that will emerge from beyond the Euphrates River (Revelation 9. 16) and 'wipe out a third of the world's population'. The founding of the European Common Market, now the European Union, is also included in this schema: 'we believe that the Common Market and the trend toward the unification of Europe may well be the beginning of the ten-nation confederacy predicted by Daniel and the Book of Revelation'.[56] The final stage of European unification, economic and monetary union, will result in the creation of a revived 'Roman Empire', whose leader will be the 'future fuehrer', the Antichrist himself, whose dark rule must overshadow the earth before the last battle or Armageddon. This leader will be given power to control the economies of the world and everyone will come to wear the 'mark of the beast' as a tattoo on their person. As Lindsey suggests 'in our computerized society, where we are all "numbered" from birth to death, it seems completely plausible that some day in the near future the numbers racket will consolidate and we will have just one number for all our business, money, and credit transactions'.[57] The new world economy and world government will be accompanied by a new global cult as people all over the world turn to idol worship. Lindsey again finds evidence that this is already happening as many of his fellow Americans turn towards astrology and various Eastern-influenced cults. The American Dream for Lindsey has long gone sour; America as the 'city set on a hill' of postmillennialist imagining is replaced by a sinful and pagan America whose people are more and more turning away from the Christian faith and towards the dark.

The end of all these dark happenings will occur in a two-stage process. First, those who remain faithful to Jesus Christ as the true Lord of human history will be raptured, taken up into heaven before the seven-year countdown to Armageddon. In the tradition of the Rapture, which Lindsey recounts, individuals will go missing from their workplaces, their beds or their cars in an instant moment of time when God calls all the elect to be with him in heaven so that they will not have to pass through the last seven years of the 'Great Tribulation'. Second, the world will be caught up in the last great conflagration of Armageddon, or 'World War III', which will happen as a result of the escalation of the crisis in the Middle East. Armageddon is only mentioned once in the Bible, in Revelation 16. 16, and seems to refer to the 'Mount of Megiddo' on the plain of Jezreel in the middle of Palestine. The battle will be so vast that it will cover hundreds of square miles north and south of Jerusalem in 'blood so deep it will approach a horse's bridle'. And the conflict will not end there: 'all the cities of the nations will be destroyed' by the unleashing of nuclear weapons which will 'scorch the earth' and 'rent it asunder' – again as the Bible is said to predict. Only when it seems 'that all life will be destroyed on earth' will Christ return to earth and save those who are left from extinction.[58] Then the promised 1,000-year reign of the saints on earth will commence.

To most European ears, and to many Americans, Lindsey's 'interpretation' of the Bible and of recent political events will seem extremely far-fetched and fantastical. However, *The Late Great Planet Earth* has sold over 40 million copies and is one of the most influential religious texts in America today. Ronald Reagan read it and he read events in the light of it, as witness his interpretation in 1971 of Gaddafi's coup in Libya:

> That's a sign that the day of Armageddon isn't far off … Everything is falling into place. It can't be long now. Ezekiel says that fire and brimstone will be rained upon the enemies of God's people. That must mean that they'll be destroyed by nuclear weapons.[59]

The dispensationalist identification of Russia as a key actor in the end times fuelled the Reagan administration's full-on engagement in the Cold War, and that of some of his predecessors. And Reagan was not alone. More than one-third of Americans believed at that time in the inevitability of a nuclear conflagration, seeing it as part of a divine plan for the end of history which no one nation could do anything to prevent; one-quarter of them also believed that God would spare them from this conflagration because of the Rapture.[60]

One of Reagan's religious mentors, the premillennialist television evangelist James Robison, who was later to pray with George W. Bush on national TV during his Presidential campaign in 1999, declared that peace activists were really heretics because 'any teaching of peace prior to [Christ's] return is heresy ... It's against the Word of God; it's Antichrist'.[61] Analogously, environmental activists were seen as communists and heretics by members of the Reagan administration. Ronald Reagan's first Secretary of the Interior, James Watt, a conservative Pentecostal, testified to a Congressional committee that he believed the return of Christ was imminent. This belief clearly influenced his and Reagan's anti-ecological agenda under which so many environmental regulations were torn up.[62] Bush's links with dispensationalists like Robison and Franklin Graham indicate that he too is a dispensationalist, although his advisors have carefully prevented any reference to such beliefs in his speeches and interviews. But on the environment, on the 'free' market, on Israel, on cuts in federal support for public services and welfare and vast increases in military spending, Bush has followed the dispensationalist Reagan every step of the way. Even the American invasion and occupation of Iraq in 2003, and its provoking of a resistance war within Iraq and terrorist acts against the invading nations, is interpreted by dispensationalists as an end time event, because Revelation 9. 14 – 15 speaks of the release of 'four angels which are bound in the great river Euphrates' who will destroy one-third of men on the earth.[63]

The political leadership of America, which once saw itself as the new Zion, is now mostly converted from postmillennialism to premillennialism in its attitude to the Holy Land: instead of rebuilding Zion in America, America is now committed financially and strategically to rebuilding Zion as the State of Israel. Bush again has acted in a way consistent with this approach, declaring in the first days of his presidency that it was time to take the pressure off Israel and allow the Israelis to deal with the 'Palestinian problem' as they see fit.[64] Since then the Israelis have destroyed the nascent economy and security apparatus of an albeit corrupt Palestinian authority, and driven a vast, heavily fortified wall across hundreds of miles of Palestinian territory, separating Palestinians from their own farms as well as from illegal Israeli settlements. The resultant mass unemployment and malnutrition amongst Palestinians have created unprecedented anger and despair and have generated a new wave of suicide bomb attacks on Israelis.

Making the Middle East safe for a newly aggressive and assertive Israel was also a central aim of the Bush administration in its war and subsequent occupation of Iraq. Egypt, Iraq, Iran, Syria, the Lebanon, even Saudi Arabia after its involvement in the September 11 attacks on the United States, are all said to threaten Israel and America. In this perspective the installation in Iraq of an American economic regimen of privatised public services, and a democratic polity subservient to American corporate, financial and strategic interests, is the core rationale for the American invasion and occupation of Iraq. With an emasculated, privatised and 'democratic' Iraq remodelled along American lines, and acting as an example to other Arab nations, and with a long-term American military presence, the Bush administration intends to make it possible for Israel to defeat the Palestinians, and more especially for Ariel Sharon and his successors to achieve their dream of settling all the 'Biblical' lands of the West Bank and East Jerusalem, and, finally, to rebuild the grand Temple of King Solomon in Jerusalem. For only when the temple is rebuilt can those last acts of history, which the Book of Revelation is said to have predicted, take place. Far from advancing peace in the Middle East, this Zionist foreign policy will only fuel the ire of Islamists and hence perpetuate the 'war on terror'. But given that the end times are indeed a time of perpetual war, this is by no means to be feared, for a final conflagration in the Middle East will bring history to its promised apocalyptic end.

Dividing the Spoils of the End Time

Premillennial dispensationalism is a powerful cultural and religious force in modern America. Among its most insidious effects has been the erosion of the Puritan belief, enshrined in the American Constitution, that because all people are creatures of God, they are all, as the Constitution declares, 'created equal'. In the dispensationalist vision, humanity is divided up into the wicked and true believers. A society deeply influenced by the bad theology of the 'rapture' is a society ideologically prepared for the extreme inequality and social division that have been the consequence of the imposition of neo-liberal 'free' market capitalism since the Reagan administrations of the 1980s. Dispensationalist pessimism about the possibility of forming a fairer society partners the religious fervour with which extreme corporate capitalism has been imposed on American communities, and through the agency of such American-based organisations as the World Bank and the International Monetary Fund, on countries all over the world.

Extreme capitalism has seen the big cities of America fractured by violence and extreme inequality in the last 30 years, while the rich increasingly retreat to their gated communities. Readers may imagine that poverty in the richest nation on earth is not poverty as traditionally understood. But 33 million Americans live below the federal poverty line and over eight million live in homes where they regularly miss meals because of lack of funds.[65] Infant mortality amongst poor Americans is higher than it is in many 'developing' countries. Thousands of poor Americans died in the 2003 heat waves in Chicago and other American cities because they could not afford air-conditioning to cool their cramped apartments, while many again died from the extreme cold that hit the East Coast in early 2004 because they could not afford to heat their homes adequately. The growth in poverty is not the inexorable result of capitalism but a consequence of political decisions by America's corporate elites, to whom Bush has shown himself a loyal President. The Bush administration has cut entitlements of the poor to state-assisted health care, home heating, housing, food, educational and child-care programmes.[66] For Bush, as he indicated in his Inaugural Address, it is the duty of the rich to have compassion on the poor and not the government, and so he gives the rich tax cuts supposedly to enable them to do this. Bush again is no innovator in taking from the poor and giving to the rich. On the contrary as Paul Krugman points out, for the past 30 years tax cuts have consistently favoured the richest 1 per cent of Americans with average incomes of $230,000, while of gains to the richest 1 per cent, 60 per cent went to the richest 0.1 per cent with annual incomes over $790,000.[67] While the poor get poorer the rich are increasingly opting out of the public sphere and, as Robert Kaplan suggests, choosing to live their lives entirely within the 'corporate sphere', in gated communities where 'they give up their personal rights for the sake of economic and physical-safety advantages' that can no longer be had in the increasingly fractured public sphere. Kaplan argues that he and other Americans, 'are very willing to give up our individual rights if it means our property values will be protected, and so on'.[68]

Given the withdrawal of the rich from the public sphere, and the appalling denials of freedoms that are the daily experience of so many less-privileged Americans, given also the domination of America's democratic machinery by corporate donors and the corporate elite, the claim that the September 11, 2001 attack on America was an attack on democracy and freedom is a perverse kind of folly.[69] America is less a democracy than a plutocracy when just 13,000 of America's richest families own more wealth in the form of land, stocks and bonds than the poorest 20 million Americans: 80 per cent of the total wealth of America is now in the hands of just 10 per cent of the people, and the gap gets wider as CEOs are paid on average 1,000 times the wages of their employees.[70] Such extreme inequality corrodes democracy: the 40 per cent of Americans who have to share less than 10 per cent of America's wealth are too busy trying to scratch a living to vote in elections, often holding down two or three poorly paid part-time jobs with no health care or pension entitlements, or else so disillusioned with parties of all political hues in America that they see no point in voting. No society that excludes so many from the good life, while others enjoy incredible levels of wealth, can call itself truly democratic or 'free'. And the corrosion of democracy is not limited to the disappearance of so many voters through a sense of disenfranchisement from American politics. It is blatantly indicated in the extent to which at every level, from City Hall to Presidential elections, corporations and corporate-funded lobby groups fund and determine 'public' policy. As Ted Honderich puts it, 'one person, one vote is fine' but 'what is the rule for influence on the government after the election?'[71]

The extreme inequality that has overtaken the United States in the last 30 years has been promoted by the ideology of the 'free' market, which has been pursued with devotion and zeal by American university economists, by Wall Street financiers and New York media moguls, by Republican and Democrat politicians and by American corporations, who bankroll both parties and elections for both Houses of Congress and Presidential elections to the tune of billions of corporate dollars. But this ideology is not just the result of a shift in the balance of power between capital and labour, or even of the reversion to classical *laissez faire* theory among America's economists. It has also been advanced by evangelical and dispensationalist Christians. The Christian Right has embraced the 'free' market as an exemplar of a truly biblical economy:

> We affirm that the free market economy is the closest approximation man has yet devised in this fallen world to the economy set forth in the Bible, and that, of all the economies known to man, it is the most conducive to producing a free, just, and prosperous society for all people. We deny that central planning and other coercive interferences with personal choice can increase the productivity of society; that the civil government has authority to set the value of property; and that the Bible teaches any "just" price other than that resulting from the interaction of supply and demand in the marketplace of free people.[72]

Far from protesting at the growing evil of social division, conservative evangelical Christian leaders advocate an end to all attempts to regulate the activities of private corporations, including not only minimum wages and environmental regulations but welfare and public health programmes. They regard inheritance tax and other taxes to fund public services and welfare payouts as unwarranted and unbiblical interference in property and inheritance rights, and they call for a more punitive criminal justice system to deal with those who steal rather than work. But while petty thieves can be sent to prison for life under the 'three-strikes' policy of some conservative States, white-collar crime involving the theft of billions through the shady manipulation of company accounts goes unpunished. Both George W. Bush and Dick Cheney have been investigated for irregularities in their business affairs by the Securities and Exchange Commission, but neither individual has ever been indicted.[73]

The Gospel of Luke records that at the angelic Annunciation that she was to bear the saviour, the Virgin Mary rejoiced in the words of a hymn that promised that his rule would reverse the values of Roman imperial power: 'he has put down the mighty from their thrones and exalted the humble and weak, he has filled the hungry with good things and the rich he has sent empty away' (Luke 1. 52 – 3). But in the American Empire many evangelical Christians have embraced an economic doctrine in which the rich are blessed while the poor are sent away empty, the direct opposite of the message of the New Testament.

The combination of privatised individualism and evangelical dispensationalism – and in particular its account of individual rapture – with the adulation of Enron-style corporate capitalism is a tragic example of the capacity of perverted religion and secular ideology to distort human lives and relationships and destroy communities. The roots of this vicious combination are Lockean in shape, even if Locke never imagined the destruction his ideas would eventually produce. Inasmuch as Locke put property before community, industry before ecology, and upturned the biblical conception of creation and land as gifted by God to all people in common, he laid the foundations for the extreme division of the spoils of the New World that Americans now experience. With the failure of the American State both in the 1920s and since the 1970s to ameliorate the social and ecological effects of unbridled corporate capitalism, it is no surprise that the bad theology of Locke should be combined with the pessimistic apocalyptic of Derby, Schofield and Lindsey. Dispensationalism is a classic instance of religion as the 'opiate of the people'. It acts as an ideology, a smoke-screen, which mystifies and shrouds the roots of the extreme social division and growing violence on the streets of America in the deregulatory mania of extreme capitalism from Reagan to Bush junior. Behind the walls and security guards of corporate gated communities, or in the ghettos and deracinated working-class neighbourhoods of post-industrial American cities, rich and poor alike take refuge in the dream that they might be included in the rapture to compensate for the failed dream of a commonwealth of liberty and democracy.

3 – The Unveiling of Empire

The word apocalypse derives from the Greek word *apocalypteo* which means literally 'without veil', or unveiling.[1] The apocalyptic writers of the Old Testament sought to see beneath the surface of present events to discern their true meaning. Their intent was to discern and disclose the divine or hidden hand of God in the events that saw the conquest of the people of Israel by foreign empires after the eighth century B.C.E.[2] Biblical apocalyptic is not so much concerned with the end of the world as it is with the relation between present history – particularly imperial oppression – and the hope of the people of God for the promised reign of God. As C. K. Barrett puts it:

> The secrets in which apocalyptic deals are not simply secrets of the future – of the Age to Come; they include secrets of the present state of the heavenly world. Indeed, these two mysteries, of heaven and the future, are very closely allied, since in apocalyptic the significant future is the breaking into this world of the heavenly world, and to know what is now in heaven is in consequence almost the same as knowing what will be on earth.[3]

The primary intent of the authors of Old Testament apocalyptic was to provide encouragement to the Israelites during their occupation and exile at the hands of the Assyrian, Babylonian and Persian empires. They sought to show that the divine plan was ultimately to overthrow the nations that had conquered Israel and to establish a

direct reign of Yahweh on earth from Jerusalem or Zion. In the mean-
time, the Israelites were to remain faithful in their worship of
Yahweh as the one true God, for he would soon be revealed as the
ruler of the nations.

The Book of Daniel is the *locus classicus* of this style of apocalyptic.
It tells the story of three Israelite men who stood up to the great
Nebuchadnezzar, King of Babylon, and resisted the cult established
for all the people, including the exiled Jews, to worship him. When
the three Jews are cast into the fiery pit as punishment for their faithfulness in continuing to pray to Yahweh and not to the King, they
survive without a blemish and are consequently admired and
achieve high office in the court of the King. The lesson of this
story for its vanquished Israelite readers would have been clear: they
may have been forced into servitude and exile hundreds of miles
from their homeland, their temple in Jerusalem may have been
ruined and their cities sacked, but whatever the unrighteous
demands of their oppressors, they were to resist and remain faithful
to Yahweh. One day Yahweh would put down the emperors and
empires that had conquered Israel. Their claims to sovereignty
would be set aside and Yahweh would be revealed as the Lord of all
the nations, and all peoples would come to worship him in a restored
Jerusalem. The rhetoric of biblical apocalyptic is a translation into the
post-exilic period of the anti-imperial and anti-monarchist story that
runs right through the Old Testament. It looks to a time when
Yahweh will once again directly rule over the people of God, without the mediation of any earthly monarch or empire. It also reminds
the Israelites that Yahweh is still on the side of his chosen people,
even though they have become – as they once were in the land of
Egypt – slaves and servants to foreign powers.[4]

John of Patmos, the Christian writer of the Book of Revelation,
also used the Jewish apocalyptic panoply in composing a Christian
apocalyptic text. His aim was to encourage and inspire Christians
who were persecuted by the Roman authorities in the late first
century to remain faithful to Christ. But while adopting the symbol-
ism of Old Testament apocalyptic, Revelation is also a work of great
novelty, which presents the impact of Christian understanding on
human and cosmic history in an imaginative and visionary way.[5] As
Christopher Rowland indicates, the imaginative appeal of Revelation

arises precisely from its 'challenge to the *status quo* and its evocation of a better world, all linked to a passionate concern for present responsibility'. The writer reconceives the world in the light of the Resurrection of Christ as a New World in which good is overcoming evil, and where God and humanity dwell together on the earth:

> The book of Revelation thus shows us that the world is no longer to be accepted as it is, that what passes for reality is to be unmasked and the frequent collusion of the world of 'common sense' with evil forces revealed. Its whole drama represents a struggle for wholeness, in which the separation between heaven and earth, God and humanity are at last overcome when God tabernacles with men and women.[6]

The real meaning of Revelation is that the Roman Empire – variously the 'beast', the 'dragon', the 'whore of Babylon' – and the Roman emperor – the Antichrist – are already defeated. The Roman Empire may appear still to reign supreme, but the time is not long before all nations, and even the 'whore of Babylon', will come to acknowledge the Lordship of Christ. Revelation is in other words a powerfully anti-imperial tract. Its coded and symbolic language pointed the first Christians to the real truth of history, which is that all empires, including Rome, will ultimately fail and be supplanted by the direct rule of God through the communion of the saints.

The Sacralisation of American Empire

It is a tragic deformation of Biblical apocalyptic that in America for more than two centuries millennialism, far from unveiling empire, has served as a sacred ideology that has cloaked the expansionary tendencies of America's ruling elites. They use millennialism to veil their construction of an empire in which the many are in service to the power and wealth of the few. Instead of an unveiling, we have here a veiling, and apocalyptic becomes an ideology that masks the truth of imperial oppression both at home and abroad.[7] So effective is the ideological veil that mystifies American power that many Americans have no conception of the imperial character of US foreign policy either in the present or in the last 200 years, and they are prevented from discovering it by the US mass media, which are in almost complete thrall to the corporate elite who rule the empire. But former US army general Andrew Bacevich suggests that 'during the twentieth century the United States came to play a role that cannot be understood except as a variant of empire'.[8] With the end of the Cold War, talk of American empire has come in from the cold and passed from communist and leftist critique to become a part of 'the lexicon of everyday discourse about U.S. foreign policy' in the United States.[9] As the historian Arthur Schlesinger put it, 'who can doubt that there is an American empire? – an informal empire, not colonial in polity but still richly equipped with imperial paraphernalia: troops, ships, planes, bases, proconsuls, local collaborators, all spread around the luckless planet'.[10] The essential aim of American empire was to 'open the world to American enterprise' for without an open world the American system of political economy, with its inbuilt expansionist logic, could not function effectively.[11]

The view that America works best in a world shaped by American military power and subjected to American economic exploitation is now at the core of American foreign policy. With the evident failure of America as a 'redeemer nation' in Southeast Asia, a new realism entered into American foreign policy deliberation in subsequent decades. The analysis goes that America was drawn into the Vietnam War primarily in the interests of stopping communism rather than advancing its own economic interests. Vietnam, Cambodia and Laos were after all part of the Francophone world and few American companies were involved in the region; furthermore there was no oil. In the 15 years of American involvement in Vietnam, Laos and Cambodia, more than one million people were killed or wounded, and in the subsequent genocide of the terrible Pol Pot, whose rise was brought about by the horrific carpet-bombing and destruction of Cambodia by Nixon and Kissinger, millions more died. The mistake in Southeast Asia, according to the new realism, was that the US intervened in three countries when it had no clear economic interests at stake. This realism was crisply encapsulated by Casper Weinberger as 'a belief in overwhelming force employed decisively on behalf of American interests'.[12] President Clinton's Secretary of State Madeleine Albright expressed a similar sentiment when she explained an American cruise missile attack on Iraq: 'If we have to use force it is because we are America. We are the indispensable nation. We stand tall. We see farther into the future'.[13]

Paul Wolfowitz, one of the major figures in the George W. Bush administration, worked in the Pentagon under the administration of George Bush Senior. He elaborated at that time in much more open terms than any previous military strategist an openly imperial and self-interested policy, which did away with the former pretence of America as a redeemer nation acting disinterestedly on the world stage for the sake of humanity. In the wake of the successful trouncing of Iraq by the American military and its allies in the first Gulf War, Wolfowitz wrote a controversial Defence Planning document, in which he suggested that American foreign policy in future should be directed toward seeing off all potential competitors for American superpower dominance on the world stage. America should present itself as the sole world power able to defend the interests of the advanced industrial nations and should devote itself both militarily and diplomatically to 'deterring potential competitors from even aspiring to a larger regional or global role'.[14]

The Bush Senior administration rejected the Wolfowitz approach, but later in the 1990s key figures in the George W. Bush administration, including Dick Cheney, Donald Rumsfeld and Richard Perle, teamed up to embrace and further elaborate the Wolfowitz doctrine. Under the banner of the Project for the New American Century, they stated that their goal was 'to promote American global leadership' and 'to shape a new century favorable to American principles and interests'.[15] In the first year of the new century the PNAC issued a document entitled 'Rebuilding America's Defenses', whose key findings read like a precise account of the military engagements and foreign policy of the administration of George W. Bush. They declare that the first core mission of the US military is 'to defend the American homeland', and after September 11 the Bush administration established the 'Homeland Defence Force'. The second core mission is to 'fight and decisively win multiple, simultaneous major theater wars' and since September 11 the United States has engaged in two major wars in the different 'theaters' of Afghanistan and Iraq, while providing 'military assistance' in the Philippines, Columbia and Haiti.[16] The document suggests that despite the end of the Cold

War, there is an urgent need to increase defence spending if America is to preserve its dominant place in the world order, something that George W. Bush promised to do in his Inaugural speech, and on which he has followed through. The report commends the development and deployment of 'global missile defences', which is essentially the revival of the Reagan-inspired anti-ballistic missile defence system known as 'Star Wars' – again an initiative of the George W. Bush administration.[17] The document also recommends that America polices much more actively the proliferation of 'weapons of mass destruction' and argues for military interventions in Iraq, Iran, Syria and North Korea in this regard.[18] Again the list of miscreant nations is remarkably close to the 'axis of evil' that Bush identified after September 11, 2001.

These new defence initiatives are designed to preserve a global *pax Americana*, which can provide 'the geopolitical framework for widespread economic growth and the spread of American principles of liberty and democracy'. This geopolitical framework is said to be threatened by events in East and Central Asia, by the rise of China, and by events in the Middle East. US forces should be redeployed from their Cold War bases in Northern Europe and Northeast Asia to the Persian Gulf and Southeast and Central Asia, locating permanent American bases in the areas where *pax Americana* is most threatened.[19] Now again it is intriguing how close these plans are to what has actually happened since 2001. US forces are now deployed in considerable strength in Afghanistan, Kazakhstan, Iraq and Kuwait as well as Saudi Arabia. The only gap in the strategy is Southeast Asia, although an American force was sent to the Philippines soon after September 11, 2001.

The Bush administration moved swiftly after September 11, 2001 to translate the PNAC strategy into executive action with its publication of the National Security Strategy. The document announced that America under Bush will use its unique strength and influence in every region of the world to pursue 'a distinctly American internationalism that reflects the union of our values and our national interests'.[20] The means to achieve this will be a vastly enhanced military budget which will enable America to strike pre-emptively at any potential threat, any rogue state, any nation that harbours terrorists and any nation that threatens to develop weapons of mass destruction. The PNAC therefore anticipates both the new aggressive, unilateral and pre-emptive military strategy of the Bush administration after September 11, 2001 and its openly imperial pursuit of global economic and military dominance.

Despite the new doctrine of pre-emptive strikes and the 'war on terror', the Bush administration's pursuit of global hegemony is not in itself novel. Bush's predecessor in the White House, William Jefferson Clinton, actively sought to manage the cultural, economic and technological innovations driving globalisation in such a way as to put America in the driving seat of the global economy.[21] Clinton established as the central goal of his administration the effort to control and dominate the new and increasingly borderless global economy, and the information revolution that was advancing it. The two major economic projects of the Clinton era – the creation of the North American Free Trade Area, and the World Trade Organisation – were both central to this strategy. Clinton had no dispute with the Republican speaker of the House of Congress, Newt Gingrich, who said that by dominating the new era of globalisation, America would become 'a country unmatched in wealth, power, and opportunity'.[22] America would be able to dominate and mould globalisation in its own image and after its own interests not only through its prowess in computers, satellites and software, which dominated the information revolution, but through the ubiquity of American brand names, entertainment products and economic and political values.[23]

Like Clinton, Bush and the Bush White House see globalisation – the opening of borders to American investment and trade – as the means for spreading American values, and in particular the American understanding of freedom, for 'the expectation of freedom is fed by free markets and expanded by free trade, and carried across borders by the Internet'.[24] The real difference between Bush and his predecessors is not over the right and necessity for American global dominance, but in the extent, and especially since September 11, to which Bush sees its pursuit as a matter of all-out war against any potential source of opposition, including dissent at home as well as terrorist and 'failed states' abroad. To be sure, as Gore Vidal and Noam Chomsky tirelessly point out, Carter, Reagan, Bush Senior and Clinton all used American military power to bomb or invade other sovereign states including Grenada, Nicaragua, Panama, Libya,

Somalia and the Sudan without reference to the United Nations.[25] But September 11 was the event that enabled the Bush administration uniquely to turn the war for markets dominated by American corporations into a military crusade. September 11 gave the Bush White House the same opportunity to press for American 'full spectrum dominance' that the Japanese, the Nazis and the Russians had given his predecessors. As Bacevich says, the new war 'on behalf of freedom and against evil akin to Nazism relegitimated the exercise of American power', and further 'Bush's war against terror and for freedom was at its core a war on behalf of the American project of creating an open and integrated world'.[26]

More than two hundred years ago, at the dawn of the European Enlightenment, of which Americans believe themselves the true inheritors, Immanuel Kant penned an essay entitled 'Perpetual Peace'.[27] It was Kant's belief that the light of reason, and the supplanting of religion by constitutional rule drawn up on rationalist lines, would bring an end to war and ultimately produce the perfect world, the paradise on earth, which the Enlightenment was said to presage. It is a strange irony then that finds a Christian President of a secular Republic using the apocalyptic language of crusade, sacred charge, universal good and axis of evil, to prosecute a pre-emptive military campaign without territorial limit against a predominantly Islamic enemy in defence of Enlightenment notions of freedom. Throughout the 'war on terror', Bush in his famous doublespeak declares that 'America will lead the world to peace'.[28] But if peace means the absence of conflict and the pacifying of enemies, then American actions in the 'war on terror' would seem only to have stirred up more hatred against America and its allies.

The Intellectual Roots of the New Imperialism

The new imperial realism of PNAC and its militaristic pursuit by the Bush administration has not developed in an intellectual vacuum. It has been in the making for a long time. It reflects a major shift in American political and social thought in the last 40 years, which may first be glimpsed in the ideas of philosopher Friedrich Hayek, the political theorist Leo Strauss and the economist Milton J. Friedman.

Almost the whole programme of the self-styled 'neo-conservatives' who run George W. Bush's administration can be traced back to the ideas of Hayek, Strauss and Friedman, and a number of them, including John Ashcroft and Paul Wolfowitz, were students of Strauss in Chicago.

The core idea of Friedrich Hayek's critique of socialism in *The Road to Serfdom* is that State action directed toward the moral improvement of society is bound to result in oppression and tyranny.[29] Writing during the Second World War and with the exemplars of Hitler and Stalin still stalking the world stage and visiting evil on millions of people, Hayek argued that the State is intrinsically violent and coercive and that therefore the best that can be done with it is to minimise its influence and legal power. Citing Friedrich Hoelderlin's statement that 'what has always made the state a hell on earth has been that man has tried to make it his heaven', Hayek sees State action to improve the human condition, whether to help an individual in poverty or to prevent a company from harming the environment, as invariably coercive, restrictive of individual freedom, and therefore immoral.[30]

Leo Strauss added another dimension to Hayek's perspective when he proposed in his teaching and writing in the University of Chicago in the 1950s and '60s that it was a fundamental error to view the political ends and capacities of the modern nation-state in moral terms. Unlike the complex and dispersed political structures of the era of the Greek city-states, the first era of democracy, the modern democratic State is characterised by a tendency to centralise and monopolise power, and to coerce those who would resist this process of power concentration through its monopoly of violence, both in terms of police power and the military. The good society for Strauss was therefore not a product of State power, for it is not possible to coerce people to be good. Neither is it possible to create a society or social systems to promote the good unless first the people themselves become good. Virtuous individuals, not the regulatory State, lie at the heart of the good society.[31] Only individuals of good character can decide to act together to create moral communities. Statist efforts to engineer a better society through redistributing wealth or providing services to advance collective well-being are therefore doubly misguided. The modern nation-state is too large, and too coercive to be capable of engineering the good society. When it purloins the wealth of individuals to do what the State is singularly ill-equipped to do, it undermines the freedom and the responsibility of moral individuals, and of moral communities or 'small platoons', to achieve the good society for themselves.[32]

The economic logic that flowed from Strauss's political vision of the virtuous individual and Hayek's account of the malign State was taken up by the Chicago economist Milton Friedman and, under his influence, by the Reagan administration. What was needed was not wealth redistribution but entrepreneurialism, not state action to ameliorate poverty but virtuous citizens who would know how to avoid poverty for themselves and how to assist those who still suffered from it should they happen to be their neighbours. What is now called 'compassionate conservatism' became the new welfare, and the State was portrayed as an illegitimate interloper into the freedoms of families and communities to help themselves. In sum, neo-liberal economics represented a return of nineteenth-century *laissez faire* economic dogma and the abandonment of the idea that the State is even capable of doing good. Administrations since Reagan, whether Republican or Democrat, have consequently rolled back Federal government spending on welfare, health care, education and public works, while increasing Federal government spending on policing, prisons and the military. The State's only truly legitimate role in neo-liberal perspective is to prevent criminal activity and promote 'security', and especially to protect property and the wealth of private citizens or American corporations, whether at home or abroad.

Both the moral and strategic elements of neo-liberalism are clearly evident in the speeches and policies of the Bush administration. But Bush adds another crucial component to the emergent neo-imperial agenda, and this is a combination of dispensationalist apocalyptic rhetoric and more mainstream elements of American Protestant social ethics, especially the 'Christian realist' tradition of Reinhold Niebuhr. In his Inaugural Speech, Bush suggested that Americans had been too dependent on the State to achieve the good society, and that this had undermined the realisation of self-reliant, virtuous and active citizens who play their part in responding to the needs of their neighbours rather than relying on the state to provide for them:

Government has great responsibilities for public safety and public health, for civil rights and common schools. Yet compassion is the work of a nation, not just a government.

In his opposition to welfare and Medicaid, to public funding of abortions and stem cell research, Bush claims that God is on his side in a battle of good over evil, which opposes noble and compassionate individuals and active citizens with an overweening and immoral state. He also suggests that Americans in the past had a stronger tradition of service and self-sacrifice than they sometimes realise in the present. The challenge he suggests is to move from the cynical goal of 'service of self' to the moral call of service to the common good, and against the forces of evil:

America, at its best, is a place where personal responsibility is valued and expected. Encouraging responsibility is not a search for scapegoats, it is a call to conscience. And though it requires sacrifice, it brings a deeper fulfillment. ... Our public interest depends on private character, on civic duty and family bonds and basic fairness, on uncounted, unhonored acts of decency which give direction to our freedom.

Bush then declares an intention to encourage individuals and faith-based organisations to respond to the suffering of helpless, poor and unemployed Americans:

Some needs and hurts are so deep they will only respond to a mentor's touch or a pastor's prayer. Church and charity, synagogue and mosque lend our communities their humanity, and they will have an honored place in our plans and in our laws. Many in our country do not know the pain of poverty, but we can listen to those who do. And I can pledge our nation to a goal: When we see that wounded traveller on the road to Jericho, we will not pass to the other side.[33]

Private virtue, individual acts of kindness, personal compassion, religiously motivated charity, these are the marks of the America Bush wants to see. The framework for their realisation will be a

society that respects private property and individual freedom, which
limits the pecuniary demands of the state on the wealthy – he
specifically promised to 'reduce taxes' in the speech even while
claiming that Americans have a duty to tackle 'deep poverty' –
and which promotes compassion through private charity and
encouragement for religious groups to do what they can do better
than the State:

> Where there is suffering, there is duty. Americans in need are
> not strangers, they are citizens, not problems, but priorities.
> And all of us are diminished when any are hopeless.
> Government has great responsibilities for public safety and
> public health, for civil rights and common schools. Yet com-
> passion is the work of a nation, not just a government.

Bush's rhetoric manifests that strange conundrum in neoliberal
or what is now called 'neo-conservative' thinking, when he uses
human suffering to evoke the action of the good citizen, while
promising tax cuts and military spending to benefit the rich and the
corporations and to enforce the 'message of freedom' on parts of the
world that still resist it. Bush's conception of public action, like that
of Hayek and Strauss, is that it is intrinsically coercive and therefore
morally dubious, while only private individuals and their religious
and charitable enterprises may be compassionate and ameliorate
human suffering. The paradox, and indeed the inconsistency, is
however that he has not chosen to reduce State spending. On the
contrary, he has created the biggest budget deficit in US history – 374
billion dollars at the time of writing and rising by 1.6 billion dollars
a day – through a quixotic combination of tax cuts and a vast
military budget.[34] This is no minimalist State, but one whose
gargantuan appetite for the money of its citizens and the resources
of the world knows no bounds.

The story Bush wants to tell about American values and virtues
is also a false one. His rhetoric evokes a society of sacrificial and
compassionate neighbours, but decades of rampant consumerism,
technological idolatry and extreme individualism have fostered a
deeply demoralised culture, as Richard Stivers powerfully argues
in *The Culture of Cynicism*.[35] With the number of abortions as well as

executions and incarcerations at record levels, America appears to be embracing a culture of death as celebrated by so many of the darker Hollywood movies, apocalyptic novels and necrophilic creations of postmodern artists. As critics of globalisation point out, the creation of a putatively borderless market in which there are fewer barriers to American investment and influence is globalising this culture of death.[36] As American corporations buy up natural resources, public services and even water in Latin America and beyond, the ideology of so-called 'free' global markets is producing a situation where the poor are excluded from the most basic of life's necessities by the global market. When economies collapse under the economic burdens imposed by America's bankers and corporations, the consequence is mass hunger in countries such as Argentina, once a relatively orderly and prosperous country.[37] According to UNICEF just 10 per cent of America's annual military budget would be enough to prevent the millions of deaths that occur around the world every year as a consequence of hunger and easily treatable diseases. But military spending and subsidies for energy corporations figure much higher in American interventions in the global market than the ending of human suffering.[38] Again we come to that strange conundrum in Bush's inaugural speech, where he uses human suffering to evoke the action of the good citizen, while promising tax cuts and military spending to benefit the rich and the corporations and coercively spread the 'message of freedom'. His conception of public action seems intrinsically to involve coercion and violence, while only private individuals and their religious and charitable enterprises may be compassionate and ameliorate human suffering.

Bush's extreme division between public coercion and war and private compassion and piety sheds an important light on the relationship between church and state that his administration is fostering. Bush and his supporters are accused of seeking to break down the traditional separation of church and state, and in a sense this is so. In addition to the Office for Faith-Based Initiatives, the Bush White House holds more prayer-meetings and Bible studies among its staff than any previous administration. Bush's Attorney General John Ashcroft holds prayer and Bible study with staff in his office on a daily basis. Richard Land of the Southern Baptist Convention, a political appointee at the heart of the Bush administration, is critical of secular humanist efforts to 'sanitize the public square of traditional religious perspectives'.[39] Land argues that Christian Americans, and those of other faiths, have a right to gain a hearing for their faith perspectives and values in the public-policy arena, and American children should be able to 'exercise their religious convictions' in public schools.[40]

Does all of this amount to a religious remoralisation of the public arena? Are Americans now ruled, whether they like it or not, by an incipient theocrat? Well, clearly Bush and the Christians on his team do not see themselves as theocrats. Richard Land says that there is a clear difference between individuals who work or speak for religious and confessional organisations and those running for public office. The project is not to Christianise the State, but to reduce its influence over the 'private' lives of Americans, the intent being to empower Americans and their families and faith communities to reclaim the moral terrain of compassion and social service from the State, whose welfare and medical programmes apparently promote 'dependence' and fecklessness rather than good citizenship. In its critique of American public culture and public services as tending morally to disempower and even corrupt individuals, the Bush administration not only reveals its religious zeal for neoliberal economics, but also the influence of the premillennialist perversion of Christianity, which has captivated such large swathes of American conservative Christians.

The contradiction in the Bush and 'neo-con' position is that the prioritisation of individual freedom, private property and personal virtue over democratic and collective efforts to pursue social justice and the common good is by no means a position that can be described as traditional, or conservative, or as promoting a society of virtuous individuals empowered to charitable works. It cannot even be described as conservative, for a truly Burkean or Jeffersonian conservative republicanism included an understanding, however patriarchal, of *noblesse oblige* and of the claims of the common good on the wealthy. As we have seen, under the influence of neoliberal capitalist dogma, the wealthy have retreated into enclaves and gated communities so that they hardly encounter poor people in their neighbourhoods or professional or corporate workplaces, let alone find opportunities to help them out. Wealthy philanthropy, encouraged by tax breaks, is more often directed at maintaining one of the grand institutions of American society – not least the universities and think-tanks in which its higher echelons are educated and socialised – than on charitable works in poor neighbourhoods.

Here is one of the deep unresolved conundrums of the growing influence of the Christian Right on American political economy, of which the election of Bush is just the latest in a series of events that can be traced back to the Reagan era. Bush and the neo-cons win adulation from conservative Christian Republican voters for freeing corporations and wealthy individuals from regulatory or tax burdens, for rolling back New Deal welfarism and for punishing single parents, the unemployed and other 'feckless' individuals with welfare cuts and other punitive measures. Clinton and Gore of course went down this same road, but they did not garner the conservative Christian vote because they were not committed on such core conservative Christian issues as abortion, sexual morality and Israel. That Bush's successor in the White House, either in 2004 or 2008, Democrat or Republican, is likely to go down the same path is just another indicator of the power of the alliance of the religious right and neo-liberal economics, which has formed around what Joseph Stiglitz calls the 'Washington Consensus'.[41] But the question is whether compassionate conservatism is, as Bush and his conservative Christian supporters believe, truly a move away from secular humanism in American politics. It looks to American workers and the poor, and to the victims of the Washington Consensus overseas, much more like the reassertion of the secular power of liberalised corporate capital over workers and ordinary citizens, albeit dressed up in the transcendent garments of apocalyptic crusade, piety and virtue.

Bringing On the Apocalypse

We have seen thus far that the pessimistic turn of American social and political thought in the latter half of the twentieth century parallels the turn of American apocalyptic and millennial theology from the optimistic postmillennialism of Jonathan Edwards or the Social Gospel movement, to the end-of-the-world premillennial scenarios of Darby and Lindsey, and the Moral Majority. The question arises whether there is any relationship between these parallel shifts in economic and religious cultures. The obvious link is that both neo-liberal, or what is now called neo-conservative, political theory and premillennial theology are deeply pessimistic about the possibility of a moral America or a better world. For both, the dream of a righteous America, of America as a 'city set on a hill' has failed. Both also view American power more in terms of self-interest rather than the promotion of global cooperation. Bush has even attempted to raise tariffs on imports, such as steel from Europe, to protect industry at home, even though his country is formally committed through the World Trade Organisation to 'free trade'.

The Bush administration has also sidelined the United Nations with its pre-emptive strike policy, and has opposed international cooperation on such matters as climate change and arms limitation. Its approach to arms reduction is to threaten to invade countries it suspects may possess, or may intend to develop 'weapons of mass destruction', while it goes on stockpiling such weapons on its own behalf and selling them to its currently perceived allies, though of course they – like Saddam Hussein – may turn bad in the future when they cease to serve American interests. Dispensationalists are, like Bush, deeply critical of international gatherings of nations, and especially the United Nations and the European Union, which they view as indicative of end time accounts of a pernicious world government that will eventually invite the Antichrist to head it up. For dispensationalists, as for Bush, American power is best when used unilaterally, because it has a unique role to play in the end time in both making the Middle East safe for Israel and in promoting the kind of global winner-takes-all in which history will come to an end.

There is an intriguing synergy here between the kind of individualistic perspective on apocalyptic history that views the end of history fatalistically as just approaching inexorably in the midst of wars and rumours of wars, and the understanding of society as best managed not by purposive, and certainly not by moral, government but rather by the invisible hand of the market, which connects and mediates all the individual decisions of purchasers and providers of goods and services. For the premillennialist, righteous individuals will be mysteriously and suddenly plucked from their beds or workplaces by the divine hand and so rescued from the coming conflagration of Armageddon at the 'Rapture'. For the free marketeer, individuals will be redeemed by the invisible hand of market forces. In neither case can collective action decisively affect their fate.

It is in the light of the dual effects of these two kinds of fatalism – dispensationalist fatalism and the ideology of a 'free' market, which is in reality a market rigged to maximise corporate power at the expense of citizens in and beyond the United States – that the increasingly brutal as well as self-interested assertion of American imperial power on every continent in the last few years can be better understood. The US corporate elite increasingly see themselves as engaged in a planetary war for the maintenance of their own prosperity and way of life, and for the directing of all human history to American ends. In this war there are no holds barred, nothing is anymore unthinkable, even the first use of nuclear weapons. The United States under Bush has not only turned its massive military budget towards a new Star Wars anti-ballistic missile system but it has also begun to invest vast sums in the development of a new generation of usable, battle-field nuclear weapons.[42]

The depths of the dark side of the new demoralised conception of social, and especially of American, power that the synergy of these two ideologies has brought about in the Bush administration are great indeed, and the Bush administration itself has done everything in its power to prevent this darkness from being lit up, whether by Congressional investigations or the media. And this darkness includes the events that surround the September 11 tragedy itself. As we have seen, the PNAC had been arguing for some years that there was an urgent need for America to increase its military spending dramatically, to refocus its strategic thinking on homeland security, by which it meant economic as well as military security, to move against potential threats and to use the military to advance American interests in the oil-rich regions of the Middle East and Central Asia. The imposition by force of American-style democracy and privatisation regimens in the Central Asian region was advanced in 1997 by Zbigniew Brzezinski, who had been National Security Advisor under the Carter Administration. Brzezinski suggested that 'the three grand imperatives of imperial strategy are to prevent collusion and maintain security dependence among the vassals, to keep tributaries pliant and protected, and to keep the barbarians from coming together', and in the context of Central Asia this meant militarily asserting American primacy in the region.[43] However, Brzezinski observes that garnering public support for the requisite militarisation of American geopolitical strategy in this distant region would be very hard involving as it would a major shift in the priorities of the Pentagon, the State Department and other agencies of American government. Brzezinski's account of Empire is very reminiscent of an earlier account of Roman imperial strategy by the Austrian political economist Joseph Shumpeter:

> There was no corner of the known world where some interest was not alleged to be in danger or under actual attack. If the interests were not Roman, they were those of Rome's allies; and if Rome had no allies, then allies would be invented. When it was impossible to contrive such an interest – why, then it was the national honour that was being insulted. The fight was always invested with an aura of legality. Rome was always being attacked by evil-minded neighbours, always fighting for a breathing space. The whole world was pervaded with a host of enemies and it was manifestly Rome's duty to guard against their indubitably aggressive designs.[44]

This way of looking at the world is powerfully evident in the rhetoric of the Bush administration and in the militarisation of American geopolitical strategy first commended by the PNAC. But the problem for the Bush administration was how to give such a strategy some kind of legal legitimacy. The PNAC had suggested that what was needed was 'a new Pearl Harbor', or in other words an attack of some kind on the American homeland. That another Pearl Harbor came along in the shape of the terrorist attacks was therefore fortuitous for an administration which until this point had lacked legitimacy, and therefore had little chance of being able overtly to pursue its ambitious geopolitical designs. After September 11, however, everything changed.

There can be no question that in one sense much did change on that day, but it is a matter of record that the geopolitical designs of the Bush administration did not change on that day but simply passed from a wish list into an activated programme under the new aegis of the rapidly announced 'war on terror'. The Bush administration brought forward enabling legislation within days of the attacks both to suppress resistance to this project at home – in the form of the draconian Patriot Act – and to advance regime change and prosecute pre-emptive strikes against any state or region of the world deemed hostile to the United States. The opportunity to suppress dissent at the geopolitical and imperial hegemony of the United States was extremely timely, as only weeks before September 11 hundreds of thousands of demonstrators had gathered in Genoa to challenge the legitimacy of the institutions through which America exercised its economic and imperial hold around the world – the International Monetary Fund, the World Bank and the World Trade Organisation. Similarly, American intentions in Afghanistan before September 11 would have been extremely hard to achieve, but afterwards the military invasion and occupation of the country was rapidly advanced under the guise of the 'war on terror', although Osama bin Laden was himself never caught, and though most of his associates did not actually come from Afghanistan but Saudi Arabia.

The coincidence between the events of September 11 and the need for a major security crisis to enable the Bush administration to achieve its geopolitical intent adds urgency to the question of just how much the Bush administration knew about the possibility of attacks on New York and Washington before they actually took place, and whether or not they might have been prevented. American intelligence and civil aviation agencies had known since 1995 that bin Laden and Al-Qaeda had intentions to crash hijacked planes into the World Trade Center in New York, and certain other sites of strategic significance in the United States. In 2000 and 2001 knowledge that a plan was coming to fruition was indicated in regular intelligence briefings at the Whitehouse under both Clinton and G. W. Bush. The FBI had warnings from a number of its operatives in 2000 and 2001 that Arabs attending flight schools in Florida, Phoenix and elsewhere seemed more interested in learning to steer planes in the air than either taking off or landing them. US and Israeli intelligence received warnings of the likelihood of an attack in 2001, and all US security agencies were warned of an impending Al-Qaeda attack in the weeks before September 11. Furthermore, American intelligence agencies were closely monitoring telephone calls between Al-Qaeda cells both within and outside the United States. In particular ABC news reported that they recorded a large number of telephone conversations made to the hijackers in the United States by bin Laden's chief of operations, Abu Zubaida, in the days immediately preceding the attack, though the content of the recordings has never been made public.[45] Suspicion of the possibility of an attack was so strong that, according to a *Newsweek* report, a number of Pentagon officials cancelled plans to travel by air on September 11.[46]

The failure of the US Intelligence Services to forewarn the American people of the possibility of attacks on September 11 has been explained under various scenarios – a failure to join up reports from the flying schools to central intelligence authorities, a lack of coordination between the CIA and the FBI, a failure of communication between the Intelligence agencies, the Federal Aviation Authority and the White House. The Bush administration is not keen to shine the light of day on these matters and it acted powerfully and swiftly after September 11 to prevent any of the papers, phone calls, intelligence briefings and other information that the White House received from the intelligence services in the months and weeks prior to the September 11 events from being reviewed by the Congressional investigation into these events, although one such Presidential briefing, in August 2001, referring to a possible Al-Qaeda attack, was finally published under pressure from the Congressional investigation in March 2004. Bush has also signed an unprecedented Presidential order that blocks access to the Presidential papers of any American President for the lifetime of that President.

How much or little the Bush administration knew before September 11 we may never know. What we do know is that in the days leading up to the attacks, a short-term plan for the invasion and occupation of Afghanistan, and a medium-term plan to invade and occupy Iraq were both already on the desks of members of the administration. They also had plans to extend America's military presence in the Central Asian region in order to lend support to American corporations in their designs on the considerable oil reserves in the Caspian region. All of these plans have come to fruition in the months and years since September 11 under the aegis of the 'war on terror'.

The 'war on terror' is something far more than a conventional policing action against certain individuals or groups who planned and resourced the terror attacks on the American East Coast. Behind it lies a long-planned geopolitical strategy to establish American military supremacy in the Middle East and Central Asia, and indeed the wars in Afghanistan and Iraq have seen the establishment of a number of new bases in the former Soviet republics of Kazakhstan and Tajikistan. It has been combined with a campaign to suppress resistance to American imperial power both at home and around the world. The invasion and occupation of Afghanistan and Iraq as part of the alleged 'war on terror' has allowed the United States and its corporations long-term secure access to the under-exploited oil reserves of Iraq, and to newly discovered reserves in the Caspian region. However, this war is certainly not just about oil. A far larger geopolitical and imperial strategy lies behind the war on terror and the events leading up to it. As Bacevich puts it, the war on terror is 'a conflict waged *on behalf* of the American imperium, a war in which, to fulfil its destiny as the New Jerusalem, the United States, as never before, is prepared to exert its authority as the New Rome'.[47]

Sacrificial Violence and the Imperial Cult of Liberty

That Empires demand sacrifices in human lives is well known to those who have charted the wars of imperial conquest through human history. Imperial power is the most deadly of all human political and economic arrangements and yet throughout human history emperors and empires have arisen to dominate large regions of the earth and large numbers of subject peoples. Babylon, Persia, Rome, Spain, Portugal, Britain, France, Belgium, Holland, Germany, Japan, the Soviet Union, China, the United States – the list is long and the list of the victims of empire is, in biblical parlance, as countless as grains of sand on the sea shore. These empires have also and often spawned religious cults to legitimate and sanctify their violent sacrifices. The cult that often serves this purpose in America is civil religion, which, in partnership with American millennialism, has served very effectively to sacralise the 'war on terror' and the larger neo-conservative imperial agenda.

Jean Jacques Rousseau might be said to have originated the concept of civil religion when he suggested in *The Social Contract* that there is 'a purely civil profession of faith of which the Sovereign should fix the articles, not exactly as religious dogmas, but as social sentiments without which a man cannot be a good citizen or a faithful subject'.[48] Such a faith does not compete with other religions, but rather it is grounded on tolerance of all religions 'so long as their dogmas contain nothing contrary to the duties of citizenship'. Civil religion of this kind was seen by Rousseau, as by Emile Durkheim, as providing the ritual focus for citizen commitment to the new society, a kind of social cement for the modern Republic.

Rousseau's ideas were embraced enthusiastically in America. While children in American public schools are not supposed to participate in public prayer, they do participate in a daily patriotic ritual before the American flag in which they repeat a vow of allegiance to American values. Similarly, would-be citizens must salute the flag and profess that they own the values and beliefs that make a person an American. As Robert Bellah argues, Americans through their history have developed 'a collection of beliefs, symbols and rituals with respect to sacred things and institutionalized in a collectivity' that amounts to a civil religion:

> American civil religion has its own prophets and its own martyrs; its own sacred events and sacred places; its own solemn rituals and symbols. It is concerned that America be a society as perfectly in accord with the will of God as men can make it, and a light to all the nations.[49]

American civil religion is the religion that is America, and at the core of this religion are the rituals of the American flag. Carolyn Marvin and David Ingle argue that the flag is the primitive totem that lies at the heart of a sacrificial system binding American citizens together as a nation. Drawing on the totemic theory of Durkheim, they propose that the flag is 'the emblem of the group's agreement to be a group'.[50] The flag is marked as magical and sacred by legal attempts to outlaw the burning of the flag, by rituals that require children to salute the flag in school, in uniformed organisations, and on camps, by its placement in the sanctuary of many churches as well as in all government and court buildings, above all by its use to wrap the coffins of America's war dead, and its precise ritual folding and gift-ing to the partner or parents of the slain as a lasting totemic reminder of the victim. The sacrificial system of which the flag is the totem is 'endlessly re-enacted in patriotic life and ritual', from the everyday ceremonial saluting of the flag to special events such as Presidential election campaigns, sustained with masses of flag-waving supporters and images of the flag on hustings, and the use of the flag by America's military in America's wars. But while the structure of the mythic life of the nation, which the flag rituals sustain, is familiar to Americans, the secret that the totem conceals is that

> blood sacrifice preserves the nation. Nor is the sacrifice that counts that of our enemy. The totem secret, the collective group taboo, is the knowledge that society depends on the death of its own members, *at the hands of the group*.[51]

The very existence of the religion of America, and its requirement that Americans offer up their adult offspring for its numerous and regular wars, is obscured by the mythology of American individual-ism. As the overt 'defining myth of America', individualism dis-guises the collective requirement of human sacrifice by identifying the victims of this violent blood-letting as 'sacrificial heroes' who freely choose to risk their lives in a heroic and virtuous fashion for the noble cause of America.[52] The taboo that the enduring myth of American individualism helps to maintain is the totemic need for violence which is at the heart of American nationalism.

The anthropologist René Girard argues that violent sacrifice is at the core of all ritual systems. This is because rituals with a sacrificial element – not all sacrificial rituals involve the death of a victim – are means that societies utilise to contain competition and rivalry, and to prohibit murder and violence outside of legally and ritually defined contexts. The individual who is chosen as the victim is in effect a scapegoat for the community. In order to deal with crises that seem to threaten the community's identity – sickness, climatic events, sibling or group rivalry – the scapegoat is burdened with the threats or shortcomings that the group experiences and is persecuted or cast out, shamed or killed.[53] Of course, modern Americans do not consciously see themselves as inhabiting such a sacred and sacrificial victim system. Blood sacrifice is seen as a feature of primitive societies – for example, of native American communities – rather than of the modern enlightened and progressive society that is America. But Girard finds that mimetic violence, scapegoating, and sacrificial systems exist in almost all societies, including the modern. He argues that the modern combination of ritual victimage with science and technology is far more dangerous than primitive victimage systems, because technologies of mass slaughter threaten humanity not just with the occasional ritual killing of individuals, or even large numbers of individuals, but with complete annihilation.[54]

In their account of blood sacrifice in America, Marvin and Ingle acknowledge their debt to Girard when they suggest that the 'collective victimage' associated with the American flag 'constructs American national identity'. They identify an ambiguous relation of the denominational religions of America to this collective victimage system. Officially, the United States gives freedom to all religious groups as denominations or sects and this freedom seems to indicate that there is no religious monopoly in America. But this is ironic, because while denominationalism gives up the claim of religious monopoly to the State, it sustains the reality that the State in America is in effect the deity of American civil religion because only the State, and not the deity, is capable of demanding sacrifice. The State, and not the denomination, has the monopoly on violence and on killing:

> The first principle of every religious system is that only the deity may kill. The state, which does kill, allows whoever accepts these terms to exist, to pursue their own beliefs and call themselves what they like in the process. In the broadest sense, the purpose of religion is to organize killing energy. This is how it accomplishes its social function of defining and organizing the group. By this standard, nationalism is unquestionably the most powerful religion in the United States.[55]

While it is taboo to admit that blood sacrifice is the organising principle of the United States, it is clearly indicated in the extensive mobilisation of the flag in military institutions and rituals, including the complex death rituals that require the return of the bodies of

American war dead to the soil of the United States shrouded in the flag, revealing the true proximity of the flag rituals of the Stars and Stripes to the enduring practice of bloody sacrifice.

There could be no more powerful illustration of the extent to which the flag is the transcendent symbol at the heart of the American victimage cult of nationalism than the mass display of the flag in the outpouring of patriotism right across America after the events of September 11. So many people displayed the Stars and Stripes outside their homes that those who chose not to do this were subjected to accusations of a lack of patriotism by their neighbours and friends. As cars and coat lapels were also used for flag display – George W. Bush and his team all began wearing flag badges on their clothing after September 11 – the association between the violent death of Americans in New York and the Pentagon and the patriotic display of the Stars and Stripes has now become culturally ubiquitous in America post-September 11.

This revived cult of the flag powerfully illustrates a central feature of Marvin and Ingle's thesis, which is that it is the violent death of *Americans* and not of America's enemies which is the true sacrifice that is effective in uniting the nation around its totem flag. This insight may also indicate why Americans have been so quick to fall away in their support of the Bush administration in its decision to go to war in Iraq, because while there were tens of thousands of Iraqi dead, there were, thanks to America's overwhelming technological superiority, less than 100 Americans killed in action before the formal phase of the war was declared over, though many more have died since. According to Marvin and Ingle, 'not winning or losing but serious bloodletting is the important factor in ritual success'.[56] Bush's decision to prevent TV footage being shown of the bodies of dead servicemen returning to US air-force bases from the Iraq war may therefore in a strange way turn out to have been counterproductive. The Bush administration clearly believes it was such pictures that turned the tide in the Vietnam War. But there is a strong argument that it was actual reporting of the inhumanity of the war as it affected Vietnamese civilians, and especially photojournalistic images of this inhumanity – such as the little girl filmed running from her napalmed village as the skin fell off her back – which more than anything else galvanised opposition to that war. And so the decision to embed journalists with the troops in Iraq, and the terrorising of those not so embedded, may turn out to have been the more effective piece of news manipulation.[57]

The argument that the civil religion of America is a totemic sacrificial system involving regular militarised conflict and death helps explain why America has always been prepared to commit so many of its people, and so much of its resources, to the military, and to weapons that kill. More than 6 million people served in the Korean war, almost 9 million in the Vietnam War; half a million were engaged in the first Gulf War, and almost as many in the second Gulf War. In these four wars America had more than 110,000 war dead, and 250,000 wounded. None of these were wars that involved any threat to the territorial integrity of the United States. But they served a larger purpose, in advancing the religion of America.

If this thesis is correct then the religion of America is truly a dangerous and death-dealing religion. How is it that American Christianity has so thoroughly acceded the ground to the American nation-state in the maintenance of this cult of blood sacrifice around its totem? As Marvin and Ingle argue, a core part of the answer to this lies in the church–state relationship carved out by the Founding Fathers, which left the churches in charge of the faith and religious experiences of Americans, and the State in charge of their bodies. This division of labour was underlined by nineteenth-century American pragmatic philosophers such as Dewey and William James, who insisted upon the confining of religion to the inner life of humanity while the public realm of politics was supposed to be ordered by pragmatic judgement and reason. James, who was the author of the modern conceptualisation of religion as experience, defined religion in his *Varieties of Religious Experience* as 'the feelings, acts, and experiences of individual men in their solitude, so far as they apprehend themselves to stand in relation to whatever they may consider the divine'.[58] Under the influence of this conception, religion was effectively privatised, and shorn of its capacity to engage with the public and political life of America. This pragmatic shift accompanied of course the rise of evangelical pietism in mainstream American Protestantism. The outcome was that increasingly American Protestantism in the twentieth century was shorn of its political and social teaching.

This may also help to explain how uncritically most religious groups have embraced the core symbol of American civil religion, despite its use to sacralise America's imperial wars. The vast majority of Protestant churches and Jewish synagogues display the American flag in or around their church buildings, and many place it in the Sanctuary. Denominational religious services will include reference to such key civil religious festivals as Memorial Day, Thanksgiving, and the Fourth of July, and the more recently inaugurated Martin Luther King Day. American churches also participate in the American dream and celebrate the American way of life in a whole range of ways, from incorporating reference to consumer products in church magazines to celebrating in religious services the prosperity or career advancement of their members as testimony to divine blessing. The phenomenon of the megachurch takes this celebration to new heights when the church building becomes a mall surrounded like other malls by a massive car park and offering everything from sports and leisure facilities and shopping outlets to computer chat rooms, cafés and counselling and therapy rooms to its members, as well as a cinema-style worship auditorium where again the flag is typically prominently displayed.[59]

The pervasive influence of the flag and civil religion on American Christians is indicated also by the role the churches played in the swell of patriotic feeling and national mourning that occurred after September 11. It was notable that President Bush used an address at the prayer service held on September 14, 2001 in the National Cathedral in Washington DC both to praise the fortitude of Americans in their response to the tragedy and to indicate an intent to 'rid the world of evil', an intent to which not even Jesus Christ ever laid claim: 'Just three days removed from these events, Americans do not yet have the distance of history, but our responsibility to history is already clear: to answer these attacks and rid the world of evil'.[60] This hubristic statement in this ritual context indicated that Bush was prepared to go even further than Reagan in hitching civil religion to his sense of divine mission in taking up the battle against 'America's enemies'. Bush, like Reagan, believes that America alone stands fully and with strength against the evils of totalitarianism and tyranny. In just the same way conservative Christian evangelist Timothy LaHaye, head of the American Coalition for Traditional Values, argues that were it not for America 'our contemporary world would have completely lost the battle for the mind and would doubtless live in a totalitarian, one-world, humanistic state'.[61]

This contiguity between conservative evangelicalism and civil religion indicates the roots of American civil religion in Protestant Christianity. But the dogmas of civil religion are significantly different from orthodox Christianity, neglecting as they do Trinitarian belief, and in particular the Incarnation of Jesus Christ, who resisted evil non-violently and was put to death at the hands of Empire. It stresses instead the Deist account of a distant creator God who sets the world in motion, and whose divine purposes for human history, and in particular American history, are revealed as a kind of latent providence. This God is only encountered directly through individual religious piety, and in particular through individual appropriation of the effects of the atoning death of Christ on the individual. But in the public world, America's God is a divine Father of the nation who prospers America and fights with her against her enemies, and who receives the bloody sacrifice of America's own with gratitude. As Robert Bellah argues, American civil religion seems to function most effectively when it appeals to a 'transcendent religious reality', a reality that is 'revealed through the experience of the American people'.[62] It is to this sense of the transcendent significance of the experience of being American that Bush, like all recent American Presidents, often appeals in his speeches. America's God is a God who acts on the world *in* and *through* America, and through America's military.

The sacrificial system of American civil religion and its heroic cult of the individual soldier as hero has its roots in the pietistic individualism and apocalyptic religion that has marked American culture from its traumatic beginnings in Virginia and New England. Liberty in their very own New Jerusalem was won for American Europeans at the cost of other human lives, as territorial expansion required the expunging of native Americans and Mexicans, and the nascent colonial economy required the enslavement of hundreds of thousands of Africans and Caribbean peoples to run the plantations of the new colonial aristocracy. Liberty, including religious liberty, won at the cost of so much oppression and violence, necessarily involved an individualisation of Christianity because the original political message of Christianity was clearly cast in such a way as to include all classes of people, from slaves to princes, in its promise of redemption and freedom. Only by interiorising and privatising the spiritual and social ethic of Christianity, by domesticating it, could the Christian faith be allied with American civil religion and turned toward the service of American neoliberalism and imperialism and its sacrificial cult.

This analysis goes some way to explaining the strange combination of personal piety and vicious corporate-sponsored imperial violence that characterises the Bush administration. Religious leaders who have met the President, and prayed with him in the Oval Office, testify to the sincerity of his religious beliefs. There is no doubting that without his religious conversion he would not be in that office today, since it was his new-found faith that helped him overcome alcohol and drug dependence. For secularists, the hypocrisy of private belief and public venality just confirms their preference for atheism over Christianity and their belief that Christianity all along has been an authoritarian religion that modernity has done well to throw off, and that religion in general is the source of more wars and violence than of community and reconciliation. Thus Gore Vidal declares that the trouble with Bush and Tony Blair is that they are both 'Jesus lovers' and Richard Dawkins notes that Bush is a good advert for 'drunks for Jesus'.[63] But the combination of personal religious experience and a sacralised cult of liberty advanced by imperial violence is far more deeply rooted in the American psyche than these comments would imply.

Bush is the latest flowering of the Jamesian turn of American Protestantism towards religious experience as the only real domain of spiritual authenticity, a turn which left the violent reality of the Civil War, a slave-based society, a corporately controlled economy and the sacrificial cult of the flag to flourish without hindrance from sustained prophetic criticism. Premillennial apocalyptic has provided a narrative of American and world history that chimes neatly with this experiential, individualistic and sacrificial turn in American religion. The 'rapture' will pluck individuals from a world on a downward spiral of violence and wickedness in high places and low. The more violent things get in the social world, the more wars and rumours of war the federal government sponsors through its foreign policy, the more sacrifices are offered up of American lives in the battle for the end, the nearer comes the hoped-for moment when the individual is finally saved from the coming conflagration of the end time.

4 – The 'War on Terror' and the True Apocalypse

When George W. Bush was invited in 2003 to be the first US President to make a full State visit to the United Kingdom, he travelled with an entourage of 700 people. The streets through which his entourage processed were cleared of all ordinary people so that they could not wave an American flag or hold up a placard of protest as he drove through London behind 5 inches of plate glass in the Cadillac Deville flown over for the purpose. His limousine drove in the midst of a procession of dozens of black cars and jeeps containing US secret service, armed militia, Presidential staff, and the keeper of the nuclear button that the President carries with him at all times in case of a sudden need arising for him to rain America's vast arsenal of nuclear weapons on a miscreant state. This was truly an imperial procession, the like of which London had never before witnessed throughout its long history.

How is it that the America of the Pilgrim Fathers, whose practice of democracy took its rise from the Puritan Congregation, has come to be ruled by an imperial president whose powers include the ability to commit the military to war, and secret service agents to subversion, in any terrain on the globe without initial recourse to Congress or any other branch of American government? In 1943 in the midst of American engagement in the Second World War, Edward Corwin, a noted Professor of American constitutional law, observed how much economic, military and political power President Franklin D. Roosevelt had gathered into the White House to enable him to organise the United States in its engagement in the war. Corwin warned that there was a great danger that the balances and safeguards against the abuse of power that were built into the Constitution of the American Republic would be undermined by the emergence of 'the leadership principle', the same principle America was engaged in attempting to overthrow in Germany and Japan.[1] As the American historian Walter LaFaber put it:

> The danger revolved around a centralized government domi-
> nated by a president who, due to his immense personal
> popularity and control of the broadcasting media, could exert
> extraconstitutional powers until he fatally weakened the basic
> document [the American Constitution] itself. The executive
> would then become, as recent scholars have phrased it, a
> "plebiscitary Presidency," in which the president exploits
> mass communications to bypass both constitutional and con-
> gressional restraints – even the restraints of the party system –
> to rule.[2]

What Roosevelt did after Pearl Harbor was in effect to declare a national emergency and by so doing to draw all the powers of the American constitution to himself and to the White House. But this emergency device did not disappear with the end of hostilities with Germany and Japan. On the contrary, a new emergency was immediately declared against the Soviet Union and then Chinese communism, allowing the Presidency to continue to conduct foreign policy covertly and without proper democratic scrutiny. As Corwin warned in 1943, 'there is always a tendency, even in democracies, for the emergency device to become the norm'.[3]

With the putative end of the Cold War, the overt need for emergency powers disappeared but September 11 occasioned a new emergency and, just like the Cold War, no end to the 'war on terror' is conceivable on the terms in which the war was announced, for all terrorists, and not merely the international terrorists who had targeted America, are included within its purview. Nationalist move-ments and opponents of governments which themselves often rule by terror are all implicated if they use violence to challenge or over-throw a government aligned with American power and interest. The war on terror thus includes Palestinians who resist the illegal Israeli occupation of their lands and the imprisonment of their people in the new laager behind Israel's wall; it includes opponents of American-supported military dictators in Latin America, Asia and the Middle East; it includes nationalist groups such as the Kurds in Turkey, Armenians in Central Europe and the Basques in Spain. It would have included the African National Congress if it had been declared in the 1980s, though they are now the legitimate government of the Republic of South Africa, and it would have included the Irish Republican politicians who have held ministerial office in Northern Ireland since the end of the troubles in 1998. It would presumably also have included the Iraqi Kurds and Shias who fought to over-throw the government of Saddam Hussein in 1992. To declare war on all those people who aspire to freedom from oppressive dictator-ships, or who struggle for the independence of their homeland is not only to declare a war that can never be won, but is to confuse the real enemy – international terrorists associated with Al-Qaeda – with millions of others who had not, until the 'war on terror' was declared, seen their struggles in terms of opposition to America.[4]

The announcement of a wide-ranging 'war on terror', which pragmatic American commentators are now beginning to admit is by definition unwinnable, had of course a different end in view than merely a police action against Al-Qaeda. This was a new imperial war to advance American 'full spectrum dominance' across the world, as envisaged by Bush's neo-conservative promoters and advisors long before he gained access to the White House. As if to confirm that the true intent of the war was precisely to generate a permanent state of emergency, the Bush administration rapidly came forward not only with war plans against Afghanistan and Iraq, but with clamp-downs on human rights, privacy and freedoms of assembly and dissent of American citizens in the homeland, while resident aliens lost all rights to *habeus corpus*, and could be imprisoned indefinitely without recourse to the courts.

For any who still doubted that America had suspended the normal behaviour of civilised nations in war, during the course of the invasion of Afghanistan the US Defence Secretary Donald Rumsfeld chillingly suggested that it would be fine for enemy com-batants to be summarily executed in Afghanistan. Vice President Cheney announced that those suspected of complicity with terrorism

– in other words, those arrested in the course of the American invasions of Afghanistan and Iraq – would be treated neither as criminals nor as prisoners of war but as 'enemy combatants'. Under this extrajudicial category he declared the intent to hold incommunicado, to indefinitely incarcerate, interrogate, judge, punish and even execute those regarded as the enemies of America without recourse to formal judicial procedures.[5] The concentration camp facility on an American naval base at Guantanamo Bay in Cuba where these combatants would be interrogated and incarcerated was built, appropriately enough, by Halliburton, the company of which Cheney had himself been CEO until becoming Vice President.

The concentration camp was invented by the Spanish and the British in the midst of their colonial wars and it was, as the Italian philosopher Giorgio Agamben notes, an exceptional institution outside the normal realm of law, just as were the concentration camps used to intern communists by the Germans in the 1920s.[6] The concentration camp was a state response to a declared exception that necessitated the suspension of normal constitutional and juridical procedures. When the Nazis took power in 1933 they maintained and extended the camps, and then proceeded to suspend constitutional articles concerning personal freedoms, freedom of assembly, privacy of postal and telephone communication.[7] However, these legal changes were not declared as part of a state of emergency. They were instead simply passed into 'normal' law. The parallels with the emergency actions of the Bush administration in its 'war on terror' are there for all to see. Neither the Patriot Act, nor its hastily written and ill-conceived equivalent in Britain, involved a legal claim of emergency or exception. On the contrary, these anti-democratic laws, which grant extra-judicial powers to hold citizens and immigrants without trial to the executive and the police, have passed into the statute books the assumption of perpetual war between sovereign states and terrorists since September 11 which necessitates the permanent suspension of normal legal arrangements.

Agamben argues that the occasion for the exception becoming the rule, and for the repeated turn of democratic modernity to forms of totalitarianism, arises from the hidden script of sovereign power over bodily life in modern capitalist and technologically ordered societies. As Michael Hardt and Antonio Negri propose, modern sovereignty is essentially capitalist sovereignty and this is 'a form of command that overdetermines the relationship between individuality and universality'.[8] The result is a combination of individuation and totalisation in the expression of modern sovereignty, which is transforming political and bodily existence, turning democratic societies into 'post-democratic spectacular societies' wherein they come to resemble their implacable enemies.

The war on terror, Guantanamo Bay and the Patriot Act shatter the American dream of prosperity and freedom gained originally at the expense of native Americans, and more recently at the expense of other imperial victims. As Ronald Dworkin argues, America is consequently not only facing a terrorist threat but another threat from within:

> In its response to this great threat, the Bush administration has ignored or violated many fundamental individual rights and liberties, and we must now worry that the character of our society will change for the worse. The administration has greatly expanded both surveillance of private individuals and the collection of data about them. It has detained many hundreds of prisoners, some of them American citizens, indefinitely, in secret, and without charge or access to a lawyer. It threatens to execute some of these prisoners after trials before a special military tribunal where traditional safeguards to protect the innocent from conviction will not be available.[9]

The Patriot Act and other emergency measures are subverting democracy and the rule of law within America, and this calls into question the claim that America is uniquely placed to lead the world towards the paradise of liberty that a global market will bring in its wake. As with the original American dream, *pax Americana* is being given effect through the spreading of a violent frontier both in suppression of freedom at home and by means of the 700 military bases that America maintains around the world. The hypocrisy will not be lost on America's enemies: to America's imperial outside, the dream looks less like freedom and more like bondage.

The Empire of Liberty and the Peaceable Kingdom

Michael Hardt and Antonio Negri compare the new American Empire and its controlling hand on the global economy with the Roman Empire before the Punic Wars:

> Empire is emerging today as the center that supports the global-ization of productive networks and casts its widely inclusive net to try to envelop all power relations within its world order – and yet at the same time it deploys a powerful police function against the new barbarians and the rebellious slaves who threaten its order. The power of Empire appears to be subordinated to the fluctuations of local power dynamics and to the shifting, partial juridical orderings that attempt, but never fully succeed, to lead back to a state of normalcy in the name of the "exceptionality" of the administrative procedures. These characteristics, however, were precisely those that defined ancient Rome in its decadence, and that tormented so many of its Enlightenment admirers.[10]

In the American empire local compromised juridical arrangements of a kind that would not be permitted in the imperial homeland deliver the pliant submission of subjugated populaces as cheap labour for imperial corporations, and their natural resources to furnish and sustain the luxuriant wealth of the homeland. Imperial suzerainty is also maintained by international financial institutions such as the World Bank and the International Monetary Fund, and the recently established World Trade Organisation. But like Rome, American empire cannot rely on these forms of sovereignty alone. It requires, and is sustained by, a constant state of crisis that calls for the maintenance of a warrior class who are the beneficiaries and allies of the military–industrial complex. As we have seen, this state of constant conflict is not alien to the American Republic, any more than it was to the Roman. On the contrary, the instantiation of power conflict at the heart of the federal constitution – with its three-fold balance of powers that is nonetheless traduced by the leadership principle – provides the dynamic principle of federalism in the unfolding of American imperialism.

When the empire or the interests of its agents are threatened, war to defend the overt ideology of freedom, and the covert cult of sacrifice, is initiated. American civil religion and American apocalyptic religion combine to give a sacred gloss to the necessity of war. Bush and his speech-writers are not inventing a new discourse, but drawing on the tradition of the violent Republic that came to believe that in spreading the 'eagle's shadow' across the world it truly spread the kingdom of God.

Whether in secular or religious guise, this ideology of freedom is too thin, too negative in its account of freedom actually to sustain the social spaces it is supposed to symbolise and represent. American intellectuals have therefore been stunningly unable to resist the violent script that the declared 'crisis of liberty' has brought forth as the war on terror. The 'war for freedom' is not only announced in the subjugated spaces of the global imperium but in the democratic spaces and institutions of the homeland. Even library records, to say nothing of emails, phone calls and credit card records, can be examined by the state in its pursuit of the security of the homeland under the terms of the Patriot Act. And yet there has been only limited resistance to the indefinite suspension of civil liberties and the imperial war on terror.[11]

The American cult of liberty fails to resist the imperial cult of violence – and may even promote it – just because it offers a narrative of freedom that is negative rather than positive in its delineations. Freedom from tyranny, freedom from history, freedom from interference in 'my' property rights, especially by the former (native American) inhabitants of my property – these are the classic freedoms that American liberalism, now dubbed neo-conservatism, affirms. But such a narrative of freedom seems to require, rather than to resist, the idea that human relations are intrinsically competitive and violent. The negative account of freedom requires the coercive state in order to keep the old empire at bay and the original inhabitants of the new one from spoiling the property claims of the new settlers.

As we saw above, this Lockean account of freedom promotes a description of society that can only conceive of politics in coercive and negative terms, just in those terms that characterise the imperial discourse of Bush and his speech-writers. Lockean liberalism, American liberalism, gives an account of how individuals can assert their independence from history and from other people, but it has no account of how individuals live in families and communities that form them to be people who are capable of living fulfilled and compassionate lives. As Hauerwas puts it, the political and social arrangements of liberalism are designed to free Americans from history and from luck so that they 'can be what they want to be', so that they can claim to choose their own destiny, and so that they can shop for whatever they desire; but 'the means necessary to secure such "freedom" in an egalitarian manner creates societies that make our lives all the more determined by powers we do not recognize as powers'.[12] The powers that the American state has acquired over its citizens through the succession of states of emergency that its imperial defence of liberty has occasioned since 1898 are exactly of this kind. In the name of liberty they undermine the conditions for a truly non-coercive peace.

American liberalism has colluded with apocalyptic religion in the construction of an imperial ideology of liberty because it has confined Christian thought and practice to the non-political, to the 'private', the 'personal' and to 'religious experience' or piety. It does this because American liberalism looks for the redemption of the human condition not in divine revelation or spiritual worship, but in an account of individual choice aided by the theoretically autonomous mechanism of the free market, and a minimalist democratic polity. Modern politics, the modern idea of political sovereignty, is then at least in theory autonomous from religion and morality. But the kind of religion that flourishes best in the autonomous market society is therefore precisely the kind of con-servative apocalyptic religion that has overtaken mainstream Christianity across great swathes of the United States. American Christianity is rendered incapable of resisting either the idolatry of liberty, masked by the imperial cult of sacrifice, or the extremes of elite wealth and mass poverty that the empire promotes both at home and abroad. Christianity when it is confined to the private sphere and to religious experience cannot save, cannot be truly evangelical. As Oliver O'Donovan puts it, 'Rule out the political questions and you cut short the proclamation of God's saving power; you leave people enslaved at points where they ought to be set free from the power of sin – their own sin and other people's'.[13]

From Paul of Tarsus to Augustine of Hippo, the early Christians believed that politics was at its core about the non-coercive quest for justice and peace in a sinful world. The born-again Christian, George W. Bush, tries to hitch this Augustinian Christian conception of politics as the quest for peace to his declarations of war. Ideologues in his administration even adopted Augustine's account of Just War to claim that their attacks on Afghanistan and Iraq met the requirements of just-war theory. But as there is no envisaged end, and as there are no clear limits to the declared 'war on terror' it signally fails to meet just-war criteria. Furthermore, neither the invasion of Afghanistan nor that of Iraq was a war of last resort as Augustinian just-war theory requires: both the Taliban and Saddam Hussein offered the Bush administration everything that it asked of them and more before America bombed and invaded Afghanistan and Iraq.

The new strategic paradigm of full spectrum dominance realised in pre-emptive strikes against all possible opponents to American hegemony cannot easily be reconciled with Christian just-war theory. These are imperial wars, as one of the Bush administration's neo-con acolytes declared:

> The conquest of Iraq will not be a minor event in history: it will represent the introduction of a new imperial power to the Middle East and a redefinition of regional geopolitics based on that power. The United States will move from being an outside power influencing events through coalitions, to a regional power that is able to operate effectively on its own.[14]

As another put it: 'once we cross the Tigris and Euphrates River, we may have started down the road to a Pax Americana through an American Imperium from which there is no return'.[15]

The famous painting entitled 'The Peaceable Kingdom' by the American folk artist Edward Hicks, which hangs in the Brooklyn Museum, shows the potentially far-reaching effects of divine shalom as conceived by the prophet Isaiah in the Old Testament. Hicks portrays Isaiah's vision of peace between species, where the lion lies down with the lamb and a child plays over the whole of an asp. In the background, Hicks depicts a peace treaty between native Americans and colonial Americans in Philadelphia. But outside the idealised world of Hick's painting, few treaties between the Indian and the Yankee were ever honoured by the Yankee. The tragedy of Christian history, including Christian history in North America, is that the Church and Christians have too often failed to practice the non-coercive ethic of a just and peaceable kingdom announced by Jesus Christ. Consequently, the Christian conception of politics as the non-coercive quest for justice and peace would be as shocking and subversive to the apocalyptic advocates of *pax Americana* as it was to the Jewish and Roman authorities in first century Palestine. The reason it is shocking as well as subversive is because of the captivity of the Bible in North America, and in the West more generally, to the privatisation of religion and the correlative domination of the 'free' market and consumerist capitalism.

I argue in what follows that the key to reforming the apocalyptic subversion of true Christianity in America is the recovery of the truly anti-imperial message of the Bible, and of Christianity's founder, Jesus Christ. The Bible, and biblical apocalyptic, rightly interpreted provide powerful resources for Christians to resist and critique American imperialism, and to challenge the sacralisation of this imperialism in the name of a debased religion of freedom and sacrifice shrouded in Christian apocalyptic language.[16]

Jesus and Empire

Jesus Christ was not born to greatness, nor was he born in a great city. He was the child of a subject people in a distant outpost of Empire whose parents were, according to two Gospel accounts, on a journey to the town of Joseph's birth in response to a summons to an imperial census. The purpose of the census was to enable Rome's client king of Judea, Herod Antipater, to collect more tribute from his subjects on Rome's behalf. Jesus' father was a migrant worker from Judea but had to return there in order to be registered. Like the American Empire today, Rome ruled its vast territories not through its own bureaucracy – the Empire was far too big for that – but mostly through client rulers and local elites who were delegated by Rome to keep order and to collect taxes.[17] Palestine thus fitted the classic pattern of Roman imperial rule.

The mention of the Emperor Augustus, and of the deeply unpopular tribute, in the birth narratives of Matthew and Luke firmly places the events of Christ's life, death and resurrection in this imperial context. Such censuses were central to the imperial economy as they were the means by which the Empire determined the amount of poll tax to be imposed on each province. It is a matter of historical record that the census in 6 A.D., which is most likely the census referred to in the Gospels, provoked a riot because it was seen as challenging the Israelite recognition of the singular sovereignty of God and the expression of this sovereignty in Israelite theocratic arrangements.[18] In addition, the tribute was producing real economic immiseration in Palestine. The Palestinian economy at this time was largely a barter economy and few peasants made enough surplus to produce an actual cash return, but cash was the only means in which the tribute could be paid. Consequently many peasant farmers fell into debt and lost their lands.

The reference to tribute so early in the Gospel of Luke indicates to the reader that from the outset the first Christians interpreted the coming of Christ as a public and political event that challenged Roman imperial rule in Galilee and Judea.[19] There are two further incidents concerning Jesus' attitude towards the tribute recorded in the Gospels. One concerns the payment of the poll tax or head tax in Galilee, which Jesus discusses with Peter (Matthew 17). Paying this head tax was in effect an acknowledgement that the body of the person paying it was under the dominion, the rule, of the emperor, and it was also a way in which the high priestly caste asserted their rule over the recalcitrant Galilean peasantry.[20] Jesus when asked by Peter if he and his disciples are bound to pay the tax declares that 'the children of God are free' (Matthew 17. 26) from such obligations. By declaring that they are free from this obligation, Jesus not only challenges Roman rule but he challenges the complicity of the priests and the Temple system in Rome's tyranny. The God who demands tribute as evidence of enforced loyalty is not the God whom Jesus describes to his followers as 'abba Father'. In his refusal to pay the tax then, Jesus is challenging both the political economy of imperialism and the transformation of the Israelite God of justice into a kingly and patronal theology that props up and legitimates the Empire and its client rulers.

The second tribute incident (Mark 12. 13 – 17) is better known. Jesus is asked by the Pharisees and Herodians in Jerusalem whether it is lawful to pay tribute to Caesar. This is a trick question with which they aim to catch him out, for under Jewish law it was certainly legally dubious to make payment to an emperor who had set himself up as a god in a cult that challenged the worship of Yahweh. In addition, the matter of tribute was at the heart of the imperial dynamic of Jewish society at the time. The peasantry and the poor on whose very bodies and lands the tribute was levied were universally opposed to the tribute. Not only was it contrary to Torah but it was a cause of growing indebtedness and hence landlessness. Those who administered the collection of the tribute – the priestly class who included the Herodians – were of course supportive of the tribute not least because it was a means of asserting their own power over the people; a power that was conferred on them as clients of imperial rule. The question was 'a test of loyalty that divided collaborators from subversives' and in reply Jesus already steals a march on his opponents because he demands that they show him the imperial coin – the Denarius – in which the tax was paid, for apparently neither he nor his disciples carried the coinage of Empire.[21] Once Jesus' opponents hold up the coin they are already at a disadvantage. He then asks them to indicate whose image it displays, and by so doing he indicates the traditional reason why many Jews including Jesus and his followers refused to carry the coin, for the image was of course that of Augustus, the current Caesar. Jewish law clearly proscribed the making of images for worship, and since the head of Caesar represented the imperial cult, it was clearly wrong to look on it or to carry it on one's person. That Jesus ironically requires the Rabbis actually to name the famous image, and the inscription to Caesar on the coin, are in themselves a defeat for his opponents. The question already names Jesus' opponents as idolators since they possess the coin and he does not.[22] In the context of the asymmetry of power that characterise his relations with the priestly authorities, Jesus uses what James Scott calls the 'weapons of the weak' – irony and jest. In his response 'give unto Caesar that which is Caesar's, and to God that which is God's' Jesus quietly challenges imperial authority while pointing up his opponents as wicked collaborators.

Jesus' famous reply to his interlocutors has often been misinter-
preted as indicating that it is not the business of Christians to resist
imperialism. It has also often been read as indicating that Jesus is
telling his opponents to pay the tax. But read in the imperial and
religious context in which they were uttered, these words indicate a
clear apocalyptic dualism between God and Caesar. Caesar's rule or
God's rule is the stark reality that Roman rule presented to the Jews
at the time of Jesus. The answer in its context was crystal clear, for
his hearers would have understood that a tax levied on the land and
people of Israel was clearly not a tax that should have been paid, for
Israel belonged to God. Only God could require tribute from the
people of Israel and only to God is such a debt owed; certainly not
to Caesar. But Jesus' reply not only resists the collaborators, those
who ruled the people of Israel on behalf of Rome. It also makes clear
that he does not wish to side with those who take up arms violently
to resist Roman rule. He does not call for an open revolt against the
tribute, but rather for Israelites to acknowledge where their true
loyalties lie.[23]

At the trial of Jesus he is arraigned both for the tribute incident
and because of other perceived challenges to the ruling authority of
the Priests, and hence of Rome, related to a number of incidents that
took place around the Temple in Jerusalem. Before Jesus was born,
King Herod had overseen substantial building works at the Temple
in Jerusalem, enlarging and enhancing this symbolic centre of the
Jewish religion as a way of sacralising and legitimating Herodian
collaboration with Roman imperial rule.[24] Since the Temple was the
focal point of the worship of Yahweh as the God of gods and the only
true king and lord of the people of God, it was always an ambiguous
location from the point of view of the Romans, who in most
provinces had successfully rooted out local cults and substituted
the cult of Caesar. But because of the fierce loyalty of the Jews to
their religion, the Romans left the Temple in place on the basis of
assurances from Herod and the priestly class that they could use
their religion as a device for assuring order and stability while at the
same time collecting and returning tribute to Rome. The result was
that the Temple became the focus for considerable peasant unease
and indebtedness because not only were they required to hand over
a considerable proportion of their annual production to the Temple,

but the Temple was also the place where the payment of the Poll Tax or tribute was organised by the Priests on behalf of Rome. Many of the peasants could not afford to pay both kinds of tax, so they abandoned the Temple tax in favour of the tribute, as non-payment of the latter resulted in violent confrontations with Roman legionaries. But by not paying the Temple tax the peasants became religiously indebted, and hence ritually unclean in the eyes of the Priests. In addition, they could not rely on the protection of Yahweh for their crops and fields. Tithes were required of Israel in acknowledgement that God had gifted the land to Israel: its flourishing was only guaranteed when the Israelites met their obligations to the Temple and to God.

Into this context Jesus commences his preaching with the liberating announcement in the Synagogue in Capernaum that the Jews are freed from debtor jails because the Jubilee year, the 'acceptable year of the Lord', when all debts were traditionally supposed to be forgiven, had arrived (Luke 4. 18 – 21). From the outset of his ministry, Jesus preaches liberty from the economic oppression and religious exclusion that Roman imperial rule had imposed on the Jews in Galilee and Judea. By collaborating with the Romans, and by abusing the ancient practice of the collection of tithes to the extent that peasants fell into debt contrary to the clear teaching of the Torah, the Temple religion and the religious authorities had betrayed the justice and mercy of God in the eyes of the Zealots who resisted Roman rule, from among whom Jesus drew a number of his own followers. This is why from the outset we see that Jesus is in conflict with the religious authorities in Israel. His healing miracles, his revisionist interpretations of Old Testament teaching, and especially his challenges to the Temple authorities indicated that while he did not support violent resistance to Rome, he did condemn and resist the priestly collaboration with Rome's imperial rule.

The first clear challenge in the Gospel of Mark to the Temple authorities occurs in the story of the healing of the paralytic. Jesus heals the paralytic man who is brought before him with the words 'my son, your sins are forgiven'. The scribes who are present were offended at these words because in their view the only place where sins could be forgiven was the Temple in Jerusalem. There is a double irony here as Dominic Crossan suggests:

There is, first and above all, a terrible irony in that conjunction of sickness and sin, especially in first century Palestine. Excessive taxation could leave the poor people physically malnourished or hysterically disabled. But since the religio-political ascendancy could not blame excessive taxation, it blamed sick people themselves by claiming that their sin had led to their illnesses. And the cure for sickness was, ultimately, in the Temple. And that meant more fees, in a perfect circle of victimization.[25]

Jesus is in effect announcing in his person that the brokerage of religious and economic power by the Temple authorities was crumbling. Instead of depending on the Temple the people are invited to rely on Jesus for a new and direct access to divine power.

Instead of the Temple system Jesus offers the free grace of God both to heal illness and social disease and to forgive sins. Disease in first-century Palestine was an indicator not only of physical malady but of poverty and of religious exclusion. The sick were regarded as religiously unclean, and very often their illness was linked with their indebtedness and poverty. But their indebtedness made them unable to make the requisite payments to the Temple to be cleansed and healed. The sick were caught in a vicious circle of imperial and ritual victimage. In healing the impoverished sick in first-century, occupied Palestine Jesus is in effect challenging the monopoly on religion and economic power that the Temple authorities claimed for themselves by 'reconstituting those healed as members of the people of Israel's God'.[26]

The second incident concerning the Temple, where the challenge to its collaboration with the Romans is particularly evident, concerns the incident that occurs just a few days before his trial and death, when Jesus physically challenges the traders and money-changers from the outer courts of the Temple in Jerusalem, overturning their tables and chasing them out, declaring that 'my house shall be a house of prayer while you have made it a den of thieves' (Luke 19. 46). He then foretells the destruction of the Temple to his disciples, saying that 'no stone will be left one upon another'. Again this incident needs to be read, as William Herzog suggests, in the context of the transformation of the Temple into a bank as a result of its central role in the imperial taxation system.[27] The high priestly families who ran the Temple were also the local rulers and tribute collectors of the imperial authorities: they had turned the Temple into the central bank of colonial Palestine and the chief instrument in the theft of the wealth of the people of Israel by the Roman imperial power, and in their consequent indebtedness and poverty. Those around the Temple, of course, benefited substantially from the impoverishment of the rural farmers. Archaeological digs around the Temple mount in Jerusalem have revealed that Temple officials and servants in Jerusalem did extremely well in the new unequal imperial economy of Judea. They lived in considerable luxury and enjoyed great wealth, while the people in the countryside lived in penury and debt.

After three years of healing the maladies of the rural poor and declaring their debts forgiven, Jesus goes in person to the Temple, the local source of their imperial oppression, and demands that it abandon its collusion in the imperial economy. In targeting the money changers, Jesus identified those who most truly symbolised the system of imperial economic oppression that the Temple stood for. Jesus is acting in the light of the demand of the ancient Torah that 'there shall be no poor among you' so long as the commandments of God are observed by the Israelites (Deuteronomy 15. 4 – 6). The reason the poor are in the land is because the law is being ignored and the religion of Israel traduced from announcing divine abundance and blessing to imposing penury and scarcity. The cleansing of the Temple, and Jesus' foretelling of its destruction, indicate that Jesus is announcing a new era in which the old religion of Israel is being replaced with a new religious order, which he calls the 'kingdom of God'. This new order of the kingdom represented a radical challenge to the old order of empire focused on the Temple as the political and economic centre of Roman imperial power over the Jews.

The Kingdom Came

But if the Kingdom came in Jesus Christ how is it that postmillennialist Puritans came to believe that they were the first truly to establish the kingdom in human history as they occupied and subdued the 'virgin' lands of America and its first inhabitants? How is it that premillennialists still view the reign of God in the Kingdom of Christ as a deferred event? Part of the answer can be found in the history of biblical interpretation. Under the influence of nineteenth-century German New Testament scholars Johannes Weiss and Albert Schweitzer, and in the context of a sharp rise in apocalyptic thinking and writing in American Christianity and American culture, many American theologians in the late nineteenth and twentieth centuries adopted a millennial frame for their accounts of the historical Jesus. They argued that the Kingdom of God was for Jesus and for the first Christians a future event, as indicated in the apocalyptic sayings of Jesus and in the disciples' apparent belief in the imminent second coming of the ascended Lord. On this view, Christ was a millennial prophet who preached that the kingdom would come only after his return as the judge of human history.[28]

However, in Christian tradition at least until the twelfth century, and again in recent theological scholarship, the orthodox account is that the Kingdom had already come in the person of Christ. Modern scholars point to a number of incidents and sayings in the Gospels, which clearly point to this interpretation, and to teachings of St Paul and the fathers of the church, which confirm it. One of the most telling of the gospel sayings of Jesus for understanding the time of the kingdom concerns the challenge that Jesus receives when he casts out a demon from a man possessed. The scribes and Pharisees accuse Jesus of working this miracle not by divine power but by the power of the devil. Jesus rejects their claim and says that on the contrary the power at work in his presence and ministry was truly the 'finger of God'. The finger of God is a phrase used in the Old Testament to indicate the specific action of the Spirit of God on behalf of God's people. And Jesus says that if the finger of God is active in their midst, then truly the kingdom of God is already among them (Luke 11. 20).[29] Jesus is clearly indicating that the new religious and social order to which his miracles and teachings point is not some distant apocalyptic reality but on the contrary is already present and becoming real in the lives of his followers and in the peasant villages in which he has already declared the coming of the reign of God.

That the reign of God had come in Jesus is again clearly indicated in Jesus' frequent assumption of the role of mediator or broker of the justice and favour of God to the people of God throughout his ministry. Jesus invites his followers to address God with the intimate Aramaic word for father, *Abba*, indicating that through his teaching they can find direct access to divine mercy and favour. This new era undermines the role of the Temple as brokerage house for divine grace and for Roman economic and political rule over the peasants. The Kingdom of God is a new society in which the people may receive forgiveness of their sins because God has drawn near to them in Jesus Christ. The distant law-giver brokered by the high priests is replaced by a God of love and mercy.[30]

In this perspective, the kingdom of God, the time of the direct reign of God over God's people, does not indicate a future apocalyptic cataclysm after which this reign will begin, as millennialists believe, but rather the new order that the wandering itinerant preacher and radical rabbi Jesus Christ was already establishing in the peasant society of occupied Palestine in the first century. As Stephen Patterson puts it:

> Wandering radicalism does not proclaim the [future] *coming* of the kingdom, it brings it directly to the front door. With the knock of the itinerant radical, the old world has already passed away, and the kingdom of God has arrived.[31]

Peasants who were released from the requirement to submit tribute to the Temple were to use their new freedom not for license or lawlessness, but to develop a new kind of society in which love for God and neighbour, even for enemies, became the rule. Christ's announcement of the Kingdom of God inaugurates a society where peasants no longer have to compete with tyranny, or with one another, to meet their needs and to fulfil the justice of God. Instead of mimicking their rulers, and 'using debt to gain control over others' they are to enact a new ethic and practice of forgiveness.[32] In answer to Simon Peter's question 'how many times shall I forgive' Jesus replies 'seventy times seven' (Matthew 18. 22). Those who want to live according to the kingdom ethic are to stop keeping a record of the sins of others. Equally they are to stop using the law courts or the Temple to resolve conflicts or to cover up their unwillingness to forgive the debts and sins of their neighbours. Instead they are to make peace before they get to court, and before making their offerings at the altar (Matthew 5. 24 – 5). The ministry of the Son of Man is a ministry of service that rejects the quest for domination of imperial society – 'it shall not be so among you' (Mark 10. 43). Just as Jesus 'came not to be served but to serve and to give his life as a ransom for many' (Mark 10. 45) so the disciples are to lay down their lives in service of one another. This new ethic, which rejected dominion and conflict, critiqued the Torah tradition of 'an eye for an eye' or tit for tat. Jesus' announcement of the reign of God, his offer of divine forgiveness, had only one condition attached to it: that those who embraced, and were embraced by, this freedom were themselves to forgive sins, to stop counting wrongs, to avoid conflict and to abandon the spiral of violence. The king of the Jews did not fight violence with violence and so he also instructed his disciples not to pay back evil for evil, and not to resist the rule of Rome with violence.

Jesus not only taught but exemplified the practice of the Kingdom in his meal feasts with his disciples to which were invited sinners, tax collectors, prostitutes and even Pharisees. No-one was excluded from table fellowship with the Lord so long as they repented of their sins and forgave the debts and sins of others. When the Pharisees ask Jesus 'when the kingdom of God was coming' at one such meal, he declares quite plainly 'the Kingdom of God is not coming with signs to be observed; nor will they say, "Lo, here it is" or "There!" for behold the kingdom of God is in the midst of you' (Luke 17. 20 – 21). Against the apocalyptic prophets who sought signs in the skies that would accompany the destruction of the imperial conquerors of Israel, Jesus declares that the kingdom was coming quietly, and had already arrived. The only sign that would be given to the people is the sign of 'the Son of Man lifted up', 'just as Moses lifted up the serpent in the wilderness' (John 3. 14), the sign in other words of the Crucifixion of Christ on the torturous Roman cross.

The apocalypse for Christians is not then a future event. The apocalypse has already come, in history, in the life of Christ. The imperial order, the law of domination and death, has already been challenged, is already overcome. The fallen powers that oppress the people of God are already cast down, already defeated, in the events of Christ's incarnation, his ministry of healings and miracles, his teaching and wisdom, his trial and death, and above all his resurrection and ascension. As St Paul puts it, 'Christ led captivity captive' when he submitted himself to trial and crucifixion. And, in the Resurrection, God vindicated God's son and showed through the event of the empty tomb on the public stage of history that he had triumphed over the powers.

This is not to gainsay that there are sayings in the New Testament that point to the likelihood of an imminent return of Christ from heaven. But it is to indicate that this expectation of return, of the parousia, did not mean that the kingdom of God was delayed until *after* this future return of Christ as judge of the world. No, the gospels and epistles of the New Testament provide clear evidence that the Jewish peasants of first-century Palestine, and the early Christians in cities such as Rome, Corinth, Ephesus and Philippi understood the teaching of Jesus about the Kingdom to indicate that it had already arrived in his person, in his coming, and that it was already taking shape in the villages and communities that heard his message and preferred it to the teachings of Jewish priests or the Gentile cult of Rome.

That there was a clear conflict between the teaching of Jesus and the teachings of the priests, between the followers of Christ and the rule of Rome, between the ethic of the kingdom and the ethos of the empire, is not in doubt in the New Testament documents. It was not though a future conflict, it did not point to a mythical confrontation but rather to the trial of Jesus before the Jewish and the Roman authorities. Jesus' sayings about conflict and the need for endurance to the end point to the fact that those who dwelt in the kingdom were already in conflict, as he was, with the powers that be. But this conflict was different from a violent rebellion, because in the Kingdom there is resistance but there is no violence; there is subversion, the governing authorities are mocked, but they are not put to the sword. This conflict was different because its leader was different. He did not organise a violent rebellion against Rome in which he was proclaimed as the rebel leader of the people. Nor did he, as some of his followers hoped he would, adopt the mantle of the longed for Messiah who would, like King David of old, vanquish the enemies of Israel and destroy the violent power of Empire. The conflict is resolved not in armed struggle, or the sacrificial shedding of warrior blood, but in the sacrifice of the life of one righteous man for the life of the world, a sacrifice that put an end to the need for blood sacrifice in the Temple or on the battlefield, which subverted the rule of violence of the *Pax Romana*.

With the mention of sacrifice we perhaps arrive at the heart of the complex relationship between Christianity and Empire, both in Roman times and in the time of the American Empire. Modern American apocalyptic Christianity lends sacral legitimacy to the imperial war on terror. The flag rituals of America as the new Rome require the regular blood sacrifices both of its enemies and of its own young men (and latterly women), while American civil religion presents these deaths as sacrifices hallowed by America's God, who for most Americans is the God of Christians and Jews. But the first Christians were, like their Lord, committed to non-violence. They did not believe it was possible to fight in an army and follow Christ. Nor did they believe it was appropriate to resist the tyranny of Rome with violence. Christians who were martyred by Roman religious persecution went to their deaths in the torturous spectacle of the amphitheatre, or at the hands of violent mobs, without inciting their Christian brethren to take up arms against their persecutors. But that their beliefs and practices were seditious, that the early church truly challenged the empire is not in doubt. Paul and Silas are delivered up to the mob at Ephesus because their teachings were 'turning the world upside down' and this was bad for trade, and bad for the imperial and idolatrous cults of Caesar and Diana. The Apostle Peter was crucified upside-down because he was the head of a church that challenged the authority and power of Rome and whose political and social arrangements subverted the class and economic structures of empire. The reign of God began in Jesus Christ and was taken up in the early church; the first Christians embraced the radical rule of their founder and launched it on the Roman world.

How is it that the non-violent teaching of Jesus came to be purloined and misused, just as the Temple religion was purloined and misused, in the cause of empire? How did a pacifist religion become a religion of holy war? How do American Christian evangelicals become advocates of violent Zionism, of apocalyptic war in the holy land? To arrive at an answer to this question we will need to investigate a little further the origins of the non-violent, non-coercive ethos of early Christianity, and then examine its transformation into an imperial cult after the momentous conversion of the third-century Roman Emperor, Constantine.

The Victory of God and the True Christian Apocalypse

The desolate disciples of Jesus in the days after his Crucifixion became the bold founders of a Church that would grow rapidly from its small beginnings as a subversive Jewish sect to become the official religion of the Roman Empire. Christian historians trace the origins of the Christian movement to the events that took place on what they call the first Easter morning. Without the disciples' emergent belief that their rabbi and leader, Jesus Christ, had risen from the dead it is impossible to account for the boldness of their witness to Christ on and after the day of Pentecost.

The first witnesses to the empty tomb, and the angelic announcement that Christ was risen were not propitious, at least from a Jewish or first-century point of view, for they were women, women who had gathered on the third day as tradition required to anoint the body of their loved one. Women were not capable of acting as legal witnesses in the culture of the time and so it is significant that the New Testament still does not hesitate to name them as the first witnesses of this momentous event. If the Gospel writers had written their accounts of the resurrection simply to persuade sceptics, rather than to attempt to describe what actually happened, it is unlikely they would have named the women around Jesus as the first witnesses. After the discovery of the empty tomb, the Gospel writers, and the Book of Acts, recount a series of miraculous appearances of the risen Lord to his disciples, and then his Ascension, where he was said to have taken his rightful place at 'the right hand of God'. On the basis of these appearances, the disciples came to believe that Jesus truly was the Messiah, the promised one who would deliver the people from tyranny and sin, and they began to worship him as the Lord of heaven and earth. As Christ explained to the disciples the meaning of the events surrounding his trial, death and resurrection – for example, to the disciples on the road to Emmaus – the disciples arrived at a more sophisticated and really remarkably novel understanding of what was the true mission of Jesus, and what he intended them to do once he finally departed.

At the heart of the first disciples' understanding and subsequent preaching about the one they had come to know as the Christ, and who they would come to worship as God, was the realisation that in the life, death and resurrection of Jesus Christ God had acted decisively within history to change its course and its meaning for ever. They understood that salvation had come to the Jews in these events and it was their apostolic and Spirit-inspired mission now to announce this salvation to the house of Israel, to preach that God had rescued them from sin and from the corruption of their Temple-based religion through its usurpation by the client–patron system of the Roman Empire. Their preaching indicated that God had acted to rescue his people, but he had not done this, as most Jews expected, by publicly overthrowing their oppressors. Instead, God did it through becoming one with them in their oppression in the life of Jesus of Nazareth. And God triumphed over the evil powers that oppressed the Jews in the triumph of the cross and the resurrection of Jesus Christ. As N. T. Wright puts it:

> First-century Jews looked forward to a public event … in and through which their god would reveal to all the world that he was not just a local, tribal deity, but the creator and sovereign of all … The early Christians … looked back to an event in and through which, they claimed, Israel's god had done exactly that.[33]

As the disciples in Jerusalem preached this message of a cosmic cataclysm, which had changed the course of history for the people of Israel, so the apostle Paul, after his Damascus road encounter with the risen Lord, began to preach the same message to the Gentiles. According to Paul, God was in Christ from the beginning of creation. In appearing in human form, God adopted the cloak of humility and through following the way of the cross God triumphed over the powers that dominated and oppressed the people of God, and the Gentiles also.

The new Spirit religion of early Christianity began not as a result of a hoax or a wish dream, but as a consequence of a world-changing

event, an event that shook the foundations of history and contravened all that we know conventionally about human life and death:
the Resurrection of Jesus Christ from the dead. Only such a cataclysmic
event could explain the power and confidence that the disciples
acquired so soon after the death of their leader, only such an event
could account for the rapidity with which they began to worship him
as the Lord of heaven and earth. Jesus had led his disciples throughout the three years of his ministry to expect a cataclysmic event that
would dramatically establish the kingdom in the life-time of the
disciples.[34] As he said to his disciples before his journey to Jerusalem
'Truly I say to you, there are some of those who are standing here
who will not taste death until they see the Son of Man coming in His
kingdom' (Matthew 16, 28). On another occasion, speaking of the
church that would be founded after his death he says 'I will give you
the keys of the kingdom of heaven; and whatever you bind on earth
shall have been bound in heaven, and whatever you loose on earth
shall have been loosed in heaven' (Matthew 16. 19). The clear implication is that the kingdom is already anticipated in his actions and
sayings and among those who follow him, and that the birth of the
church after the cataclysm of his death and resurrection represents
the new time of the kingdom.

According to the teaching of the apostles in Jerusalem, and the
teachings of St Paul, the apostle of the Gentile church, the apocalypse
that had been foretold by Daniel and the other ancient Israelite
prophets, the new era when God would directly rule his people –
when he would 'turn their hearts of stone into hearts of flesh, and
write his laws on their hearts' (Jeremiah 31. 33) – had already come.
Jesus Christ was the true apocalypse. Most of the Jews who lived
under the Roman imperial rule hoped desperately for the coming of
the messiah.[35] They interpreted their scriptures to indicate that God
would come in power to overthrow their oppressors, and establish
a new kingly rule on earth in which the people of God would be
vindicated, their Temple religion restored and cleansed of its imperial
corruption. This was the meaning of apocalypse for the Jews, and in
particular the meaning of the book of Daniel that so many modern
apocalyptic Christians have turned to once again as a source of a new
millennial belief system. But the kingdom that was bodied forth in
Jesus Christ and in the Church his disciples founded was not like the

kingdom that the Jews hoped for and expected. It did not involve the violent overthrow of Roman imperial power, it did not forcibly remove the corrupt Temple authorities from their place at the head of the Jewish religion. On the contrary, Christ appears in history as a servant king, as one who is put to death by the empire rather than resisting it with the sword. The victory of God does not come through a war or the triumph of a divine or angelic army. It comes through the Cross and Resurrection of Jesus Christ, and the out-pouring of the Spirit of God at Pentecost. What is the significance of this change in perception from the violent apocalypse that the Jews expected to the peaceable kingdom that Jesus announced and that the early Christians took up in their new conception of themselves as the church of God, the Spirit-filled body of Christ? What is the meaning of the true apocalypse, and how is it that millennialist Christians have, like the Jews of Second Temple Judaism, turned back to an expectation of a violent apocalypse, and reinvented Christ as an apocalyptic prophet, a latter-day Daniel?

Douglas Harink suggests that St Paul, and not the writer of the Book of Revelation, is the key apocalyptic theologian of the New Testament, and that through a close engagement with his writings it is possible to recover the true meaning of the Christian apocalypse for this founder of the Gentile churches and so for the first Christians. The Christian apocalypse does not indicate the end of the world in a mighty conflagration called Armageddon, nor the resettling of the land of Israel as the Zionists would have it. On the contrary:

> Simply stated, "apocalypse" is shorthand for Jesus Christ. In the New Testament, in particular for Paul, all apocalyptic reflection and hope comes to this, that God has acted critically, decisively, and finally for Israel, all the peoples of the earth, and the entire cosmos, in the life, death, resurrection, and coming again of Jesus, in such a way that God's purpose for Israel, all humanity, and all creation is critically, decisively, and finally disclosed and effected in the history of Jesus Christ.[36]

This history displays all the marks of traditional Jewish apocalyptic, barring violent war. It indicates that God acts decisively to achieve salvation, that the powers that enslave the people of God in history are in a war with God that they will lose as God liberates the people from the powers, bringing about a new restored humanity and a new creation. It indicates that in Jesus Christ the powers that rule the world, and the people of God, both meet their judge, the one by whom their fidelity or otherwise to the reign of God is measured. It indicates that the liberating action of God in Christ is final and unsurpassed; 'there is no reality, no historical or mythical figure, no system, no framework, idea, or anything else that transcends the reality of Jesus Christ'.[37] It indicates that the God who made the world has truly disclosed, revealed, Godself (the Greek word 'apocalypse' is best translated as 'revelation') and in so doing has finally and definitively revealed the goal and purpose of the cosmos. In this perspective, the true Christian apocalypse critiques and resists the attempts by American Christian millennialists to turn the American project, and especially the American imperial project, into an apocalyptic struggle for American national security and democratic freedoms.

The Epistle to the Galatians is a key locus for Paul's account of the true Christian apocalypse. The Galatian Christians had been visited by Jewish Christians from Jerusalem, who had suggested to them that their cleaving to the revelation of Jesus Christ was not enough for their salvation and that in addition they had, as Gentiles, to take up certain features of the Torah of Israel, to submit themselves in other words to the ritual requirements of the Jewish religion, and in particular to the practice of male circumcision, or else they could not really be followers of Jesus Christ. Paul when he hears of this attempt to interfere with the church he founded is very angry. 'Who has distracted you from the freedom of the Gospel?' he asks. Against the Judaisers, Paul declares that there is one event and one event only that has delivered them into the Kingdom of God and the new era that has begun, and this is the event of Christ's crucifixion: 'it was before your eyes that Jesus Christ was publicly exhibited as crucified' (Galatians 3: 1). The Galatians, like Paul, have been redeemed or rescued by this event and not by any action of theirs, and certainly not by the ritual requirements of the Torah. For it is Christ who rescued the Galatians from the powers that rule the world, and these powers include the religion of the Torah, which, though it was able to show that they were sinners, was unable to redeem them.

But why is Paul so insistent that only Christ, Crucified and Risen, is the source of their salvation? Why is it that no action of theirs can be said to complete this apocalyptic event? Well, according to Paul, the Galatians are confronted with a sharp division in their lives: either they are chosen as the children and heirs of God or they are slaves of the powers, 'the weak and beggarly elemental spirits' (Galatians 4. 9) who rule the world and once ruled their lives. The Galatians imagine they are free, that they can go on choosing to jump from one realm into another. But to choose to follow the old gods is to choose 'immediate exit from the new creation' back into the place of enslavement to the powers. For Paul, the Christian apocalypse means that no other form of society, no other religion, no other Torah, no other politics can claim the loyalty of the Galatians if they have been chosen and adopted as the 'Sons of God'. If they are sons then they are 'claimed by God in Christ to be God's own people', as Peter, the first disciple of the Lord, puts it in his own epistle. If they are sons they are free, but this freedom is not a freedom to choose again their old ways. The freedom of the Christian is a new kind of servitude, one that issues in a new kind of community, a new kind of politics, a new kind of society, a new kind of virtue. The shape of this virtue is the 'fruit of the Spirit', which includes 'love, joy, peace, faithfulness, gentleness, goodness, patience, meekness and self-control' (Galatians 5: 3). This list of the Christian virtues is unlike a Roman heroic ethic or an Aristotelian aristocratic ethic. It indicates that the shape of the Christian life, the freedom into which Christians are invited by the apocalypse of Jesus, is the Spirit-given ability to fashion their lives and communities after the life and death of Jesus Christ. The shape of the Church is a cruciform shape. As Christ gave up his life for the world, so Christians are to submit their interests to one another, to avoid conflict and dissension and violence, and to embrace love and gentleness and service in the 'unity of the Spirit'.

Straightaway when we put matters like this, the opposition between the imperial American account of freedom and the New Testament account of freedom becomes apparent. According to George W. Bush, America is attacked by its enemies because they envy America's freedoms. To defend these freedoms blood is spilled on the battlefields of Afghanistan and Iraq, and tens of thousands of lives are sacrificed. But what kind of freedom is it that demands so much blood spilt, and what kind of freedom is it that requires that it is imposed on foreign nations through the technological superiority of Abrams tanks and the death-dealing weaponry of cluster bombs and Depleted Uranium shells? It is clearly a different kind of freedom to Christian freedom, which involves the avoidance of violent means and violent ends, for in the Christian apocalypse the struggle between good and evil is in the most important sense already over. Christ through the cross and resurrection has already overcome, already demonstrated the triumph of right over might.

The American account of freedom is imperial when it requires that Christians submit their bodies to the imperative of the flag, and allow their or their children's blood to be spilt in America's wars. Similarly when education or public health programmes, which could increase opportunities and reduce infant mortality in poor American communities, are sacrificed for burgeoning military budgets, human life is sacrificed for the idol of national security. The requirement that these sacrifices be made is in conflict with the Christian claim that the sacrifice of Christ was a sacrifice that put an end for ever to the need for blood sacrifice. It is also in conflict with the form of service, the kind of freedom that is the shape of the new life made possible in God's kingdom.

American Christians are faced with a clear division in their loyalties that is just as serious as the conflict between the Judaisers and Paul in the church at Galatia. If they are called to give up their lives and their taxes in the bloody wars of the American imperium then, despite the offer of religious freedom implicit in the Church–State separation of American society, the American Republic makes a claim on Christians that is in direct conflict with their worship and service of Jesus Christ and the Church. As Harink puts it:

> American Christians (and Christians of any other nation) can no more give their bodies to the flag and nation than the Galatian Gentiles can let themselves be circumcised. With Paul, the only marks which Christians may bear in their bodies will be "the marks of Jesus" (Galatians 6. 17). The national flag in the church sanctuary is the mark of the beast on the Christian body.[38]

The sacralisation of American political arrangements is such that for many American Christians 'the first subject of Christian ethics in America *is* America' and Christian social ethics becomes 'not simply a theory of government but a theory of society that is imperial in its demands'.[39] These imperial demands have only one outcome for Christians who would embrace the American account of freedom – that they must submit, and therefore really abandon, their loyalty to Christ in favour of their loyalty to the American empire. By the very nature of the Church as body, and as an assemblage of bodies, it is not possible to hive off parts of the bodies of Christians – the military parts, the tax-paying parts, the voting parts – from the worshipping and believing parts. But this is what the civil religion of America and its alliance with millennial evangelicalism seems to require. It sets up a division of labour between the coercive activity of the State and the inner piety of Christians. Such a division requires that Christianity become a private religion of the heart, of spiritual comfort and psychological interiority – the religion, in fact, of American evangelicalism – while the State is free to pursue its militarist and imperial wars without prophetic criticism or resistance from conservative evangelical Christians.

The body of Christ, if truly it is the ecclesial embodiment of Christ, will therefore resist all definitions of religion or Church as private or personal, and of State as public and political, because the body of Christ is itself a polity and its first responsibility is not to baptise American values, or America's imperial wars. For Hauerwas, the first political task of the Church is to exemplify in its own life an alternative politics that resists the imperial demands of the cult of America on the bodies of American Christians. This involves witness to the sovereignty of the Ascended Christ and heavenly King in the lives and communities of Christians. Such witness will involve commitment to peaceableness, for it is precisely over the question of violence that the Christian is most tested in a world that claims that Christians

> must be willing to choose sides and kill in order to preserve the social orders in which they find themselves. As Christians when we accept that alternative it surely means that we are no longer the church that witnesses to God's sovereignty over all the nations, but instead we have become part of the world.[40]

Hauerwas suggests that Christians must resist the world at this point if they wish to follow the example of their Lord because he

> would not employ violence to avoid death at the hands of a state. Just as that oppressive regime could not prevent his authorization of God's kingdom so neither as Christians do we believe any worldly power can stop us from living true to God's peaceable kingdom.[41]

Does this mean that Christians are to cut themselves off from the world, that they have nothing to say to the dilemmas of a state faced with acts of terror that seem to threaten its very existence? On the contrary, Hauerwas suggests that the world needs the Church to be the non-violent Church, to exemplify the peaceable kingdom, if the world is to come to see that there is an alternative to hate and terror and war. This is why after September 11 Hauerwas was one of the very few well-known public voices in America calling for a non-violent response. Hauerwas spoke and wrote, argued and debated the reasons for his pacifist stance up and down the East Coast, in magazines, journals, books, lectures and on the internet. The idea that a theologian who goes to so much trouble to put in the public domain a set of extremely unpopular arguments for the legitimacy of pacifism is a sectarian, or is commending a withdrawal from the world, is laughable.

Christians who resist apocalyptic wars launched in defence of the free market, liberty and democracy may easily be identified as sectarian fanatics, but so long as they are non-violent this identification is not a problem: 'Christians who insist on "the politics of Jesus" cannot but appear like Islamic fundamentalists – not a bad place to be from my perspective'.[42] The worst kind of fanaticism is that promoted by the ruling elites of America, who have become so zealous in their pursuit of 'liberty' that they adopt the methods of the terrorist, and even turn the fanatic into a terrorist. The School of the Americas in Georgia for more than 30 years trained foreign militia from Latin America, Indonesia and the Philippines in the methods of terror including assassination, car-bombing, kidnapping, and torture. Liberal intellectuals, such as Harvard Law Professor Alan Dershowitz, have even suggested that America may be justified in using torture if it would prevent a terrorist atrocity and have thereby seemed to justify the extensive use of interrogation techniques and forms of incarceration on American army bases in Afghanistan and Iraq, and in Guantanamo Bay which the United Nations convention on torture recognises as torture.[43] There is also extensive evidence from independent human rights groups that American troops have used torture, including sleep deprivation, beatings, sexual humiliation, and even electric shocks, on those detained in Afghanistan and Iraq.[44] Against that background, the witness of apocalyptic pacifism to the non-violence of Jesus and His Kingdom seems all the more urgent.

5 – The Warrior Ethos and the Politics of Jesus

The parallels between the global reach and military superiority of the American Empire in the early twenty-first century with the Roman Empire in the third and fourth centuries are irresistible. Like the Roman Empire, America aspires to control and direct human history, and the 'neo-cons' in particular intend to turn the twenty-first century into 'the new American century'. As we have seen, America manages its imperium not so much by direct rule as by client–patron relationships, and through rapid deployment of a highly mobile military force, which uses the extensive network of American military bases to launch technologically sophisticated and fearsome raids on 'failed states' and terrorists identified as opposing the imperium. American neo-conservatives suggest that this new empire-lite needs a new warrior ethos if it is to be effectively defended, analogous to the violent ethos of terror with which Rome used its legionaries to police its empire, and to control the history of its own time. Robert Kaplan quotes Livy with approval when he said 'It is better that a wise man fear you than that foolish friends praise you' and suggests that 'we [the United States] and nobody else will write the terms for international society'.[1] The military have not been slow to take up this new concept of imperial service, and American soldiers now receive instruction in the new 'warrior ethos'. The ethos calls for extreme fitness, total commitment to military aims, an inner dedication to the demands of conflict, and the willingness to kill. It is inculcated in the form of a new 'soldier's creed', which says 'I will always place the mission first. I will never accept defeat.

I will never quit. I will never leave a fallen comrade'.[2] The extensive targeting of civilians and civilian infrastructure in the wars in Afghanistan and Iraq, and the continued killing of civilians since the formal end of hostilities in both countries, would seem to indicate that the uncompromising stance of the warrior ethos has been adopted in the 'war on terror'. American troops are not even required to keep a record of civilian deaths, although an independent and reputable website run by American academics has so far recorded over 10,000 civilian deaths in Iraq alone.[3]

Rome's warrior legionaries were accustomed to killing and terrorising civilian populations. The word decimation refers to the legionaries' practice of killing one in ten males in an imperial province, as a standard strategy for terrorising and subduing a newly conquered populace. That the Roman Empire was founded on violence and terror is easy to forget, given the labelling of its rule as *Pax Romanum*; but this peace was an enforced peace, a subdued peace, a violent peace.

At the heart of the warrior ethos of America, like that of Rome, is the virtue of courage, a virtue frequently invoked by George W. Bush in his post-September 11 rhetoric:

> In the sacrifice of soldiers, the fierce brotherhood of fire-fighters, and the bravery and generosity of ordinary citizens, we have glimpsed what a new culture of responsibility could look like. We want to be a nation that serves goals larger than self. We've been offered a unique opportunity, and we must not let this moment pass.[4]

Bush sees the terror attacks as an opportunity to revive traditional virtues, but as with the heroic virtues of Greece and Rome, the virtues he invokes seem to rely upon war and responses to it for their realisation. As Jean Bethke Elshtain puts it 'the problem with the tradition of civic virtues can be succinctly stated; that virtue is *armed*'.[5] Aristotle thought courage was at the heart of the virtues because the Greek city state – the *polis* – was built on war and only those who fought its battles, and had thus displayed heroic virtue, had the right to become citizens in the public assembly.

Bush is certainly right that war is instructive. War might even make us wise, for it faces us with great suffering and great opportunities for sacrifice and solidarity. When my parents tell stories of living through the blitz in London in the Second World War they have a light in their eyes, and they seem to express the hope and glory of life in the midst of war that makes life in peace-time look pale by comparison. Their children and grandchildren are to learn the virtues elsewhere than on the battlefield, for the modern nation-state system is supposed to have done away with the need for war and to provide schooling in citizenship in other ways. But far from the era of democratic nation-states seeing the end of war, the most democratic century, the twentieth, was also among the most violent in history. As Jean Elshtain observes, 'the nation-state, including our own, rests on mounds of bodies'.[6]

The Church as Counter-Culture to Empire

For the first three centuries of the Christian era, Christians were forced to make a choice between fealty to the warrior ethos of Caesar and fealty to Christ. From its inception, Christianity was at odds with the warring Roman imperium because the first Christians understood that the battle that needed to be fought to overcome fear and hate had already been won. Certainly, courage was needed in this battle, and Christ displays great courage in the gospels. But it is not the conventional courage of the warrior; instead the gospels speak of the meekness of Christ, of his humility and patience in enduring the way of the cross. Christians were exhorted to display the same virtues that Jesus displayed and they did not imagine that the result would be peace with the empire. The important thing was that they practised peace with one another. When there was disagreement or conflict they were taught to confront and confess sin, and then to forgive and be reconciled.

The conflict between Rome and early Christianity did not arise so much from the fact that the Roman authorities had put Jesus to death, as from the subversive challenge of communities formed by the Christian story to the warrior ethos of Rome. What St Paul called the 'kingdom of the Son' was a political and spiritual order that represented a radical challenge to the imperial cult and to the quest for power and control over the hearts and minds of all those who lived within Rome's imperial orbit. Paul himself was eventually tried before the Emperor and put to death. His teachings and those of the sects he founded were viewed as a real threat to the cult and power of Empire. This threat was closely tied to the fact that Christian courage was different from Roman courage.

Christians were exhorted to be virtuous but their virtues of patience, of endurance in the face of suffering, of humility in the face of power, and of non-violence in the face of evil were counter-cultural to Roman civic virtue. The consequences of confessing Christ as Lord included constant threats to their homes and property, exclusion from the upper echelons of imperial society, its client rulers and their service classes, and for some martyrdom. In the face of these threats, the writer to the Hebrews, like the writer of the Book of Revelation, exhorts his readers to endurance: 'you shared the suffering of the prisoners, and you cheerfully accepted the seizure of your possessions, knowing that you possessed something better and more lasting. Do not then throw away your confidence, for it carries a great reward. You need endurance, if you are to do God's will and win what he has promised' (Hebrews 10. 34 – 36). It was not that Christians lacked courage, but that their courage was of a different kind to the warrior's and it was therefore bound to be subversive of a polity sustained by courage learned in war.

The first Christian churches could not help but be a counter-culture within the Empire. They operated as open societies, though they met not in public places but in small private houses and formed networks of believers who of necessity supported one another and shared their resources with one another in the face of imperial persecution, theft and violence. Despite their violent treatment by Rome, Christians remained true to their founder and refrained from armed resistance, because the early Christian ethos was modelled on the life and teachings of Jesus. Just as Christ had followed the way of non-violence leading to the cross, so Christians also were called to 'take up the cross' and to avoid conflict both in their own communities and with their neighbours.

This modelling reflected something deep within the Christian story, which was the revolutionary idea that the sacrifice of Christ, and his resurrection from the dead, had put an end to the need for blood sacrifice for all time. As René Girard suggests, rituals of sacrifice and the scapegoat are fundamental to most religious and cultural systems, including those of modern nation-states and empires.[7] The Jewish religion was no different in this respect to other religious systems. But while the God of Israel had required blood sacrifice – of animals not humans – as part of the covenantal system for righting wrongs and maintaining social order, St Paul and the other New Testament writers viewed the death of Christ on the cross not only as an example of non-violent resistance to evil, but also as constituting the end of the sacrificial system. Christ was in the words of the Book of Revelation the 'lamb that was slain' and he was also *vicit agnus noster*, 'our victorious lamb'.[8] The first Christians understood the death and resurrection of Christ as having a unique finality, which demonstrated within history that the distorting rule of sin and death that the Jewish sacrificial system was instituted to correct was dethroned, disempowered, in the victory of Christ in his crucifixion and resurrection.

This radical conception of salvation as victory over sin and death, and over the fallen powers that ruled the world, meant that the early Christians did not need to institute a cult to compete with the corrupted cult of the Temple or the mystery religions and imperial cult of Rome. Instead, their meetings were social and spiritual gatherings in which no animals were slain. The rituals of the first Christians were based around prayers and psalms, readings from scripture and the sharing of a meal of bread and wine. The element of sacrifice was excluded precisely because there was no longer a need for scapegoating or bloodshed.

The root of violence is fear: fear of the other, fear of the stronger, fear of cataclysm, fear of not having enough, and these fears drive the mimetic violence of rivalry of which Girard speaks. As Wendel Berry observes, fear is the weapon the Bush administration uses to garner support for its perpetual war while wilfully neglecting the real causes of terrorism and war in the global inequality and injustice created by the vast consumer economy of the United States.[9] Since September 11, 2001 the Bush administration has constantly stoked public fear with terrorist warnings. In St John's account of the salvation wrought by Christ, 'perfect love casts out fear' (1 John. 18),

and, according to St Paul, Christ has taken away the root of fear and
of violence which is the 'dividing wall of hostility' (Ephesians 2. 2)
and so the need for sacrifice was removed for all time. As the writer
to the Hebrews put it, 'we have a great high priest who has passed
through the heavens' (Hebrews 4. 14) having 'offered himself
without blemish to God' (Hebrews 9. 14). The writer sees Christ as
having offered the perfect sacrifice of a sinless victim which brings
to an end the need for blood sacrifice for all time. Now that 'the
veil of the temple is torn in two' (Mark 15. 38), the holy of holies
is no longer a shrine hidden from the people; instead the new
people of God are the living stones (1 Peter 2. 5) that constitute the
new temple, the sanctity of their communities creates the new
holy of holies. A new ethic of love, justice and peace is practised,
which through the rituals of confrontation, confession, penitence
and forgiveness provide lived demonstrations of the possibility
of true reconciliation between ruler and ruled, between enemies,
between residents and aliens. This puts an end to enmity and hence
to systems of violent sacrifice meant to resolve it. As Hauerwas
puts it:

> The sacrifice to end sacrifices was made by God through the
> sacrifice of his son, and the ending of sacrifice means that we
> don't continue to sacrifice other people to make the world come
> out all right. Justice has been done. We've been given all the
> time in the world to announce that God would not have God's
> kingdom wrought through violence.[10]

Despite their resistance to the warrior ethos of empire, Christians in
the first century sought nonetheless to live peaceably not only with
one another but with Rome. St Paul, the Jewish Apostle who often
speaks of his own status as a Roman citizen, while condemning
Roman idolatry and Jewish collaboration with Rome, nonetheless
commended the Imperial authorities to the Christians of Rome as
those who served the purposes of God in maintaining order and
punishing wrong-doing (Romans 13). Christians were not to resist
legitimate authority and they were to pray for the state that it might
be saved from corruption and tyranny. But despite this benign
attitude to the authorities, Christians soon found themselves in

conflict with Rome and, by the early second century, persecution and violence against the early Christians were endemic.

It was for the encouragement of a number of increasingly embattled Christian communities in Asia Minor that the Christian Apocalypse of St John of Patmos, the Book of Revelation, was written. This book is full of the language of war and violence and redolent of the cultic and sacrificial symbol system that the victory of Christ over death had put to an end. But the purpose of the writer was not to encourage Christians to engage in warfare themselves but to explain to them that the battle between the fallen and sinful powers that rule the world, and the angels and spiritual powers that reign in heaven has already been fought and won in the death and resurrection and ascension of Jesus Christ. The war of the lamb brings about a peaceable victory. But Christians are given no guarantee that this victory will prevent them from suffering for their faith, or even being martyred. The only guarantee that is offered is that which is already revealed on the cross and in the resurrection; history has been redeemed, and the kingdom is already present in history. Therefore Christians do not need to try to control history's outcome. Christ is 'alpha and omega', the beginning and the end of the world; time stood still on the cross and was redeemed on the third day, and the power of evil and of death itself are overcome in the resurrection. This was the secret that the writer of the Christian Apocalypse revealed to his readers. Though the Romans did not know it, their empire was bound one day to come to acknowledge Christ as Lord, and to worship with Christians the God of the Jews who was revealed as the saviour of the whole world, and not just of the Jews, in Jesus.

The Crusade Against 'Evil' and the Defeat of the Powers

When George W. Bush first announced his 'war on terror' to the world, he declared that wherever terrorists and their supporters were hiding, the United States would root them out in a holy crusade against wickedness whose apocalyptic purpose was to 'rid the world of evil'. He withdrew the language of crusade after journalists and religious leaders pointed out to him how offensive this word was to Muslims, and how indeed it would only lend credence to the claims of Osama bin Laden that America was engaged in a Zionist crusade to dominate the Middle East, to erase the Arab presence from the Holy Land of Israel, and to humble the aspirations of Muslim people to freedom from American hegemony. But something more lies behind Bush's claim to be capable of 'ridding the world of evil'. Anyone who can make such a claim clearly believes that they themselves are incapable of truly being evil; only the enemy is truly evil. 'I' or 'we' are righteous, capable of doing great good but not of deep wickedness. As Wendel Berry suggests, the idea that in opposing evil, or even ridding the world of evil, as Bush promised to do in his speech in the National Cathedral on 14 September, 2001, Americans can as a nation consider themselves good is doubly problematic. First because it adopts the very self-deceiving delusional anathemas of those whom America claims to be opposing, and second because it completely neglects the teaching of Christ that only one can properly be called good who is God.[11]

A Christian account of the good can never identify any particular political structure or strategy, let alone a national strategy of pre-emptive warfare, as unambiguously good.[12] It is precisely when the Church has come to think of itself as the supreme arbiter of divine judgement, although Christ taught his disciples to judge no one, that the Church has been most compromised in its relationships with corrupt monarchs and oppressive empires. Equally, a Christian account of evil is mistaken if it understands evil as a positive force which has entirely captured the hearts and minds of certain individuals, or groups or nations. Evil for Christians, as John Milbank affirms, is not so much a positive force as it is evidence of lack: lack of truthfulness, of decency, of faith, hope and love.[13]

The Christian account of evil takes its rise from Jesus' own way of dealing with evil as described in the gospels. This is nowhere more powerfully exemplified than in the story of the encounter of Jesus with the Gerasene demoniac. The people of the country of the Gerasenes had only two years previously been subjected to the most brutal massacre by a Roman legion, which had left many deranged with fear and grief, or what today we would call 'post-traumatic stress disorder'. Jesus' hearers, and first-century Gospel readers, would have immediately got the reference to these events when the

demon of the man possessed responds to Jesus' question 'what is
your name?' with the reply 'my name is Legion' (Mark 5. 9). The evil
Jesus challenged was that state of affairs which manifested itself in
imperial slaughter. Evil was also manifest in the debt, privation and
sickness which imperialism had visited on the Jewish people, and in
the self-deception of those who collaborated with the imperial
authorities among the Jewish people. It was not appropriate or even
effective to declare war openly on these evils, for as Jesus told his
disciples when they used swords in an attempt to resist those who
came to arrest him in the Garden of Gethsemane, the old saying still
holds that 'those who live by the sword will die by the sword'
(Matthew 26. 52). But in declaring that he would 'bind the strong
man', Jesus indicates that it is his intention to release the people of
Israel from their subjugation to the Roman authorities and their
Jewish collaborators.[14]

Jesus' strategy for dealing with evil was to expose the self-
deception of those who collaborated with it, to condemn the lies of
the Temple elites under which guise they piled up riches for themselves, and to declare that despite all appearances it was possible to
resist evil by dwelling in communities where evil was dethroned,
where instead people took up the cross of self-denial, and practised
love and justice in service of others. Jesus does not therefore ever
condemn Roman or Jewish elites, tax collectors or soldiers as classes
of people who are entirely evil. He healed the child of a Roman
centurion, he swapped wisdom sayings with Pharisees, he admitted
a tax collector to his inner circle of disciples and told another,
Zacchaeus, that as he had repented of his sins and promised to make
restitution, so salvation had come to his household (Luke 19. 9). Jesus
resisted evil by teaching his disciples to discern deception even in
their own hearts, and by embracing the truth revealed in his coming
that divine self-giving love is more powerful than the powers that
drive men and women to destroy and persecute one another. His
most angry put down of any of his disciples was when Peter
suggested that the way of the Messiah was not to be the way of the
cross but the way of triumphal victory over the Roman oppressors
of the Jewish people: 'get behind me Satan' was Jesus' response
(Mark 8. 33). There is no other end to the story than the way of the
cross; the point, which the disciples failed to see, was that this

ending was not an end but the only way to a new beginning, for in the death and resurrection of Christ evil is at last defeated and life is redeemed from fear and hatred. Through the Resurrection, Christ triumphed over the 'rulers of the present age' and 'led captivity captive' so that a new age, a new order, a new people might come into being.

The language that St Paul adopts to explain the defeat of evil in the cross and resurrection of Christ is that of the 'principalities and powers' and the 'elemental spirits of the universe'. These are angelic and creaturely beings or influences, which keep men and women in slavery, subject to their rules and under their tutelage, 'following the course of this world' and 'the ruler of the power of the air' (Ephesians 2. 2). Life under the sway of the Powers characterises the state of sin that made those who were not of the Kingdom 'children of wrath' before they were made alive together with Christ (Ephesians 2. 3 – 4).[15] According to Walter Wink, Paul's language of the Powers does not just indicate fallen angels, but rather points to the formal institutions and social structures that give shape to human social life: these include states, classes, nationalisms, tribes, democratic systems and bureaucracies, religious institutions and symbol systems, ideologies, moral codes and customs, and economic organisations including corporations and markets as well.[16] The Powers are not absolutely evil, and nor are they entirely outside of the purposes of the good God who created them. Though part of God's good creation, they are fallen, and prevent persons from realising a truly free and loving existence because, as John Howard Yoder puts it, 'they have absolutized themselves and they demand from the individual and society an unconditional loyalty'.[17] The enslavement of humanity to the fallen Powers finds divine response in the Crucifixion and Resurrection of Christ, in which God 'disarmed the principalities and Powers and made a public example of them, triumphing over them' (Colossians 2. 15). It is in being the Church that Christians witness to the triumph of Christ over the Powers and indicate that their dominion is at an end.[18] Critical witness to the demise of the Powers arises first and foremost not from Christian talk about freedom or justice but from the alternative form of community life that is the Church. As Yoder puts it:

All resistance and every attack against the gods of this age will be unfruitful, unless the church herself is resistance and attack, unless she demonstrates in her life and fellowship how men can live freed from the Powers. We can only preach the manifold wisdom of God to Mammon if our life displays that we are joyfully freed from its clutches. To reject nationalism we must begin by no longer recognizing in our own bosoms any difference between peoples. We shall only resist social injustice and the disintegration of community if justice and mercy prevail in our own common life and social differences have lost their power to divide.[19]

This does not mean that Christians can neglect the Powers. On the contrary, the Powers that dominate the public realm are part of God's design for creation and human society and intended for the good of all, though they have become at the same time the oppressors of all.[20] The State in particular is a servant of God and this is why St Paul in Romans 13 indicates that Christians are not to resist the State so long as it sustains good order and punishes evil-doers.

According to Yoder, this dual understanding of the nature of the Powers – as ordered for good but fallen and therefore, often, evil – runs prophetically counter to the concept of power that is core to modern accounts of power and weakness, evil and good. Such accounts are manifest in the rhetoric of Bush that America's enemies are evil while the military power of America is a force for good in the world. It is equally evident in the narrative of Robert Kagan that America serves the good in its unilateral use of its technological superiority and in its unashamed intent to win wars that Europeans are too weak to fight.[21] The truth is that there are countless wars and coups and covert actions in which American power has been used to support tyranny and genocide, from Guatemala in the 1940s to Vietnam, Cambodia and Laos in the 1960s and 70s, and from East Timor and Columbia in the 1990s to Iraq and Afghanistan in the twenty-first century.[22] The truth is that America, along with its close ally Britain, has used the indiscriminate technologies of cluster bombs and Depleted Uranium in civilian areas in all its recent wars and has not only killed and maimed thousands of non-combatants with these dreadful weapons, but left behind a legacy of genetic disorder and cancer that will be around for generations wherever American (and British) forces have utilised these dreadful weapons.[23] In such circumstances Christians must not only attempt to live out an alternative ethic but they ought also publicly to challenge and critique the State, for the powers of the State that St Paul speaks of in Romans 13 are only legitimate when it acts as a power for good, and restrains evil-doers. But when state violence becomes indiscriminate then it must be condemned and resisted.[24] It is a tragedy that so few Christians either in America or Britain have critiqued these indiscriminate technologies and their vicious short and long-term impacts on human life since the Gulf War, when they were first used extensively and appear to have had long-term effects not only on Iraqis but on US and British troops. Despite government denials of the existence of 'gulf war syndrome', hundreds of troops who served in the Gulf have experienced a raft of strange illnesses, or died prematurely.

Against the scale of indiscriminate violence regularly visited by America on its enemies – America initiated more than one hundred military campaigns since 1945 in defence of its 'interests' and is the only nation ever to have launched both chemical and nuclear weapons from airborne bombers against civilian populations – it is unsurprising that the weak adopt a terror of their own. The relationship between American power and those who resist it in the Middle East and around the world is of course a classic imperial relationship in which there is an asymmetry of power. But just because the weak are weak, this does not make their terrorist and violent response to power any less evil than power abused by the strong. The modern mythology of evil, as often embraced by Muslims as by secularists or Christians, celebrates the violent resistance of the weak to the evil of the strong. Those who resist imperialism or the abuse of power are described as heroic 'freedom fighters' even when they use the same techniques of terror, assassinations, bombings, attacks on the innocent, as the strong. Here again, the tradition of warrior virtue infects contemporary discourse. But terror is terror, evil is evil – it does not matter whether it is inflicted by a nation-state or an informal network of terrorists. In the perspective of the New Testament language of the Powers, the angel of God does not fight on the side of the strong *or* the weak when they fight evil with evil.

Bush is wrong about that and so is bin Laden; God is not a freedom fighter and neither does God send his angels to fight on behalf of America.

Jesus and the early Christians knew all about asymmetric power relationships. But by discerning that power is subverted through the weakness of the cross rather than force of arms, they understood with St Paul 'that power is weak and weakness strength' (2 Corinthians 10. 9). As Yoder puts it, this

> is no poetic paradox: it is a fact of life. What recent ecumenical thought calls 'the epistemological privilege of the poor', what comparable Roman Catholic texts call God's 'preferential option for the poor,' what Tolstoy meant much earlier when he said that the oppressed are the bearers of the meaning of history, is not poetry but serious social science.[25]

In this perspective, both the terrorists who attacked America, and the Bush administration that responds to their attacks with deception and lies to advance a series of wars whose real intent is American economic and political hegemony, and not just a policing action to punish evil-doers, are deceived by the Powers into imagining that coercion, violence and war are the means to defeat what they identify as evil and to advance what they identify as good.

In their attempts to sacralise their conflict, both Bush and bin Laden are aided in their self-deception by the doctrine of holy or just war, a doctrine which has its roots in the Old Testament, and which was recycled by Christian theologians after Constantine, and later by the prophet Muhammad. The roots of Christian just-war theory may be traced to the new imperial theology that Christian bishops adumbrated in their new role as leaders of an imperial religion. When the Book of Revelation's prediction of the conversion of the Roman Empire to the cause of the Church eventually came true with the conversion of the Emperor Constantine in the third century, Christians found themselves in the strange position of being not an embattled minority but the majority, and this new majoritarian position had the tragic consequence of deforming the faith of the first Christians into a new cult of empire.

Constantine, Christian Imperialism and Just War

Constantine acceded to the Imperial throne after a bloody civil war for the accession after Diocletian had attempted to demit it to his son Maxentius. Diocletian had sponsored an edict of persecution against the Christians in 303, which inaugurated a particularly vicious wave of executions of Christians, and destruction of homes and sanctuaries, which many pagans felt to be excessive since Christianity was growing in popularity despite persecution. In the course of a military campaign against Diocletian's ill-starred son Maxentius, Constantine is said to have had a vision of the cross which was a turning point in his battle for Rome.[26] As a consequence of the vision he instructed his troops to mark their shields with this heavenly sign in the form of the cross with a circle above it to resemble the Christian symbol of the *chi-rho*, being the first two letters of the name Christ in Greek. After doing this the battle turned in Constantine's favour and the next day he was declared emperor.

Constantine announced that he intended to adopt Christianity as his imperial cult because the vision of the cross had favoured him in battle and he wished for himself and his imperial court to convert to Christianity.[27] In so doing Constantine was also recognising the political reality. The Diocletian persecution had been neither popular among pagans nor successful in quelling the strength of the Church. The simplest thing for a successor emperor was to make peace with the ever-growing Christian Church, and enlist this successful religion in the service of the authority of empire, which is exactly what Constantine did. The Empire had become so large that it was in danger of splitting apart, and for a time there had been a multiplicity of Caesars in different parts of the Empire as a device for dealing with its sheer geographical size. Constantine resolved to attempt to reunite the Empire and he seems to have seen Christianity as the form of monotheism – he had been a monotheist for some time before his vision of the cross – that stood the best chance, because of its widespread popularity, of helping to unite the empire. As H. A. Drake puts it, the simple guiding idea behind Constantine's attempt to sacralise empire around Christianity was that there were:

sufficient grounds for agreement between Christians and pagans for the ties between emperor and divinity which were now a necessary condition for legitimate rule to be defined in terms suitable for Christians, pagan monotheists, and even those polytheists who did not insist on performance of blood sacrifices.

The problem for Constantine, as for emperors since the third century, was that Roman citizenship had been redefined around a requirement to make 'ritual sacrifice to the official gods of the Roman state', and this was something that Christians were unable to do. Given the failure of the persecution, it made sense to incorporate Christians into the new project of securing a unified empire rather than to continue to persecute them.[28] The Edict of Milan was issued only months after Constantine became emperor and in it he committed the Roman state to the principle of the freedom of religion, provided it was generally monotheist, and granted Christianity in particular legal status for the first time in its history. The Edict does not however refer to the Christian God specifically but instead to the *summa divinitas* or 'supreme deity'.

The Edict of Milan marked a milestone in Western Christian history. With it Constantine began the transformation of the Western Church from a confessional community into a civic religion that would serve as the imperial cult with which he intended to shore up the borders of the Roman Empire. This transformation prefigured the enlisting of the Christian God by first European and later American Empires, as the over-arching deity who gives sacred honour to the imperial quest to conquer and control the history of the world in subsequent eras. For Constantine there was nothing especially novel in this. All Caesars had maintained that the gods were on their side in their imperial wars and that they carried in their person the divine benison on empire. But it was a dramatic rupture for the Church when Constantine enlisted Christian symbols in the imperial war machine. The *chi-rho*, representing the first two letters of the Greek name *Christos*, was incorporated into a gilded *labarum* or wreath, which became the new emblem or logo under which Rome's imperial armies did battle. The *labarum* consisted of the *chi-rho* atop a gilded spear and a transverse bar, making the shape of the cross, and this new logo was emblazoned on the helmets and shields of Rome's armies, and those of the emperor himself. The Church also adopted the *labarum* as its new logo and it can be found inscribed in stone in the large basilicas – public temples – that became the new locus for Christian worship in Rome's imperial cities.

With the adoption of Christianity as the imperial cult by the Emperor Constantine, Christian theologians had to reckon with a newly Christianised global Empire. The first truly imperial theologian, Eusebius of Caesarea, who was promoted to Bishop by Constantine, described the unipolar world which the Christianisation of Rome was creating as the work of divine providence, which would bring the world through its singular sovereignty to an earthly and universal peace:

> And as the knowledge of one God and one way of religion and salvation, even the doctrine of Christ, was made known to all mankind; so at the same period the entire dominion of the Roman empire being vested in a single sovereign, profound peace reigned throughout the world. And thus by the express appointment of the same God, two roots of blessing, the Roman empire and the doctrine of Christian piety, sprang up together for the benefit of men.[29]

Eusebius here does not seem to celebrate war as such but rather sees Constantine's victories as victories against war. He envisages a time when the whole world will appear one 'well-ordered family', when the prophecies of an 'abundance of peace' (Psalm 72.7) and of swords beaten into ploughshares (Isaiah 2.4) will have come to pass. Eusebius engages the Christian emphasis on peace through the cross of Christ as a means of shaping his own paean to Constantine's achievements, and even as a way of imposing moral and religious discipline on Rome's unruly and capriciously violent armies.[30] But what Eusebius bequeathed to Christendom – and in this sense he was perhaps Christendom's founding theologian – was the idea of a social order sustained by military power and imperial authority, which is blessed by God and which carries in its officers, and especially its emperor, the power and authority of Jesus Christ.

Towards the end of Constantine's reign, Eusebius gave a Jubilee speech in which he described the emperor in such a way as to exalt him almost to the status of the fourth person of the Trinity. Eusebius turned to the Old Testament to justify his theological blessing of Constantine because nothing in the New Testament could give grounds for Christians to adopt an emperor as their spiritual head. In his *Life of Constantine* Eusebius tells the story of a Christian prince born in a foreign land who God adopts as the one who will become God's chosen emperor. Constantine is compared to Moses, born in the house of Pharaoh, who goes on to lead the people of God from the darkness of persecution – under the Pharaoh Diocletian – to the promised land of liberty to worship their God under Constantine.[31] As Alastair Kee argues, for Eusebius it is Constantine and not Christ in whom God saves the Empire and turns it towards God's purposes for good, and in particular the good of the Church.[32] Constantine is described after the metaphor of the imperial games as 'the victor of God', and as having a God-given omnipresence and power over his empire, being 'outfitted in the likeness of the kingdom of heaven' who 'pilots affairs below with an upward gaze'.[33]

Eusebius' lauding of Constantine as God's chosen one is indicative of the extent to which Constantine had become not only the head of the Empire but the head of the Christian Church. Constantine summoned an ecumenical council of bishops of the Church at the famous Council of Nicaea at which he presided as emperor. He instructed the bishops to compose a formulaic creed which would once and for all resolve certain theological problems that threatened the unity of the church, and hence the efficacy of Christianity as a unitive religion of empire. Constantine became also an appointer of bishops, and a deposer of sects and heretics. He was in all but name head of the Church as well as Caesar over the Empire.

Once Constantine adopted Christianity, or at least a version of monotheism that looked rather like Christianity, as the official religion of empire, Christians began to think differently about the nature of the apocalypse, and of the place of violence and war in the continuing purposes of God for human history. For the theologians of empire from Eusebius onwards, God would determine the outcome of history not in Jesus Christ but in the attempts of the Empire to shape the destiny of its subject peoples, and in Rome's wars with its outside, with the 'barbarians'. Consequently the theologians of empire turned for a theological justification of Rome's wars to the pre-Christian idea of holy or just war.

To understand the doctrine of 'Just War' it is helpful to return briefly to the Old Testament. Modern readers of the Old Testament tend to read these ancient stories of the Jews as stories that indicate a warlike God who fights with his people against those who had formerly possessed the holy land, or who would at various times in their history, conquer the people of God in the holy land.[34] The Old Testament would seem then to provide a set of stories and histories in which war is clearly and divinely intended as the way to settle disputes about history's outcome. This is not however the way that Old Testament theologians themselves understood the role of war and violence in the history of their people. It is true that when the people of Israel first entered the land of Canaan they were apparently instructed to wipe out all the people who had lived there before, since these people were put under a sacred 'ban' by God. However, Joshua, who first led the Israelites into Canaan, did not achieve his military victories by brute force. On the contrary, the Book of Joshua explains that it was when he put most of his best men aside and trusted in the Lord to win the battle for him that he eventually succeeded in subduing the Canaanites. The message was clear; it was Yahweh and not the strength of Israel's armies that gave them the victory: 'and the fear of God came on all the kingdoms of the countries, when they heard that Yahweh had fought against the enemies of Israel' (II Chronicles 20. 29).[35]

The theologians who constructed the ancient histories and the prophets who came after them constantly warned the people of God against putting their trust in 'horses and chariots' or in rulers who conquered by the size and strength of their armies. The favoured kings of Israel were not those who were the most successful in grabbing land from their neighbours; they were those who ruled, as the Prophet Zechariah put it 'not by might nor by power' but by the Spirit of God (Zechariah 4. 6). They manifested God's anointing not in their prowess in fighting, nor in their imperial ambitions, but in the character of their reign, and the quality of society which obtained under their rule among the people of God. *Tsedeq* is the Hebrew word, often translated as 'righteousness', which indicates right relations, or what we today tend to call justice: right relations between God and the people and among the people. And it was the extent to which they observed the covenant of righteousness that was the test of true anointed kingship in Israel, not success in battle. According to the Prophets it was because the kings of Israel and Judah came to trust more in chariots than in God that they were overthrown and their people sent into exile by other empires who took over the land of the promise. The leaders of the people had trusted in their own security and in the power of their armies and at the same time they had misused the gift of the land; they had stolen almost all of it for themselves so that the poor had nowhere left to live (Isaiah 5. 8). Their failure was a failure of trust in God, and a failure to be faithful to the covenant conditions for living in the land. Consequently even the land itself turned against them and became infertile (Isaiah 5. 10).[36] Their punishment was to be conquered by a succession of empires, the last of which was the Roman Empire.

Now despite this theological critique of imperial violence and war in the Old Testament, and Jesus' clear teaching and example in the New Testament that evil and the powers were defeated not by violence but by a preparedness to face even death rather than respond to evil with evil, Christians after Constantine invented a doctrine of just war which they attempted to link with Old Testament history, since they could find little justification for this new doctrine in the New Testament. Just like the American Senator in the eighteenth century who judged that the angel was in the storm that was the violent American Revolution against the English, and like George W. Bush who imagines that the angel of God fights with America's armies against its enemies, so Eusebius and his heirs judged that Constantine was the agent of God in bringing about Rome's peace in the fourth century. Later the Catholic Kings of Europe would similarly judge that God was with the Crusaders in their struggle against the Muslim inhabitants of the Holy Land and the city of Jerusalem.[37]

The problem with the invention of this new teaching is that the standard of discernment was not the standard that Christians learnt from the New Testament about how to judge the activity of God. The New Testament gives Christians no grounds for believing that God is active in war because its clear message is that there is no more need for war; in the language of the Book of Revelation the war in heaven has already ended, Michael and his angels have already put down the elemental spirits and the fallen angels that have misled the created Powers that govern the earth, and the Powers have been dethroned. They may continue to appear glorious and claim to be all-powerful, but Christians are called not to fight against them, rather to enact their defeat in their communities of worship and reconciliation.[38]

The imperial theologians who lauded Constantine as the angel of God, like the imperial theologians who laud America's 'war on terror', adopted the language of just war as the device with which to affirm the righteousness of Rome's wars. Augustine was the theologian who gave fullest expression to this belief in the era of the Roman Empire. In his classic work *The City of God* he describes how a war can be just, provided it is entered into by the Emperor with the purpose of extending and maintaining the peace of Rome:

> Whoever gives even moderate attention to human affairs and to our common nature, will recognize that if there is no man who does not wish to be joyful, neither is there any one who does not wish to have peace. For even they who make war desire nothing but victory – desire, that is to say, to attain to peace with glory. For what else is victory than the conquest of those who resist us? And when this is done there is peace. It is therefore with the desire for peace that wars are waged, even by those who take pleasure in exercising their warlike nature in command and battle. And hence it is obvious that peace is the end sought for by war.[39]

Augustine here gives first clear expression to the emergent Christian belief that wars are just provided that those who wage war have peace as the end. In the Middle Ages Aquinas expresses the same mind:

> Among true worshipers of God those wars are looked on as peacemaking which are waged neither from aggrandizement nor cruelty but with the object of securing peace, of repressing the evil and supporting the good.[40]

In his *Summa Theologiae* Aquinas gave three criteria for initiating a just war, known as *jus ad bellum*, which were, first, *just authority*, which is to say that only the legitimate rulers of the state may declare war; second, *just cause*, which is to say that a nation may only wage war when some direct injury has been done to it by another nation; and third, *right intention*, which is to say that those engaging in war must intend the achievement of peace. Revenge, the desire for plunder or for the suffering or destruction of people on the other side are always wrong.[41]

The just-war position is a central feature of the Constantinian inheritance, for it takes the imperial belief that violence is necessary for the restraint of evil and revises the earlier Christian view that all that is necessary for restraining evil is to live out the non-violent love that Christ exemplified and has made possible in the Church by the gift of the Spirit. According to Augustine, peace is the desire and the goal of the righteous Christian emperor and it is his divine mandate to use war to bring it about. Augustine did *not* thereby entertain the idea that such war was holy, nor that the Church, or the 'City of God', might engage in such wars. But, nonetheless, Augustine offers a theological warrant for the actions of Christian rulers, which has had enormous significance in the subsequent history of Christian civilisation, and in many ways might be said to be the origin of the very idea of Christian civilisation. What Constantine and his theological acolytes achieved in the fourth century was the transformation of Christianity from a pacifist and politically subversive creed and practice into an imperial ideology that would serve as bulwark of Byzantine Rome, and of subsequent would-be Christian empires, long after the demise of the Roman Empire.

Along with the Bush administration, some intellectuals in America have used the just-war theory in precisely this way in their defence of the 'war on terror'. In her *Just War Against Terror* Jean Elshtain suggests that the war on terror is a war of self-defence in response to the attacks of September 11 and is therefore morally justified. In relation to the war in Afghanistan that launched the US response, Elshtain says 'the U.S. military response in Afghanistan meets the just cause criterion of being a war fought with the right intention – to punish wrongdoers and prevent them from murdering civilians in the future'.[42] But it is hard to see how Elshtain can sustain this conclusion. The action in Afghanistan failed to meet the traditional just-war criteria either for launching a war (*jus ad bellum*), or for conduct in a war (*jus in bello*). Neither the Taliban nor the people of Afghanistan had declared war on, or attacked, America. In any case, since 1948, what Augustine and Aquinas called the only 'legitimate authority' that can declare war in international law resides not in the United States or with other nation-states, but with the Security Council of the United Nations.

In relation to the US conduct of the war in Afghanistan (and later Iraq) Elshtain's case is even weaker. *Jus in bello* criteria require that combatants use tactics and weapons that discriminate between enemy combatants and civilians. But the American and British forces clearly contravened this principle in their tactic of aerial bombardment of urban areas and villages and in their targeting of civilian infrastructure including public water supplies, communication systems and power stations (though Afghanistan, unlike Iraq, had precious little of these even before the American bombardment). The British and Americans also ignored the principle of discrimination in their deployment of cluster bombs and Depleted Uranium (DU) munitions. These weapons are weapons of mass destruction and terror, which are no more discriminating in their effects than the flying bombs used by the terrorists on September 11, and it is for this reason their use is banned by the UN.[43] Doctors and arms control experts report hundreds of thousands of cancer cases in Iraq as a consequence of the use of DU in the first Gulf War. DU has also given rise to thousands of horrendous birth defects in Iraq, and of infants born with diseases associated with uranium exposure including leukaemia, lymphoma and Hodgkin's disease.[44] It is estimated that 315 tons of DU dust was left in Iraq after the first Gulf War, and an official British report on the toxicity of battlefield DU indicated that just 40 tons of debris from DU munitions could give rise to over 500,000 deaths.[45] Cancers and birth defects among civilians are being reported not only in Iraq, but in every area where US and British troops have used DU munitions in the last 15 years including Kuwait, Bosnia, Kosovo and Serbia.

These technologies are so indiscriminate that even well-protected troops have left or been uplifted from battlefields in their thousands with a range of illnesses, and a long-term legacy of cancer, kidney

disease and genetic and nervous system disorders.[46] Pentagon reports
on DU indicate that the tiny particles that these weapons form on
impact can enter deep into the lungs and pose a major cancer risk.
Despite extensive documentation of the effects of DU on civilians
and soldiers exposed to it, and on their unborn children, the United
States and Britain again deployed them in the second Iraq War in
2003. In the State of Mississippi, one report indicated that 67 per cent
of children of Gulf War veterans were born with birth deformities
including missing eyes, ears or fingers or with severe blood or
respiratory disorders.[47] The use of these weapons in Afghanistan in
2002, and in Iraq over two US-led wars, amounts to a war crime that
has already caused the death and maiming of more people than
those for which the terrible regime of Saddam Hussein has been
held responsible. It also clearly contravenes two other *jus in bello*
principles: that the use of force should be proportionate to stated war
aims, and that the evil resulting from a war should be less than that
which would prevail if it were not fought. No one disputes that the
serious crimes against humanity for which Hussein is indicted had
ended many years before the second US-led war in Iraq. That an
American Professor of Social Ethics can argue that the terrible
and indiscriminate weapons the United States deployed in Iraq, and
its larger strategy of destroying civilian infrastructure and bombing
civilians, can be justified under the traditional Christian account of
'just war' is a powerful example of the deformation of American
Christianity by American imperialism.

Atonement and Violence

The effects of the alliance of Christianity and imperialism in early
Christianity are equally dramatic and are particularly evident in
theological and ritual changes that can be discerned in the Latin
Church after the fourth century. The cross is rarely found as an image
in Christian places of worship or in Christian mosaics and paintings
before the fourth century because the Cross was an imperial symbol
of torture and death. Instead, we find the *chi-rho* as the most
common symbol of Christian belief, along with the fish, the good
shepherd and one or two other recurring images. However, in the

fifth century the cross begins to appear as a symbol after the turn of Christianity into an imperial cult. Cross images at this time tend not to be empty, but to show images of Christ on the Cross in the form of the Ascended Christ, the divine sovereign who has taken his seat in heaven on the right-hand of God and who has triumphed over the powers. By the sixth and seventh centuries images begin to appear of the warrior Christ, as if the Christ whom Christians then worshipped was no longer the one who followed the way of non-violence, but was now one who fought with Christians against their enemies. And, by the Middle Ages, we begin to see images of a dead and tortured Jesus on crosses in Christian art.[48]

It is also in the Middle Ages that a new and influential teaching about the atoning significance of the death of Christ was put forward by Anselm of Canterbury in his book *Cur Deus Homo*.[49] Anselm argued that the death of the Son of God was a judicial transaction between God and God's Son analogous to the payment of a feudal burden. For Anselm, the salvific effects of the Incarnation lie exclusively in this transaction: Christ lived and died in order to satisfy the legal requirements of God the Father for a price of redemption to be paid for the sins of humanity, and therefore those who avail themselves of the saving benefits of the blood of Christ are those who are saved. All the analogies, the cultural context for Anselm's writing, reflected the new form of hierarchical feudalism and seignorage that had overtaken the formerly relatively non-hierarchical Anglo-Saxons and Celts of Briton as a result of the Norman conquest. Anselm's theological innovation was to place the divine necessity of violent sacrifice, and its continual ritual re-enactment by priests offering again the sacrifice of Christ at the Mass, at the heart of the Western Christian understanding of salvation history, and this profound innovation was then taken up in due course by the Reformers and by modern day Protestants and evangelicals. It is surely no coincidence that it was precisely also in the Middle Ages that the Church began itself to take on the trappings and the values of Empire; pursuing a series of vicious crusades against Muslims in the Holy Land, using violence and torture against heretics in the infamous Inquisition, and adopting a standing papal army, the remnants of which can be seen in the fortified citadel of the Vatican City in Rome to this day.

The turning of Christianity into a cult of violence has had terrible effects in Christian history and while the Inquisition may be a distant memory, America remains the most Christian nation in the West and the most violent. The violence is not just directed towards America's enemies; a student of mine told me that he returned to the United States after the terrible events of September 11, 2001 and found that his friends in Seattle, including a number of evangelical Christians, now carried guns whenever they went on public transport, and kept them in their houses for security. America punishes by execution more than any other Western nation, and Texas more than any other State. As we have seen, America since 1945 has bombed or invaded 49 countries. Violence – Rambo style, Clint Eastwood style – is the American way, it is at the heart of America's story about itself.

The problem for Christians is that violence is also at the heart of American Protestant Christianity. American evangelicals regard as one of the unchallengeable fundamentals of their religion that it was Christ's sacrificial and violent death on the cross that turned back the wrath of God from those who confess the Lordship of Christ. Millennialist evangelicals also believe that violence will be visited by God against all those who do not so confess Christ and who consequently remain in a state of wickedness. A millennial businessman and missionary interviewed by the psychologist Charles Strozier declared of his God, 'when he looks down on New York City, I honestly don't know why he doesn't wipe it out'.[50]

Millions of evangelical Americans believe their God is a violent and a wrathful God and that history will end in violence. Ending the lives of those who are evidently wicked serves the purposes of God, and may even help to bring the end of history nearer. So it is that the Southern states, where judicial killing is most widely practised, are also the most evangelical states. The very same states which teach the doctrine of creation alongside evolution in their public schools are those states who execute the largest number of criminals. If religion is mimesis, and evangelical conservative Christians are committed to a view of their salvation that is intrinsically violent – which sets the necessity of violent punishment in the heart of the being of God, which even sets God as Father violently against God as Son on the Cross – then the violence of America is in some ways an enactment of Christian violence.

Now, of course, by no means are all evangelicals committed to the violent course that the American judicial system and American gun ownership and America foreign policy involves. There are many radical evangelicals who strongly critique the dangerous complicity of conservative Christianity and judicial and imperial violence. They include powerful and prophetic voices such as Jim Wallis of the Sojourners Community, Tom Sine and Ron Sider, who have long advocated a radical evangelical social ethic of justice and peace, and have prophetically denounced America's imperial ambitions and her wars. Evangelical religion is certainly not alone the root of violence. Of course not. There are many elements in America's history that have set it on a violent trajectory, including the terrible genocide against Native Americans, the Revolutionary war with Britain, the Civil War and in the twentieth century the technological prowess of America in its development and manufacture of arms and weapons of mass destruction. But my case is that there is still a problem about Christianity, atonement and violence that needs to be confessed and repented of, especially if Christians are to cleanse their faith from its violent imperial legacy.

Jesus charges the disciples at his final resurrection appearance in the Gospel of Luke to witness to a gospel of repentance and forgiveness of sins to all the nations. This is the Christian witness, this is what the true apocalypse means – not war or violent punishment, but confession, change of life, forgiveness of sins. Spreading this message may bring Christians into conflict with the governing powers, but when such conflict arises the Christian response will be peaceable if Christians truly remain faithful to the victory over sin and evil that was won in the death and Resurrection of Christ. This victory involved the first Christians in a clear conflict with the violence and wealth of the Roman Empire. The Gospels clearly and unambiguously depict Jesus as a non-violent teacher. He teaches non-violence and he acts out non-violence, peaceableness, in his person and in the way of the cross. Living out the way of non-violence in a violent imperial culture means that he is killed though he is innocent. It is precisely as the *innocent* victim that Christ's death opposes the violence of those who oppose the reign of God. As the Mennonite theologian Denny Weaver puts it, 'his death unmasks the powers of evil, and renders empty their claim that

peace and order are founded on violence'.[51] The reign of God is
not founded on violence because God is revealed in Christ as a
forgiving and loving God. Violence is a consequence of the Fall of
humanity but it is no longer to play a part in God's way with God's
world.

The option of non-violence for the Church is not then simply an
option – it is a requirement if God truly reigns:

> those who believe in the Resurrection perceive the true nature
> of power in the universe. Resurrection means that appearances
> can be deceiving. Regardless of what appears to be the case
> from an earth-bound perspective the Resurrection demonstrates
> the power of God's rule over all evil'.[52]

This recognition commits Christians who live in the midst of violent
empires not to the necessity, but to the ultimate and divine impossi-
bility of violence as means to redeeming the human condition. Those
Christians who claim that only through war can peace be attained
are committed to another view of the atonement, a view that has
to dismiss the non-violent teaching of the Jesus of the Gospels as a
perfectionist ethic, only good for monks, sectarians, and pacifists
who care not for the fate of the innocent, who would not resist
tyranny. But it would be completely wrong to understand the Jesus
of the Gospels as one who commends non-resistance to evil. As we
saw in the last chapter, it was precisely his resistance to the evils of
empire and in particular of religious complicity, the sacralisation of
empire in the Jewish Temple, which entailed his following the way
of the Cross, and it is precisely in Christ as Risen victor that
Christians understand that evil is overcome, overthrown, not by
violence but by the reign of a non-violent God.[53]

The Politics of Jesus and the Politics of Empire

At the heart of America's imperial war machine and of the sacrificial
violence that sustains it are capitalism, fear and national pride. If the
ethics and example of Jesus are the norm for Christian ethics, as Yoder
suggests they should be, we are faced not only with a contradiction

between Jesus' peaceableness and America's imperialism but also between Jesus' justice and American capitalism. From the outset of his ministry, economic exclusion of the kind sustained by American capitalism is critiqued in Jesus' announcement in the synagogue in Capernaum of the biblical Jubilee. The Gospel announcement of Jubilee represents a standing critique of the tendency of capitalism when it becomes the dominant governing force in human societies to generate great extremes of wealth and poverty. Against these tendencies, which were equally a feature of the impact of Roman imperialism on first-century Palestine, Jesus trained his disciples not to worry about what they would eat or what they would wear. In the new society he inaugurates, those rich in this world's goods are to share with those who have nothing. The Jerusalem church enacted this ethic when they saw to it that 'no-one claimed private owner-ship of any possessions' and they shared their goods with one another according to need (Acts 4. 32 – 5). Justice was central, not epiphenomenal, to the communities of the first Christians, hence St Paul's admonitions to the Gentiles in the churches he founded to contribute to collections he was making on behalf of the Jewish Christians who were suffering poverty and famine in Judea (2 Corinthians 9. 6 – 15). Christ proclaims the favourable year of the Lord and he, like the apostles, directs the Christians to behave as if they have more than enough, for generous actions depend on trust in the generous providence of God who rewards gracious giving with gifts in return.

American free market capitalism displays a lack of trust in divine providence and in gift exchange, preferring instead the coerced con-tracts that allow America, and other rich nations, to maintain the gargantuan consumer economy at the cost of the well-being of other peoples and of the planet. This lack of trust indicates a basic fear and insecurity that drives individuals and nations in a fallen world to seek to control history so as to ensure history's outcome and their future security. American foreign policy, its traditional alliances with military dictatorships, and its latest branding as the 'war on terror' are clearly driven by the effects of this fear. America seeks 'full spectrum dominance' because others challenge America's extreme wealth and would struggle for fairer economic distribution of the earth's limited resources among the world's peoples.

Christ rejects the temptation to control history's outcome when he is tempted so to do by the devil in the wilderness. Instead, he follows the non-violent way of the cross, trusting that history will come out right by the grace of God. Christ's rejection of worldly power, and of the model of the kingly messiah, is a clear rejection of the Roman imperial strategy and its modern counterpart in America's imperial defense of corporate capitalism. Yoder suggests that those who pursue strategies which amass power and resources in a quest for absolute security are trying to find a 'handle on history' with which they would 'get a hold on the course of history and move it in the right direction'. The Church too is tempted to adopt this approach, to find a handle, a strategy, an ideology such as freedom or democracy, with which to move history along. But the problem with this approach is that it identifies 'one thread of meaning and causality which is more important than individual persons, their lives and well-being' and therefore 'it is justified to sacrifice to this one "cause" other subordinate values, including the life and welfare of one's self, one's neighbour, and (of course!) one's enemy'.[54] America's ritual slaughter of its young and of its enemies in its on-going imperial wars is required by the handle on history that is American capitalism. But those who would control history's outcome are faced with the unpredictability and unknowability of the consequences of their strategies. The phenomenon of 'blowback' is a direct consequence of the attempt to control history because although people try to manage history there are other agents with alternative strategies who resist the would-be controllers of history.

More fundamental for Yoder than the unpredictability of history is the question of effectiveness implicit in attempts to control history:

> Even if we know how effectiveness is to be measured – that is, even if we could get a clear definition of the goal we are trying to reach and how to ascertain whether we had reached it – is there not in Christ's teaching on meekness, or in the attitude of Jesus toward power and servanthood, a deeper question being raised about whether it is our business at all to guide our action by the course we wish history to take?[55]

When God intervened in creation to redeem history from evil, to turn it in a new direction, God did so not by coercive control, but by putting aside divine power and adopting the humility of a servant. Rather than choosing the path of a warrior messiah proffered by the disciples and the crowds in Jerusalem, Christ goes 'like a lamb to the slaughter' along the way of the cross, and turns history around. It is in this turning of history around that the real meaning of Revelation, of apocalyptic, resides. John's announcement that 'the lamb that was slain is worthy to receive power' means that

> the cross and not the sword, suffering and not brute power determines the meaning of history. The key to the obedience of God's people is not their effectiveness but their patience. The triumph of right is assured not by the might that comes to the aid of right, which is of course the justification of the use of violence and other kinds of power in human conflict. The triumph of the right, although it is assured, is sure because of the power of the resurrection and not because of any calculation of causes and effects, nor because of the inherently greater strength of the good guys.[56]

American premillennialists hope to bring forward the end of history by supporting a war in the Middle East which, as well as shoring up America's access to oil, was intended to secure the Jewish resettling of the Holy Land and the rebuilding of the Temple in Jerusalem. But the Book of Revelation points in an entirely different direction: the early Christians were to defeat evil 'by the blood of the lamb and by the word of their testimony, for they did not cling to life even in the face of death' (Revelation 12. 11). It is not that suffering, or the willingness to give up life itself, are in themselves redemptive but rather that those who confront evil while rejecting violence partici- pate in the 'triumphant suffering of the lamb'.[57] For St John the Divine, the war in heaven between the angels and the devil is already won in the triumph of the lamb and all that remains is for the down- fall of the dragon to become visible in the downfall of Empire. But for George W. Bush, and his millennialist and Zionist supporters, the angel continues to fight through the military might of American empire to bring about history's end.

The burden of Yoder's witness to what he calls the politics of Jesus is that the radical Reformed commitment of Mennonites, Quakers and others to pacifism is not an irresponsible sectarian escape from political responsibility but the only possible form of political witness for Christians who intend to model their lives and communities on the life and character of God as revealed in Jesus. It is Christian worship and ministry that are the context in which Christians model the love of God and their trust in divine providence. This modelling is enacted in the Christian performance of forgiveness and non-violence; in acts of service and rituals of reconciliation; in economic justice symbolised in the sharing ritual of the Eucharist; in incorporation into the people of God regardless of ethnicity or nationality in the practice of Baptism; in servant ministry in congregations that honour the weak and give a voice to the humble alongside the strong.[58] This modelling of the politics of Jesus is the way in which the Church witnesses to those who direct the politics and economics of the societies in which Christians live. Instead of the Christian realism of Reinhold Niebuhr in which Christians are required to embrace an ethic of coercion and violence in the realm of the state and confine the love ethic to their piety, the Church for Yoder is the visible sign that the war of the lamb has non-coercively defeated evil and overcome the enmity and strife which threatened to destroy human society and God's creation. The Church witnesses to the triumph of love over violence by being the Church, not by conforming to the requirements of a violent state: 'the very existence of such a group is itself a deep social change'. 'If it lives faithfully, it is also the most powerful tool of social change'. This approach does not lead to sectarian withdrawal from the public domain, for the Church is not a *religious* group but a public gathering, gathered to do the business of Jesus, and 'to find what it means here and now to put into practice this different quality of life which is God's promise to them and to the world and their promise to God and service to the world'.[59] At the heart of this service is non-violence – it is precisely through pacifism that the Church witnesses to the apocalyptic realisation that history has already come out right, good has already triumphed, in the victory of the lamb and there is no need any more to go to war in the struggle to control history's outcome.

In this perspective, the differences in political and economic strategy between Marxists, Islamists, democratic nationalists, and Christians who side with the coercive power of the State are actually more apparent than real. Khrushchev, Osama bin Laden, George W. Bush and Jerry Falwell are united in their commitment to the resolution of the social problem through the choice of their favoured group of aristocrats, oligarchs or elites who, because of the superiority of their ideology, are rightly charged with using 'the power of society from the top so as to lead the whole system in their direction'.[60] Bush and his Islamist enemies are united in their desire to control history, bin Laden to reinstitute the Islamic Caliphate, Bush to suppress all dissent to American dominance and the superiority of American over all other human or ecological interests. The Islamist, the Communist, the democratic nationalist, the imperialist free marketeer are united by the belief that any sacrifice is possible, even legitimate, in the pursuit of the good cause, which they identify as directing history toward their chosen end. This is the true meaning of the apocalyptic politics of extremist Islamists and American premillennialists.

Yoder's position is that the Church is sustained in its witness to the powers that be by the recognition that the apocalypse is already come and history has in a very real sense already found its end. But does this mean, as critics maintain, that Yoder and Hauerwas intend that Christians opt out of hoping, praying and struggling for the nations in which they live also to be more just and more peaceable? Or, to put the point more positively, do Christians expect the world to own the non-violent Lordship of Christ? The answer Yoder gives is that in American and European history it is not the world that has been the problem but the Church. It is the peculiar 'deformation of Biblical faith', and not pagan or secular philosophy, which has led in the last 1,500 years to the crusading mentality that has seen Christians pitted against Islamists and Jews, and which has advanced so much war and destruction.[61] The source of this deformation of Christian faith, and of the return of the concept of holy or just war into Christian social witness, is the Constantinian inheritance. The establishment of Christianity as the religion of Empire committed the Church to alliances with those who would grasp at and seek to control history's outcome. Consequently, the

Church abandoned its early belief that victory over sin and evil is already assured, has already come to pass in the new aeon of faith in which the Church lives after the Resurrection and Ascension of Christ, and that therefore for Christians there is no more cause for war.

Justice and Peace

Samuel Huntington has famously described the conflicts that have emerged around the world since the end of the Cold War as a 'clash of civilizations'. He claims that the new wars are the wars of tribalism, as nation-states turn out to be unsuccessful in suppressing the old cultural and religious roots of fear and prejudice and war.[62] Many in America and the Middle East also view recent events, and in particular the 'war on terror' as a clash between Christian democratic countries and Muslim autocratic ones. They suggest that there was an inevitability about the events of September 11, 2001 because of the clear conflict between the open liberal values of a democratic America and the closed aristocratic, and even theocratic, societies of the Arab Middle East.[63] So long as the Middle East remains undemocratic, the argument goes, it will remain a hotbed of ignorance, poverty and terrorism. America's role in this account is clear. America had to defend aggressively its values of freedom and democracy and take its war for these values into the Middle East itself. This was precisely what Bush, Cheney and Rumsfeld did with their wars in Afghanistan and, especially, in Iraq. The Afghanistan war, while a horrible war in which civilians were targeted in their thousands by American weaponry, was nonetheless clearly directed at a country which had been harbouring Al-Qaeda, a terrorist organisation which had attacked America: it was possible to describe this war not as a pre-emptive strike but as a retaliatory action. The war in Iraq was however of an entirely different order. This was a war not only about oil – even the Afghanistan war seems to have included oil as an element in US strategy – but about trying to bomb people into accepting a value system, and a set of institutional and economic arrangements, that imperial America would impose upon them by brute force, and by colonial government.

Yoder did not live to see the tragic events of September 11, 2001 or their aftermath in the outburst of fervent patriotism and war fever right across America, both Christian and pagan, but Stanley Hauerwas, Yoder's foremost interpreter, did and he has spoken and written on a number of occasions against these dual tendencies in Bush's America. Ironically, *Time Magazine* declared Hauerwas America's 'best theologian' the day before the terror attacks, but despite this unsought accolade he continued after September 11 to denounce the warrior tendencies of American patriotism.[64] Hauerwas is on the editorial board of a journal called *First Things* and was provoked by a war-mongering and patriotic editorial to pen a response in which he considered the possibility that he and *First Things* may have to part company.[65] In that editorial, the editors had praised the response of George W. Bush to the September 11 atrocity. He had declared in his State of the Union address that 'either you are with us or you are with the terrorists. From this day forward, any nation that continues to harbor or support terrorism will be regarded by the United States as a hostile regime'. The editors of *First Things* declare that they too are convinced that America is now at war and that all right-thinking Americans will be with the Bush administration in prosecuting this war. The President had declared a war that would not end 'until every terrorist group of global reach has been found, stopped, and defeated' and they wanted to support him when he made a direct claim that God was on the side of America as it prosecuted its war on America's enemies:

> The course of this conflict is not known, yet its outcome is certain. Freedom and fear, justice and cruelty, have always been at war. And we know that God is not neutral between them. We will meet violence with patient justice, assured of the rightness of our cause and confident of the victories to come. In all that lies before us, may God grant us wisdom and may He watch over the United States of America.[66]

The editorial went on to criticise those who argued for a non-violent response to the terrorists. While the editors defended the right of pacifists to their minority position, they argued that pacifism is fine for a small monastic-oriented minority but cannot be the option of mainstream Christians. They were sneering in their dismissal of those who argued for non-violent strategies for dealing with terrorism. Such people were fraudulent in their claim that they would resist evil while refusing violence; they were irresponsible and lacking in genuine courage because they were 'refusing the call to service with its risk of killing or of being killed'.[67] Consequently the editors declare that those who refuse violence have no business criticising the military war: 'One matter that has been muddied in recent decades should now be clarified: those who in principle oppose the use of military force have no legitimate part in the discussion about how military force should be used'.[68]

For Hauerwas, the editorial was deeply troubling:

> the position taken "In Time of War" comes close to implying that the pacifist refusal to respond violently to injustice makes us complicit with evil and injustice and, therefore, immoral.[69]

The dismissal of pacifism as at best monastic indifference and at worst a fraud is offensive because the non-violent church is not an apolitical church but on the contrary a church which as a non-violent polity refuses the distinction between private religion (love) and public politics (war), which Americans have long embraced and which finds renewed advocacy in the Christian Right and the Bush administration. The non-violent church is politically responsible just because it refuses 'a strong distinction can be drawn between politics and war'. Christians are neither silent nor non-resistant in the face of evil. On the contrary, they follow the example of Christ who resisted evil and overcame evil through the way of non-violence, the way that the resurrection vindicated.[70]

How though do those who would refuse violence because they believe Christ has already overcome evil non-violently deal with violence against the innocent of the kind meted out by Al-Qaeda, or the United States? The problem is that although Christians may believe that evil is defeated, and that a new history has begun in the story of those who live in the light of evil's defeat, nonetheless the world seems to continue on its way, evil men and empires do seem still to triumph at least from time to time in the affairs of men and women; the final *eschaton* when Christ reigns and when all acknowledge Christ as Lord of history has not arrived. How do Christians live 'between the times' while not evading their responsibilities to their fellow citizens? Can Christians who adopt a non-violent politics themselves take political office for example?

Yoder's answer to this problem is beguilingly simple and yet wonderfully enlightening, not least because of the way in which it addresses the other thorny problem we have hardly touched on yet; the relation between Christians and those of other faiths, and in particular those of the other Abrahamic faiths, for it would appear that in many ways the 'war on terror' does involve conflicts between these faiths, and not least over the status of the Holy Land.

Towards the end of his life, Yoder began work on a large project in the area of Jewish–Christian relations. At the core of this project was the proposal that Jesus did not come to unseat the Jews from being the chosen people of God, or to announce that Christians were to be chosen instead of Jews. On the contrary, Christ's coming as a non-violent Messiah, who ultimately defeated the evil powers that had usurped the Temple in Jerusalem and were oppressing the Jews in their homeland, was a vindication not a denial of Jewish prophecy. The message of the Book of Daniel was not that the Jews would return home to crown a Messiah as their new earthly king who will overthrow their enemies and reinstitute their kingly temple-based religion in Jerusalem. On the contrary, Daniel is about how it is possible to be Jews and remain faithful to the God of the Covenant while living in exile among foreign peoples under foreign kings who worship foreign gods. Daniel is not so much about the end of the world, as Christian millennialists would have it, but rather the end of Judaism as a Temple and land-based religion. Daniel provides a prophetic account of the courage and faithfulness needed by Jews if they are to live true to the stories of their ancestors as diaspora Jews. Daniel is in effect a parable about how to live up to the challenge of Jeremiah, who suggested to the newly exiled Israelites in Babylon that they were to carry on their lives, building houses, marrying and giving their children in marriage, planting crops and vineyards, and they were not to turn against those they lived amongst. Instead God charges them:

seek the welfare of the city where I [Yahweh] have sent you into
exile, and pray to the Lord on its behalf, for in its welfare you
will find your welfare. (Jeremiah 29. 7)

Yoder calls this charge the Jeremianic model of Jewish existence.
After the destruction of the Temple, Jews worshipped in Synagogues
which did not have to be in Jerusalem and they were taught by
Rabbis and not Levitical priests. As Yoder says, the Jews 'from the
age of Jeremiah to that of Theodore Hertzl, depended more on
the leadership in Babylon, where living without a temple was
possible and was accepted as permanent, than on the Palestinian
institutions, distracted as they were by the agenda of Maccabean
rebellion and Herodian negotiation, and then by Roman destruction'.[71]
Jeremiah clearly anticipates the teaching of Jesus and Paul that
while Christians, like Jews, are to live in the world, they are not to
be 'of the world'; they are not called to be in charge of history, nor to
adopt national or State structures as their own for they already know
history's outcome. As Jesus memorably put it, 'foxes have holes and
birds their nests, but the Son of Man has nowhere to lay his head',
and as the writer to the Hebrews put it, 'here we have no continuing
city'. The writer of the second-century *Epistle to Diognetus* puts
memorably the relationship between Christians and the 'world':

For the Christians are distinguished from other men neither by
country, nor language, nor the customs which they observe. For
they neither inhabit cities of their own, nor employ a peculiar
form of speech, nor lead a life which is marked out by any
singularity. The course of conduct which they follow has not
been devised by any speculation or deliberation of inquisitive
men; nor do they, like some, proclaim themselves the advocates
of any merely human doctrines. But, inhabiting Greek as well
as barbarian cities, according as the lot of each of them has
determined, and following the customs of the natives in respect
to clothing, food, and the rest of their ordinary conduct, they
display to us their wonderful and confessedly striking method
of life. They dwell in their own countries, but simply as
sojourners. As citizens, they share in all things with others, and
yet endure all things as if foreigners. Every foreign land is to

them as their native country, and every land of their birth as a land of strangers. They marry, as do all [others]; they beget children; but they do not destroy their offspring. They have a common table, but not a common bed. They are in the flesh, but they do not live after the flesh. They pass their days on earth, but they are citizens of heaven. They obey the prescribed laws, and at the same time surpass the laws by their lives. They love all men, and are persecuted by all. They are unknown and condemned; they are put to death, and restored to life. They are poor, yet make many rich; they are in lack of all things, and yet abound in all; they are dishonoured, and yet in their very dishonour are glorified. They are evil spoken of, and yet are justified; they are reviled, and bless; they are insulted, and repay the insult with honour; they do good, yet are punished as evil-doers. When punished, they rejoice as if quickened into life; they are assailed by the Jews as foreigners, and are persecuted by the Greeks; yet those who hate them are unable to assign any reason for their hatred.

Christians are to be sojourners, or 'resident aliens'. This does not mean that they feel no sense of responsibility for the nations in which they dwell and the peoples among whom they live. On the contrary they are called, like the diaspora Jews, to pray for them and to seek their welfare. They are not though to desire to change the course of history to assure their own place in history for they are already citizens of heaven, they already know how history will turn out. Yoder's claim is that what Christians learnt through the impact of Jesus' teaching was also authentically the ethos of diaspora Judaism which was an 'ethos of not being in charge and not considering any local state structure to be the primary bearer of the movement of history'.[72]

The Jeremianic approach provides the real meaning to the coded language of apocalyptic for Yoder. Apocalyptic Christians are not meant to predict the end of history by reading the signs of the times or by trying to control the times, as do Christian Zionists who see the resettling of the land of Israel by force as a fulfilment of divine prophecy. Instead the true apocalyptic prophet is motivated by the recognition that God is acting, has acted in history, in certain ways that he or she is also called to seek after, model and emulate. This is not pie in the sky, abandoning responsibility to the coming end of history but on the contrary it requires the framing of lives which own and acknowledge the prior action of God in shaping history.[73]

Read in the light of the Jeremianic model of the people of God dwelling in a strange land while still remaining faithful, none of the biblical apocalypses from Ezekiel through Daniel to Mark 13 and the Book of Revelation is about either the Jews resettling Israel by force or the Russians invading Israel. They indicate instead how the suffering servant, the crucified Messiah, is a more adequate key to understanding what God is about in the real world of empires and armies and markets than is the ruler in Rome, with all his supporting military, commercial and sacerdotal networks. They indicate that history has an end and that God already knows this end and that it is revealed not to those who grasp after history to control its outcome, nor to those who greedily seize an unjust share of the resources of the earth through corporate capitalism and military power, but to those who discern the true meaning of the shape of the world and of the place of Jews and Christians in it. For Yoder, pacifism, non-violence, is not about giving up on the world, or abandoning responsibility for the world. On the contrary, Jeremianic Jews and Christians who 'seek the welfare of the city' while remaining faithful to the God who has already overcome evil, who has already shown how good trounces wickedness, have no need of a territorial nation, for God has already set aside a way of being a people. The Jeremianic community is not ineffective or irresponsible in the face of evil; it is not pie in the sky or opium for the masses, it does not cave in to empire, or unjust structures, or the rule of violence:

> to follow Jesus does not mean renouncing effectiveness. It does not mean sacrificing concern for liberation within the social process in favour of delayed gratification in heaven, or abandoning efficacy in favour of purity. It means that in Jesus we have a clue to which kinds of causation, which kinds of

community-building, which kinds of conflict management, go with the grain of the cosmos, of which we know, as Caesar does not, that Jesus is both the Word (the inner logic of things) and the Lord ("sitting at the right hand").[74]

Once we read the clues to history which we find in the life, death and resurrection of Jesus, we will know the kinds of actions as well as the kinds of communities that will be effective in resolving conflict because they are also 'with the grain of the universe' that God created and in which humans construct cultures, and nations treaties. Yoder speaks with considerable integrity here, for he was a member of a Christian communion, the Mennonites, who were not only persecuted viciously in their early history in Europe for their pacifism, but who, since their re-founding in the United States, have become notable world-wide for their ministry of reconciliation in places of conflict around the world.[75]

One clear consequence of this account of Jewish–Christian relations is that neither Christians nor Jews ought to have any investment in the resettling of the holy land by the Jews. The Zionist cause is not a sign of a fulfilment of prophecy so much as the rejection of prophecy, not a sign of faithfulness to the prophetic message of the Old Testament so much as its denial. Another more startling conclusion is that when the Jews embraced the ethos of diaspora Judaism in European Christendom for more than 1,500 years, it was they and not Christendom Christians who were being more faithful to the Jeremianic model as read through the Cross of Christ. Constantinianism involved Christians in traducing the Cross of Christ, turning their religion into a religion of empire, of nation-states, of governors. Like the Jews under their ancient Kings, Christians after Constantine came to see Christian rule as divinely authorised. Consequently they failed to witness to history's already decided outcome as displayed in the Cross and Resurrection of Jesus, and the Church ceased to be a visible sign of a different way of living. In Christendom, the true Church became in effect an invisible church where it was no longer clear who were the 'real' Christians and who were only nominal Christians who practised Christianity as the religion of empires and governors and nation-states.

Before Constantine, the Church was a visible sign, while the end of history had to be taken on faith in Christ. After Constantine, the Church is invisible, but the end of history is no longer taken on faith. Men and women themselves take it into their own hands:

> The sign that pointed towards its truth was the fidelity of the Church, the visibility of a sanctified people who modelled an alternative ethic to that of empire. But after the alliance with empire the church becomes invisible; it is necessary to take on trust that there exists a true church in a society in which allegiance to church and emperor are the same, and baptism becomes a rite of passage for membership of empire or nation and not just of adoption by the people of God.[76]

The third implication of Yoder's Jeremianic model is that when Christians embraced rule, control, history, they ended up killing Jews and Muslims. Granted, the Holocaust itself was managed by a nation in which the Church was deeply compromised by its allegiance to the Third Reich. Nonetheless, Christians stood by while the Holocaust was going on; they even worshipped in churches at the very gates of the death camps while ignoring what was going on behind the wire fences.[77] Similarly, in the terrible acts of genocide committed by Christian crusaders in the Middle Ages, Christians can see the dreadful dangers that come from believing that they are in charge of history on behalf of their God.

The Jeremianic model does not just offer Christians the possibility for repentance of their past complicities in imperial violence. It offers a way for Christians in the age of another rising empire to resist taking charge, and to hold to account those who do take charge in the name of their God. One of the deep ambiguities for Christians in the current rise of an imperial America is precisely the professed Christianity of Bush, Cheney and others in the Bush administration, and also of his closest international ally, British Prime Minister Tony Blair. Vice-President Dick Cheney's family Christmas card for 2003 bore the message 'And if a sparrow cannot fall to the ground without His notice, is it probable that an empire can rise without His aid?' The quote is from Benjamin Franklin, who was speaking at the Constitutional Convention at the end of the Revolution. He was calling for daily prayers at the regular meeting of the people's representatives in what is now called the House of Congress, in recognition that without God's aid no empire – Britain is the empire he had in mind – would ever be resisted and no fairer or truer kind of nation or government would ever come into existence. His proposal was rejected.[78] This quote used now in the context of the 'war on terror' is a direct reversal of Franklin's meaning, and it reveals the imperial ambitions of the Bush administration, as well as the idolatrous and sacral claims of its apocalyptic project to reshape the world after the interests of American corporate capital. It is a truly stunning piece of Constantinianism at its most insidious. Cheney is a master of the dark arts of Machiavellian politics, of the use of State power for the gain of the small elite who govern and control the corporate empire of the United States, and more especially of the Halliburton Corporation of which he was Chief Executive Officer until he became Vice President and in which he retains personal financial interests. Cheney in his Christmas card message claims the imprimatur, the seal of approval on the corporate empire he builds, from the infant Jesus who became the suffering servant, the prophet who resisted empire and who was crucified for criticising those who put their religion into imperial service.

Yoder's Jeremianic model does not suggest that Christians and Jews, or we might add Muslims or Buddhists or Hindus, who are pacifist and yet who 'seek the welfare of the city' can never take political office, or even work in the police force, though they cannot of course join the military. What it does suggest however is that when they take up political office, or work in a police force, or in any other profession bar that of the military, they remain accountable for their behaviour in these roles not to the world's ethos of power and violence but to the ethos of the diaspora Jew and the Church that has no continuing city, and whose community practices are modelled on the politics of Jesus.

If political leaders like Bush and Blair and Cheney worship as Christians in Churches before the Cross, they cannot in their political lives pursue an ethic that is contrary to the cruciform shape of Christian politics. If they do so, then the remedy is clear: such persons if they depart from clear Christian teaching in the exercise of their public office should be 'bound' by their fellow Christians according to the instruction of Christ (Matthew 5. 23 ff.). They must be publicly confronted and called to account for their actions before the congregation. Only when they confess and repent – that is to say indicate how they plan to change their actions in quite concrete ways – can they be reconciled and readmitted into the worship of the faithful.

The practice of binding and loosing, which Christ authorises in the New Testament, involves the practices of confrontation, repentance and forgiveness and reconciliation. They may seem arcane, and indeed few churches these days practise them in the public form in which the early Christians practised them. However they are in fact precisely the kinds of practices which Mennonites and some other Christian groups have adapted from their own religious communities in their work in peace making and conflict resolution in situations of grave civil strife such as the former Yugoslavia, South Africa, Israel–Palestine, Northern Ireland and Mozambique. They have not always met with success, but the achievements of this approach to conflict resolution have been remarkable, especially when compared with the cost in lives lost, communities destroyed and lands poisoned when warfare is used to settle disputes. Instead of seeking common ground or covering over past crimes, this approach to conflict resolution involves each side in confronting the other over its actions, each side in confession and in seeking forgiveness, and each side in committing to specific acts of penance that enable the emergence of a new, more peaceable relationship. This is not about 'hugging terrorists', as the editors of *First Things* dismissively put down their opponents' pacifist traditions. It is about taking violence and evil as seriously as God took them on the Cross, while at the same time acknowledging that the Resurrection of Christ, and the healing of the world that flows from it, make possible a new way of dealing with the roots of conflict and violence which does not involve killing or blood sacrifice.

Epilogue

Angels have become something of a cultural icon in American popular culture. Films about angels include the classic *It's A Wonderful Life*, and more recently *Heaven Can Wait*, *Angels in the Outfield* and *City of Angels*. There have been two long-running TV series about angels including *Angel*, a spin-off from *Buffy the Vampire Slayer*, and *Touched by an Angel*, and an award-winning play *Angels in America*, which was also screened as a TV film. There are also numerous books on angels with titles like *My Guardian Angel* and *All the Angels in the Bible*. The notable thing about these popular images of angels is that they symbolise the dominant strain of individualistic piety that characterises the evangelical religion adhered to by more than 40 per cent of Americans. These angels bring comfort to individuals in times of crisis and terror, they rescue them, they help them to meet their needs and to realise their dreams and desires. But they offer no prophetic message from God on the economic and spiritual corruption of modern America.

In the Bible, angels do not serve human beings or help them to realise their dreams. On the contrary, they are the servants of God and the means by which God moves, speaks with, and touches the earth. Angels such as those that appear to Abraham's servant Hagar before she conceived Ishmael (Genesis 16), and to the Virgin Mary before she conceived Jesus (Luke 1), mediate between earthly and heavenly realities and bring a prophetic and transforming message to the individuals whom they visit.[1] The more than 300 references to angels in the New Testament all refer to Christ; the angels serve the revelation of the divine Word in Jesus by announcing and affirming the redeeming actions of God on earth.[2]

The angelic and spiritual powers that visit humanity are bridges between earth and heaven, but they are ambiguous. They have no continuing presence on earth or precise form, and furthermore their influence is sometimes beneficent and sometimes malign. Both Old and New Testaments include accounts of fallen angels who serve neither God nor humanity but their own malign purposes. Whereas Mary is visited by the angel of the Lord, Jesus is tempted by a fallen angel in the wilderness. The devil tempts the Son of God before his public ministry begins to abuse ecological power by turning stone into bread; to abuse political power by establishing an empire on earth; to abuse spiritual power by throwing himself from a rocky pinnacle and forcing the angels to rescue him.[3] These temptations recall the Genesis account of the serpent who tempts Adam and Eve in the Garden of Eden, and the tempter of God's faithful servant in the Book of Job. The New Testament describes the many ways in which God in Christ overturns the spiritual powers and fallen angels under whose influence human life is drawn towards sin and evil. It is not angels who bring this about. They may announce the coming redemption of Christ, and they appear in the Book of Revelation even to do battle in his name, but only Christ himself in his life, death and resurrection is able ultimately to challenge and defeat the fallen spiritual powers that produce misrule and disorder on earth. But Christ did not promise his disciples that they would rule the world in place of the principalities and powers, only that they had a duty to witness to him, and to bind the unrepentant and to loose and forgive the repentant in the churches they would lead (Matthew 5. 23). Analogously, angels when they appear to men and women in the Bible do not offer them control over events. Rather, they offer them new ways of perceiving reality and of responding to the divine hand in events. Mary when she is told that she will bear the saviour simply responds in humility 'let it be with me according to your word' (Luke 1. 38).

The angel invoked by George W. Bush in his Inaugural Speech in 2001 is more like a prideful fallen angel than a humble servant of God. Bush invokes his angel at the end of a speech that set out a range of policies – vast increases in military spending, threats to nations that would resist American power, tax cuts to the super-rich – that indicate an arrogant intent to direct world events for the benefit of the few. We have seen in this book how conservative and millennialist Christians in America have lent this intent and these policies their loyalty and support. According to the apocalyptic vision of John of Patmos in the Book of Revelation, the spiritual powers that take body in empires and their leaders have been defeated but this does not mean that their influence is entirely at an end, and especially not their power to mislead the faithful. More than anything else, the 'antichrist' – the Roman Emperor – is revealed in Revelation as a master of deception, and his greatest achievement is to deceive Christians into acknowledging his supreme sovereignty.

If another empire is now rising at the beginning of the third millennium of the Christian era, and if there are those who fight against this empire with terror and violence, the clear import of the Book of Revelation is that Christians are to resist the temptation to give their allegiance to it, or to its violent opponents. The Lord's prayer includes the petition 'Your will be done on earth, as it is in heaven'. In heaven, God's reign is already established as it was on earth in Jesus, and as Christ now stands at the right-hand of God, the angels gather continuously around God's throne to offer God praise. In their praise and worship, Christians imitate and join with the praise and worship of the heavenly hosts. They affirm that the world they inhabit is the world in which Christ was resurrected, in which God's power was revealed against all which threatens the peace of creation, and that despite appearances the principalities and powers no longer reign.[4] There are and will still be those who would attempt to establish the kingdom by force (Matthew 11. 12) but Christians can resist them, confident in the message of the angels 'be not afraid', and of the Revelation of John, 'Behold, I am making all things new' (Revelation 21. 5).

Notes

Introduction

1 Sheldon Rampton and John Stauber, *Weapons of Mass Deception: The Uses of Propaganda in Bush's War on Iraq* (London: Robinson, 2003), p. 25.

2 Ron Suskind, *The Price of Loyalty: George W Bush, the White House, and the Education of Paul O'Neill* (New York: Simon and Schuster, 2004).

3 Stephen Mansfield, *The Faith of George W. Bush* (Lake Mary, FL: Charisma House, 2003), pp. 85 – 6 and 92 – 6.

4 Michael Moore, *Stupid White Men and Other Sorry Excuses for the State of the Nation* (New York: Regan Press, 2001).

5 Mansfield, *Faith of George W. Bush*, p. 109.

6 George W. Bush, 'Inaugural Address', 20 January, 2001.

7 Bush, 'Inaugural Address'.

8 Jacob Duche cited Clifford Longley, *Chosen People: The Big Idea that Shaped England and America* (London: Hodder and Stoughton, 2002), p. 66.

9 Longley, *Chosen People*, p. 67.

10 Howard Fineman, 'Bush and God', *Newsweek*, 10 March, 2003.

11 Bush, 'Inaugural Address'.

12 Bush, 'Inaugural Address'.

13 Bush, 'State of the Union Address', 29 January, 2002.

14 George W. Bush, Address at a prayer breakfast of the National Religious Broadcasters Convention, Nashville, Tennessee, 10 February, 2003.

15 Bush, 'State of the Union', 2002.

16 *Le Monde*, 11 April, 2003, reported that a British officer at Central Command in Qatar estimated that 'some 30,000 Iraqi military have probably been killed during the three weeks bombardment' in March. Human Rights Watch on the basis of a survey of Iraqi hospitals recorded 3,000 civilian deaths during the invasion.

17 George W. Bush, 'Victory Address on the *Abraham Lincoln*', April 2003.
18 George W. Bush's remarks at Central Command headquarters, February 2003.
19 Reinhold Niebuhr, *The Irony of American History* (New York: Charles Scribner, 1955), p. 70.
20 Christopher Columbus cited Paul Boyer, *When Time Shall Be No More: Prophecy Belief in Modern America* (Cambridge, MA: Harvard University Press, 1992), p. 225.
21 Thomas Paine, *Common Sense* (Harmondsworth: Penguin, 1976), p. 120.
22 Catherine Keller, *Apocalypse Now and Then: A Feminist Guide to the End of the World* (Boston: Beacon Press, 1996), p. 8.
23 Charles Strozier, *Apocalypse: On the Psychology of Fundamentalism in America* (Boston: Beacon Press, 1994), p. 175.
24 Jack G. Shaheen, *Reel Bad Arabs: How Hollywood Vilifies a People* (New York: Olive Branch Press, 2001).
25 Bush, 'Inaugural Address'.
26 John Gray, *Al-Qaeda and What It Means To Be Modern* (London: Faber and Faber, 2003).

1 – American Apocalypse

1 Sacvan Bercovitch, *The Rites of Assent: Transformations in the Symbolic Construction of America* (New York: Routledge, 1993), p. 147.
2 Bercovitch, *Rites of Assent*, p. 137.
3 Jonathan Edwards, *A History of the Work of Redemption* (Edinburgh: W. Gray, 1774), p. 296.
4 Ernest Lee Tuveson, *Redeemer Nation: The Idea of America's Millennial Role* (Chicago: Chicago University Press, 1968).
5 Bercovitch, *Rites of Assent*, pp. 155 – 7.
6 Bercovitch, *Rites of Assent*, p. 158, citing a sermon by the eighteenth-century preacher Jonathan Mayhew.
7 Bercovitch, *Rites of Assent*, p. 150.
8 John Quincy Adams, *An Oration Delivered on 4 July* (1837) cited Bercovitch, p. 176.
9 For an account of neoliberal economics see below chapter 3.
10 Seymour Martin Lipset, *American Exceptionalism: A Double-Edged Sword* (New York: W. W. Norton and Co., 1996).
11 A. David Lindsay, *The Modern Democratic State* (London: Royal Institute of International Affairs, 1943), p. 77.
12 Jeffrey Stout, *Democracy and Tradition* (Princeton, NJ: Princeton University Press, 2004), p. 167.
13 Thomas J. Curry, *The First Freedoms: Church and State in America to the Passage of the First Amendment* (New York: Oxford University Press, 1986).

14 Rodney Stark and Laurence R. Iannaccone, 'A Supply Side Re-Interpretation of the "Secularisation" in Europe', *Journal for the Scientific Study of Religion*, Vol. 33 (1994), pp. 230 – 52.

15 Stanley Hauerwas, *After Christendom: How the Church is to Behave if Freedom, Justice, and a Christian Nation Are Bad Ideas* (Nashville, TN: Abingdon Press, 1991).

16 See for example Ernest R. May, *Imperial Democracy: The Emergence of America as a Great Power* (New York: Harcourt, Brace and World, 1961).

17 Andrew J. Bacevich, *The American Empire: The Realities and Consequences of U. S. Diplomacy* (Cambridge, MA: Harvard University Press, 2002).

18 Michael Ignatieff, 'Why are we in Iraq?', *New York Times*, 7 September, 2003.

19 Anders Stephanson, *Manifest Destiny: American Expansionism and the Empire of Right* (New York: Hill and Wang, 1995), p. 5.

20 Winthrop S. Hudson, *Nationalism and Religion in America: Concepts of American Identity and Mission* (New York: Harper and Row, 1970), p. 55.

21 Ezra Stiles, 'The United States Elevated to Glory and Honour', a sermon at the anniversary election, 8 May, 1783, New Haven, excerpted in Hudson, *Nationalism and Religion*, p. 64.

22 William Ellery Channing cited Stephanson, *Manifest Destiny*, p. 49.

23 Michael Hardt and Antonio Negri, *Empire* (Cambridge, MA: Harvard University Press, 2000).

24 On the history of the corporation in America see further David Korten, *When Corporations Rule the World* (London: Earthscan, 1995).

25 Stephanson, *Manifest Destiny*, p. 75.

26 Albert J. Beveridge, 'For the Greater Republic, Not for Imperialism: An address before the Union League Club of Philadelphia, February 15, 1899', excerpted in Hudson, *Nationalism and Religion*, pp. 117 – 8.

27 William Appleman Williams, 'American Intervention in Russia: 1917 – 1920', in David Horowitz (ed.), *Containment and Revolution* (Boston: Beacon Press, 1967).

28 Michael Ignatieff, 'The Burden', *New York Times Magazine*, 5 January, 2003.

29 Ignatieff, 'The Burden'.

30 Albert K. Weinberg, *Manifest Destiny: A Study of Nationalist Expansionism in American History* (Baltimore: John Hopkins Press, 1935), pp. 63 – 4.

31 Woodrow Wilson cited Weinberg, *Manifest Destiny*, p. 469.

32 Robert Jewett and John Shelton Lawrence, *Captain America and the Crusade Against Evil* (Grand Rapids, MI: Eerdmans, 2003), p. 73.

33 Wilson cited Weinberg, *Manifest Destiny*, p. 470.

34 Wilson at Oakland cited Tuveson, *Redeemer Nation*, p. 211.

35 Stephanson, *Manifest Destiny*, p. 123.

36 Mike Davis, 'Furcht vor der Fünften Kolonne' cited and trans. Ulrich Duchrow in Ulrich Duchrow and Franz J. Hinkelammert, *Property for*

People, Not for Profit: Alternatives to the Tyranny of Global Capital (London: Zed Books, 2004), p. 116.

37 Stout, *Democracy and Tradition*, p. 200.

38 Steve Brouwer, Paul Gifford and Susan D. Rose, *Exporting the American Gospel: Global Christian Fundamentalism* (New York: Routledge, 1996) pp. 47 – 9.

39 Piero Gleijeses, *Shattered Hope: The Guatemalan Revolution and the United States 1944 – 1954* (Princeton, NJ: Princeton University Press, 1992).

40 National Security Council, National Security Decision Memorandum 93, Policy Towards Chile, 9 November, 1970 archived at http://www.lakota.clara.net/Library/nsaebb8/nsaebb8.htm.

41 Department of Defense, U.S. Milgroup, Situation Report 2, 1 October, 1973, archived at http://www.lakota.clara.net/Library/nsaebb8/nsaebb8.htm.

42 Christopher Hitchens, *The Trial of Henry Kissinger* (London: Verso, 2002).

43 Kermit Roosevelt, *Countercoup: The Struggle for Control of Iran* (London: McGraw Hill, 1970).

44 Mark Curtis, *Web of Deceit: Britain's Real Role in the World* (London: Vintage, 2003), pp. 310 – 11.

45 Annabelle Sreberny-Mohammadi, *Small Media, Big Revolution: Communication, Culture, and the Iranian Revolution* (Minneapolis, MN: University of Minnesota Press, 1994).

46 Curtis, *Web of Deceit*, p. 38.

47 Rampton and Stauber, *Weapons of Mass Deception*, p. 76.

48 'Interview with Zbigniew Brezinski', *Le Nouvel Observateur*, 15 – 21 January, 1998, p. 76.

49 Ahmed Rashid, *Taliban: Islam, Oil and the New Great Game in Central Asia* (London: I. B. Tauris, 2002), p. 18.

50 Ahmed Rashid, 'The Taliban: Exporting Extremism', *Foreign Affairs*, Vol. 78, No. 6, (November – December 1999), pp. 22 – 35.

51 John L. Esposito, *Unholy War: Terror in the Name of Islam* (Oxford and New York: Oxford University Press, 2002), pp. 10 – 11.

52 Rashid, *Taliban*, p. 211.

53 Malise Ruthven, *A Fury for God: The Islamist Attack on America* (London: Granta, 2002), pp. 134 – 5.

54 Rashid, *Taliban*, p. 211.

55 Nafees Mosaddeq Ahmed, *The War on Freedom: How and Why America was Attacked September 11, 2001* (Joshua Tree, CA: California, 2002).

56 Esposito, *Unholy War*, p. 11.

57 Robert Fisk, Interview with Osama bin Laden, *The Independent*, 6 December, 1996.

58 Osama bin Laden, 'Letter to the American People', *The Observer*, 24 November, 2002.

59 Shirley McArthur, 'A Conservative Total for US Aid to Israel: $91 Billion

and Counting', *Washington Report on Middle Eastern Affairs*, pp. 15 – 16 (January – February 2001).

60 Robert Fisk, 'American Billions Keep Arabs Sweet', *The Independent*, 2 March, 2003.

61 Interview with Osama bin Laden cited Esposito, *Unholy War*, p. 24.

62 Chalmers Johnson, *Blowback: The Costs and Consequences of American Empire* (New York: Owl Books, 2003).

63 Interview with Zbigniew Brzezinski, *Le Nouvel Observateur*, 15 – 21 January, 1998, p. 76.

64 Francis Fukuyama, 'The End of History', *The National Interest*, Summer, 1989.

65 On the religious right's influence on American foreign policy see Martin William, 'The Christian Right and American Foreign Policy', *Foreign Affairs*, Spring, 1999.

66 Gray, *Al-Qaeda and What It Means To Be Modern*, pp. 21 – 5.

67 Farhang Rajaee, 'Islam and Modernity: The Reconstruction of an Alternative Shi'ite Islamic Worldview in Iran', in Martin E. Marty and R. Scott Appleby (eds.), *Fundamentalisms Observed: Reclaiming the Sciences, the Family and Education* (Chicago: Chicago University Press, 1993), p. 103.

68 Jalal Al-e Ahmad as quoted in R. Scott Appleby, *The Ambivalence of the Sacred: Religion, Violence, and Reconciliation* (Lanham, Maryland: Rowan & Littlefield, 2000), p. 87.

69 Gray, *Al-Qaeda and What It Means To Be Modern*, p. 77.

70 Bryan S. Turner, *Orientalism, Postmodernism and Globalism* (London: Routledge, 1994), p. 87.

71 Gilles Kepel, *The Revenge of God* (Cambridge: Polity Press, 1993).

72 Sayyid Qutb, *Milestones* (Delhi: Markazi Maktaba Islami, 1981) p. 111.

73 Maududi, *al-Jihad fi sabil Allah* cited Ruthven, *Fury for God*, pp. 70 – 1.

74 Qutb, *Milestones*, pp. 50 – 1.

75 Gray, *Al-Qaeda and What It Means To Be Modern*, p. 25.

76 Stanley Hauerwas, *The Peaceable Kingdom: A Primer in Christian Ethics* (London: SCM Press, 1983), pp. 60 – 1.

77 Reinhold Niebuhr, *The Children of Light and the Children of Darkness: A Vindication of Democracy and a Critique of Its Traditional Defenders* (London: Nisbet and Co., 1945).

78 Robert Kagan, *Paradise and Power: America and Europe in the New World Order* (London: Atlantic Books, 2003), p. 100.

79 Kagan, *Paradise and Power*, p. 88.

80 *Irony of American History*, pp. 75, and 134 – 8.

81 Stanley Hauerwas, *Dispatches from the Front: Theological Engagements with the Secular* (Durham, NC: Duke University Press, 1994), pp. 101 – 5.

82 Gray, *Al-Qaeda and What It Means To Be Modern*, pp. 101 ff.

83 Norman Cohn, *The Pursuit of the Millennium: Revolutionary Millenarians*

and Mystical Anarchists of the Middle Ages (revised and expanded edition, London: Temple Smith, 1970).

84 Oliver O'Donovan, *The Desire of the Nations: Rediscovering the Roots of Political Theology* (Cambridge: Cambridge University Press), pp. 152 – 4.

2 – The Fading of the Dream

1   Paul A. Baran and Paul M. Sweezy, *Monopoly Capital: An Essay on the American Economic and Social Order* (London: Monthly Review Press, 1990).

2   Robert Bellah et. al. (eds.), *Habits of the Heart: Individualism and Commitment in American Life* (Berkeley, CA: University of California Press, 1985).

3   Lindsay, *Modern Democratic State*, pp. 122 – 4.

4   On the origins of the modern American corporation see further David C. Korten, *When Corporations Rule the World* (Bloomfield, CT: Kumarian Press, 1996).

5   David H. Fischer, *Albion's Seed: Four British Folkways In America* (Oxford: Oxford University Press, 1989).

6   Fischer, *Albion's Seed*, p. 411.

7   Richard Hofstadter, *The American Political Tradition and the Men Who Made It* (London: Jonathan Cape, 1962), p. 11.

8   John Locke, *Two Treatises on Civil Government*, II, para. 32.

9   Locke, *Civil Government*, II, para. 4.

10 Locke, *Civil Government*, II, para. 6.

11 Barbara Arneil, *John Locke and America: The Defence of English Colonialism* (Oxford: Clarendon Press, 1996), p. 151.

12 See further my discussion of Aquinas' views on property in Michael S. Northcott, *The Environment and Christian Ethics* (Cambridge: Cambridge University Press, 1996).

13 Will Hutton, *The World We're In* (London: Abacus, 2003).

14 Jonathan Clark, *The Language of Liberty, 1660 – 1832: Political Discourse and Social Dynamics in the Anglo-American World* (Cambridge: Cambridge University Press 1994), pp. 38 – 9.

15 Mark Noll, *America's God: From Jonathan Edwards to Abraham Lincoln* (Oxford: Oxford University Press, 2002), p. 9.

16 Noll, *America's God*, p. 49.

17 Noll, *America's God*, p. 56.

18 Ezra Stiles, cited Noll, *America's God*, p. 64.

19 See below chapter 3 for a fuller account of civil religion in America.

20 Dietrich Bonhoeffer, 'Protestantism with Reformation' in *No Rusty Swords: Letters, Lectures and Notes from the Collected Works*, edited by

Edwin H. Robertson, trans. John Bowden with Eberhard Bethge (London: Fontana, 1970), p. 100.

21   J. F. Maclear, 'The Republic and the Millennium' in Elwyn A. Smith (ed.), *The Religion of the Republic* (Philadelphia, PA: Fortress Press, 1971).

22   G. W. F. Hegel, *Lectures on the Philosophy of World-History: Introduction – Reason in History* cited Richard Rorty, *Achieving Our Country: Leftist Thought in Twentieth Century America* (Cambridge, MA: Harvard University Press, 1998), p. 21.

23   Rorty, *Achieving Our Country*, p. 19.

24   John Dewey, 'Creative Democracy – The Task Before Us', in *Later Works of John Dewey*, Vol. 14 cited Rorty, *Achieving Our Country*, p. 29.

25   Rorty, *Achieving Our Country*, p. 30.

26   Mark A. Noll, 'Introduction' in Mark A. Noll (ed.), *God and Mammon: Protestants, Money, and the Market, 1790 – 1860* (Oxford: Oxford University Press, 2001), p. 11.

27   Charles Sellers, *The Market Revolution: Jacksonian America 1815 – 1846* (Oxford: Oxford University Press, 1991).

28   Sellers, *The Market Revolution*, pp. 29 – 30.

29   Noll, *God and Mammon*, p. 12.

30   Maclear, 'The Republic and the Millennium', p. 201.

31   Roger Finke and Rodney Stark, 'How the Upstart Sects Won America: 1776 – 1850', *Journal for the Scientific Study of Religion*, 28 (March 1989) cited Noll, *God and Mammon*, p. 11.

32   David Paul Knord, 'Benevolent Capital: Financing Evangelical Book Publishing in Early Nineteenth-century America' in Noll (ed.), *God and Mammon*, pp. 147 – 70, and Kathryn T. Long, 'Turning ... Piety into Hard Cash: The Marketing of Nineteenth-century Revivalism' in Noll (ed.), *God and Mammon*, pp. 236 – 64.

33   Mark A. Noll, 'Protestant Reasoning about Money and the Economy, 1790 – 1860: A Preliminary Probe' in Noll (ed.), *God and Mammon*, p. 267.

34   Gordon Wood cited Noll, 'Protestant Reasoning about Money', p. 267.

35   Noll, 'Protestant Reasoning about Money', p. 269.

36   Henry Ward Beecher cited George M. Marsden, *Fundamentalism and American Culture: The Shaping of Twentieth-Century Evangelicalism: 1870 – 1925* (Oxford: Oxford University Press, 1980), p. 21.

37   Max Weber traces this alliance of piety and capitalism to the influence of Benjamin Franklin in *The Protestant Ethic and the Spirit of Capitalism*, trans. Talcott Parsons (London: Allen and Unwin, 1976).

38   Michael Williams, *This World is Not My Home: The Origins and Development of Dispensationalism* (Fearn, Rosshire: Mentor Press, 2003), p. 9.

39   J. N. Darby, *Collected Works* XI, p. 156 cited Timothy P. Weber, *Living in the Shadow of the Second Coming: American Premillennialism 1875 – 1925* (Oxford: Oxford University Press, 1979), p. 22.

40 Weber, *Living in the Shadow*, p. 42, and Williams, *This World is Not My Home*, p. 113.
41 Dwight L. Moody, *New Sermons* cited Williams, *This World is Not My Home*, pp. 41 – 2.
42 Shirley Anne Case, *The Millennial Hope* cited Weber, *Living in the Shadow*, p. 66.
43 Chafer, *Satan and the Satanic System* cited Williams, *This World is not My Home*, p. 53.
44 Charles Schofield, *What Do the Prophets Say?* cited Paul Boyer, *When Time Shall Be No More: Prophecy Belief in Modern American Culture* (Cambridge, MA: Belknap Press, 1992), p. 98.
45 R. A. Torrey, *What the Bible Teaches* cited Boyer, *When Time Shall Be No More*, p. 101.
46 Boyer, *When Time Shall Be No More*, p. 184.
47 Schofield Bible cited Boyer, *When Time Shall Be No More*, p. 185.
48 Theodore Herzl, *The Jewish State*, trans. Sylvie d'Avigdor (London: Nutt, 1896).
49 William E. Blackstone cited Weber, *Living in the Shadow*, pp. 138 – 9.
50 Weber, *Living in the Shadow*, p. 141.
51 Hal Lindsey, *The Late Great Planet Earth* (New York: Bantam Books, 1973), p. i.
52 Increase Mather, *The Mystery of Israel's Salvation, explained and applyed; or a discourse concerning the general conversion of the Israelitish nation, etc* (London, 1669)
53 Lindsey, *Late Great Planet Earth*, pp. 40 and 47.
54 N. T. Wright, *Jesus and the Victory of God* (Minneapolis, MN: Fortress Press, 1996).
55 Lindsey, *Late Great Planet Earth*, p. 68.
56 Lindsey, *Late Great Planet Earth*, p. 83.
57 Lindsey, *Late Great Planet Earth*, p. 101.
58 Lindsey, *Late Great Planet Earth*, pp. 152 – 7.
59 Ronald Reagan cited Boyer, *When Time Shall Be No More*, p. 142.
60 Boyer, *When Time Shall Be No More*, p. 144.
61 James Robison cited Boyer, *When Time Shall Be No More*, p. 145.
62 Keller, *Apocalypse Now and Then*, pp. 4 – 5.
63 George Monbiot, 'Apocalypse Please', *The Guardian*, 20 April, 2004.
64 Suskind, *The Price of Loyalty*.
65 These figures are derived from the World Bank's *World Development Indicators 2000* as cited Ted Honderich, *After the Terror* (Edinburgh: Edinburgh University Press, 2002), p. 8.
66 Molly Ivins and Lou Dubose, *Bushwhacked: Life in George W. Bush's America* (New York: Random House, 2003), p. 39.
67 Paul Krugman, 'For Richer', *New York Times Magazine*, 20 October, 2002.
68 Robert Kaplan, 'Manifest Destiny: An Interview with Robert D. Kaplan', *The Atlantic Online*, 16 September, 1998, http://www.theatlantic.com/

unbound/bookauth/ba980916.htm. See also Robert D. Kaplan, *An Empire Wilderness: Travels Into America's Future* (New York: Random House, 1998).

69 Honderich, *After the Terror.*
70 Figures from the *Federal Reserve Bulletin* cited Ivins and Dubose, *Bushwhacked*, p. 44.
71 Honderich, *After the Terror,* p. 108.
72 'The Christian World View of Economics', Coalition for Revival cited Laurence Iannaccone, 'Fundamentalism and Economics in the US' at http://www.gordon.edu/ace/pdf/Iannaccone_Fundamentalism.pdf.
73 Ivins and Dubose, *Bushwhacked*, p. 13.

3 – The Unveiling of Empire

1   Wes Howard Brook and Anthony Gwyther, *Unveiling Empire: Reading Revelation Then and Now* (Maryknoll, NY: Orbis Books, 1999).
2   Christopher Rowland, *The Open Heaven: A Study of Apocalyptic in Judaism and Early Christianity* (London: SPCK, 1982), p. 9.
3   C. K. Barrett, 'New Testament Eschatology' cited Rowland, *Open Heaven*, pp. 2 – 3.
4   Christopher Rowland, *The Open Heaven: A Study of Apocalyptic in Judaism and Early Christianity* (London: SPCK, 1982).
5   Richard Baukham, *The Climax of Prophecy: Studies in the Book of Revelation* (Edinburgh: T. and T. Clark, 1993).
6   Christopher Rowland, *Revelation* (London: Epworth, 1993), p. 3.
7   I owe this way of putting things to my friend Wilf Wild, who pointed out the link between veiling and ideology in a personal communication.
8   Andrew J. Bacevich, *The American Empire: The Realities and Consequences of U. S. Diplomacy* (Cambridge, MA: Harvard University Press, 2002), p. 30.
9   Bacevich, *American Empire*, p. 30.
10 Arthur M. Schlesinger Jr, *The Cycles of American History* cited Bacevich, *American Empire*, p. 30.
11 Bacevich, *American Empire*, p. 31.
12 Casper Weinberger cited Alex Callinicos, *The New Mandarins of American Power* (Cambridge: Polity Press, 2003), p. 64.
13 Madeleine Albright cited Callinicos, *The New Mandarins*, p. 64.
14 Patrick E. Tyler cited Bacevich, *American Empire*, p. 44.
15 Project for the New American Century, *Rebuilding America's Defenses: Strategy, Forces and Resources for a New Century* (Washington, DC: PNAC, 2000), p. 1.
16 On the American war in Columbia see Noam Chomsky, *Hegemony or Survival: America's Quest for Global Dominance* (London: Hamish Hamilton, 2003), pp. 52 – 4.

17 PNAC, *Rebuilding America's Defenses*, p. v.
18 Robert Fisk, 'This looming war isn't about chemical warheads or human rights: it's about oil', *The Independent*, 18 January, 2003.
19 PNAC, *Rebuilding America's Defenses*, p. 4.
20 *The National Security Strategy of the United States of America*, foreword by George W. Bush, The Whitehouse, Washington DC, September 2002.
21 Bacevich, *American Empire*, pp. 38 – 40.
22 Newt Gingrich cited Bacevich, *American Empire*, p. 39.
23 Joseph S. Nye, *The Paradox of American Power: Why the World's Only Superpower Cannot Go It Alone* (New York: Oxford University Press, 2002), pp. 78 – 81.
24 George W. Bush, 'Address of the President to the Joint Session of Congress', Washington DC, 27 February, 2001.
25 For a full list of the hundreds of American military operations since the end of the Cold War, see Vidal's essay 'Black Tuesday' in Gore Vidal, *The Last Empire: Essays 1992 – 2001* (London: Abacus, 2002), pp. 303 – 24.
26 Bacevich, *American Empire*, pp. 230, 232.
27 Immanuel Kant, *Perpetual Peace: A Philosophical Sketch, 1795*, trans. Frieden Zumewigen (London: Allen and Unwin, 1915).
28 George W. Bush, 'Remarks by the President at the Citadel', cited Bacevich, *American Empire*, p. 238.
29 Friedrich A. Hayek, *The Road to Serfdom* (New York: George Routledge and Sons, 1944).
30 Hayek, *The Road to Serfdom*, p. 19.
31 Leo Strauss, *Liberalism Ancient and Modern* (Chicago, IL: University of Chicago Press, 1995).
32 Charles Murray used Edmund Burke's phrase 'small platoon' in a plenary address on the neoconservative economic and political vision which he gave at the annual meeting of the Societas Ethica in Sigtuna, Sweden on 2 September, 2003.
33 Bush, 'Inaugural Address'.
34 'George W. Bush and the Real State of the Union', *The Independent*, 20 January, 2004, p. 1.
35 Richard Stivers, *The Culture of Cynicism: American Morality in Decline* (Oxford: Blackwell, 1994).
36 James F. Petras and Henry Veltmeyer, *Globalization Unmasked: Imperialism in the 21st Century* (Halifax, Nova Scotia: Fernwood, 2001).
37 Joseph Stiglitz clearly identifies the American-based International Monetary Fund, and other American banks, economists and corporations as those principally responsible for the economic collapse of Argentina in his *Globalization and its Discontents* (London: Allen Lane, 2002), pp. 68 – 70.
38 UNICEF, *The Progress of Nations*, cited Noam Chomski, *Rogue States: The Rule of Force in World Affairs* (London: Pluto Press, 2000), p. 136.

190   AN ANGEL DIRECTS THE STORM

39   Richard Land, 'Talking the Talk: Responses', in Michael Cromartie and Irving Kristol (eds.), *Disciples and Democracy: Religious Conservatives and the Future of American Politics* (Washington: Ethics and Public Policy Center and Grand Rapids, MI: Eerdmans, 1994), pp. 99 – 104 (102).
40   Land, 'Talking the Talk', pp. 102 – 3.
41   Stiglitz, *Globalization and its Discontents*.
42   Helen Caldicott, *The New Nuclear Danger: George W. Bush's Military-Industrial Complex* (New York: The New Press, 2002).
43   Zbigniew Brzezinski, *The Grand Chessboard: American Primacy and its Geostrategic Imperatives* (New York: Basic Books, 1997).
44   Joseph Schumpeter, *Imperialism and Social Classes* trans. Heinz Norden (Oxford: Basil Blackwell, 1951).
45   Nafeez Mosaddeq Ahmed, *The War on Freedom: How and Why America was Attacked on September 11, 2001* (Joshua Tree, CA: Tree of Life Publ., 2002), p. 88.
46   *Newsweek*, 24 September, 2001.
47   Andrew J. Bacevich, 'New Rome, New Jerusalem', in Andrew J. Bacevich (ed.), *The Imperial Tense: Prospects and Problems of American Empire* (Chicago: Ivan R. Dee Publ., 2003), p. 97.
48   Jean-Jacques Rousseau, *The Social Contract*, trans. Maurice Cranston (London: Penguin, 1968).
49   Robert Bellah, 'Civil Religion in America', *Daedalus*, 96, 1 (Winter 1967), pp. 1 – 21.
50   Carolyn Marvin and David W. Ingle, *Blood Sacrifice and the Nation: Totem Rituals and the American Flag* (Cambridge: Cambridge University Press, 1999), pp. 1 – 2.
51   Marvin and Ingle, *Blood Sacrifice*, p. 3.
52   Marvin and Ingle, *Blood Sacrifice*, p. 3.
53   René Girard, *The Scapegoat*, trans. Yvonne Freccero (London: Athlone Press, 1986), pp. 40 – 2.
54   René Girard, *Things Hidden from the Foundation of the World*, trans. Stephen Bann and Michael Metteer (London: Athlone Press, 1987), p. 136.
55   Marvin and Ingle, *Blood Sacrifice*, p. 10.
56   Marvin and Ingle, *Blood Sacrifice*, p. 89.
57   See further Jolyon P. Mitchell, *The Media and Christian Ethics* (Cambridge: Cambridge University Press, forthcoming).
58   William James, *The Varieties of Religious Experience* (London: Longman, Green and Co., 1902), p. 34.
59   On the rise of the megachurch see further Kimon Howland Sargeant, *Seeker Churches: Promoting Traditional Religion in a Nontraditional Way* (New Brunswick, NJ: Rutgers University Press, 2000).
60   President George W. Bush's address at the Washington National Cathedral Prayer Service, 14 September, 2001.
61   Timothy LaHaye, *The Battle for the World* (New Jersey: Revell, 1980), p. 35.

62 Bellah, 'Civil Religion in America'.

63 Gore Vidal in an interview with columnist Liz Smith, *New York Post*, April 4, 2003, ' Richard Dawkins,'Letter to the President', *The Guardian*, 19 October, 2003.

4 – The 'War on Terror' and the True Apocalypse

1   Edward S. Corwin, 'The War and the Constitution: President and Congress' cited Walter LaFaber, 'American Empire, American Raj', in Warren F. Kimball (ed.), *America Unbound: World War II and the Making of a Superpower* (New York: St Martin's Press, 1992), p. 55.

2   LaFaber, 'American Empire, American Raj', p. 55.

3   Corwin cited LaFaber, 'American Empire, American Raj', p. 56.

4   Michael Mann, *Incoherent Empire* (London: Verso, 2003).

5   John Milbank, 'Sovereignty, Empire, Capital and Terror', in Stanley Hauerwas and Frank Lentrucchia (eds.), *Dissent from the Homeland: Essays After September 11* (Durham, NC: Duke University Press, 2003), p. 68.

6   Giorgio Agamben, *Homo Sacer: Sovereign Power and Bare Life*, trans. Daniel Heller-Roazen (Stanford, CA: Stanford University Press, 1995), pp. 166 – 7. See also John Milbank, *Being Reconciled: Ontology and Pardon* (London: Routledge, 2003), p. 97.

7   Agamben, *Homo Sacer*, p. 168.

8   Michael Hardt and Antonio Negri, *Empire* (Cambridge, MA: Harvard University Press, 2000), p. 87.

9   Ronald Dworkin, 'Terror and the Attack on Civil Liberties', *New York Review of Books*, Vol. 50, No. 17, 6 November, 2003.

10 Hardt and Negri, *Empire*, pp. 20 – 21.

11 For examples of theological criticism see Hauerwas and Lenttruchia (eds.), *Dissent from the Homeland: Essays After September 11*.

12 Stanley Hauerwas, *Wilderness Wanderings: Probing Twentieth Century Theology and Philosophy* (London: SCM Press, 2001), p. 10.

13 Oliver O'Donovan, 'Political theology, tradition and modernity', in Christopher Rowland (ed.), *The Cambridge Companion to Liberation Theology* (Cambridge: Cambridge University Press, 1999), p. 241.

14 George Friedman cited by Robert Novak, 'The American Imperium', *Chicago Sun Times*, 10 February, 2003.

15 Robert Novak, *Chicago Sun Times*, 10 February, 2003.

16 Richard Horsley, *Jesus and Empire: The Kingdom of God and the New World Disorder* (Minneapolis, MN: Fortress Press, 2003).

17 Peter Garnsey and Richard Saller, *The Roman Empire: Economy, Society, Culture* (London: Duckworth, 1987), pp. 20 – 26.

18 William R. Herzog, *Jesus, Justice, and the Reign of God: A Ministry of Liberation* (Louisville, KY: Westminster John Knox Press, 2000), p. 228.

19 Richard Horsley, 'Liberating Narrative and Liberating Understanding: The Christmas Story', in Norman K. Gottwald and Richard A. Horsley (eds.), *The Bible and Liberation: Political and Social Hermeneutics* (Maryknoll, NY: Orbis Books, 1993), p. 161.

20 Herzog, *Jesus, Justice, and the Reign of God*, p. 220.

21 Ched Myers, *Binding the Strong Man: A Political Reading of Mark's Story of Jesus* (Maryknoll, NY: Orbis Books, 1988), pp. 310 – 1.

22 Herzog, *Jesus, Justice, and the Reign of God*, p. 229.

23 Myers, *Binding the Strong Man*, p. 314.

24 Herzog, *Jesus, Justice, and the Reign of God*, p. 122.

25 Dominic Crossan, *The Historical Jesus: The Life of a Mediterranean Jewish Peasant* (Edinburgh: T. and T. Clark, 1991), p. 324.

26 N. T. Wright, *The New Testament and the People of God* (London: SPCK, 1992), p. 472.

27 Herzog, *Jesus, Justice, and the Reign of God*, p. 136.

28 This view is now held by only a minority of American New Testament scholars. See the debate between Dale C. Allison and Marcus Borg, Dominic Crossan and Stephen Patterson in Robert J. Miller (ed.), *The Apocalyptic Jesus: A Debate* (Santa Rosa, CA: Polebridge Press, 2001).

29 Herzog, *Jesus, Justice, and the Reign of God*, pp. 208 – 9.

30 Crossan, *Historical Jesus*, p. 225.

31 Stephen J. Patterson, *The Gospel of Thomas and Jesus* cited Dominic Crossan, *The Birth of Christianity: Discovering What Really Happened in the Years Immediately After the Execution of Jesus* (Edinburgh: T. and T. Clark, 1998), p. 305.

32 Herzog, *Jesus, Justice, and the Reign of God*, p. 211.

33 N. T. Wright, *Jesus and the Victory of God* (London: SPCK, 1996), p. 108.

34 Wright, *Jesus and the Victory of God*, p. 110.

35 See the account of the apocalyptic hope of Israel in N. T. Wright, *The New Testament and the People of God* (London: SPCK, 1992), pp. 280 – 338.

36 Douglas Harink, *Paul Among the Postliberals: Pauline Theology Beyond Christendom and Modernity* (Grand Rapids, MI: Brazos Press, 2003), p. 68.

37 Harink, *Paul Among the Postliberals*, p. 69.

38 Harink, *Paul among the Postliberals*, p. 89.

39 Hauerwas, *Against the Nations*, pp. 18 – 19.

40 Hauerwas, *Against the Nations*, p. 129.

41 Stanley Hauerwas, 'The Non-Violent Terrorist', in Hauerwas, *Sanctify Them in the Truth: Holiness Exemplified* (Edinburgh: T. and T. Clark, 1998), p. 188.

42 Hauerwas, 'Non-Violent Terrorist'.

43 Alan Dershowitz, *Shouting Fire: Civil Liberties in a Turbulent Age* (New York: Little Brown and Co., 2002).

44 'Enduring Freedom: Abuses by U. S. Forces in Afghanistan', *Human*

Rights Watch, March 2004, Vol. 16, No. 3. Amnesty International reported the use of torture on Iraqi detainees in July 2003: 'U.S. Accused of Torture', CBS News, 19 July, 2003.

5 – The Warrior Ethos and the Politics of Jesus

1 See for example Robert Kaplan, *Warrior Politics: Why Leadership Demands a Pagan Ethos* (New York: Random House, 2001).
2 Joe Burlas, 'Army Chief of Staff stresses warrior ethos for all soldiers', Army News Service, 4 March, 2004.
3 See the Iraq Body Count at http://www.iraqbodycount.net/.
4 George W. Bush, 'State of the Union Address', 29 January, 2002.
5 Jean Bethke Elshtain, 'Citizenship and Armed Civic Virtue: Some Questions on the Commitment to Public Life' cited Stanley Hauerwas and Charles Pinches, *Christians Among the Virtues: Theological Conversations with Ancient and Modern Ethics* (Notre Dame, IN: University of Notre Dame Press, 1995), p. 150.
6 Elshtain, 'Citizenship and Armed Civic Virtue' cited Hauerwas and Pinches, *Among the Virtues*, p. 151 and also Hauerwas, *Against the Nations*, p. 148.
7 René Girard, *Violence and the Sacred*, trans. Patrick Gregory (Baltimore, MD: John Hopkins University Press, 1977).
8 Cf. the sub-title of John Howard Yoder's *The Politics of Jesus: Vicit Agnus Noster* (Grand Rapids, MI: Eerdmans, 1972).
9 Wendel Berry, 'Thoughts in the Presence of Fear' in Berry, *Citizenship Papers* (Washington, DC: Shoemaker and Hoard, 2003), pp. 17 – 22.
10 'Interview with Stanley Hauerwas', 8 November, 2001, in *Sojourners Commentary* at http://www.sojo.net/index.cfm?action=news.display_archives&mode=current_opinion&article=CO_010702h
11 Wendel Berry, 'A Citizen's Response to the National Security Strategy of the United States of America', *Orion*, Vol. 22, No. 2 (March – April 2003), pp. 18 – 27.
12 Berry, 'A Citizen's Response', p. 20.
13 Milbank, *Being Reconciled*, pp. 21 – 2.
14 This is the core theme of Ched Myers' commentary on the Gospel of Mark, *Binding the Strong Man*. See esp. pp. 164 – 7.
15 John Howard Yoder, *The Original Revolution* (Scottdale, PA: Herald Press, 1971), pp. 142 – 3.
16 Walter Wink, *Engaging the Powers: Discernment and Resistance in a World of Domination* (Minneapolis, MN: Fortress Press, 1992).
17 Yoder, *Politics of Jesus*, p. 146.
18 Berkhof, *Christ and the Powers*, cited Yoder, *Politics of Jesus*, pp. 150 – 1.
19 Yoder, *Politics of Jesus*, p. 151.

20 Yoder, *Politics of Jesus*, p. 147.
21 Kagan, *Paradise and Power*.
22 On East Timor as well as Columbia see further Chomsky, *Hegemony or Survival*, pp. 52 – 4.
23 Caldicott, *The New Nuclear Danger*, pp. xi and 149 – 55.
24 Yoder, *Original Revolution*, pp. 77 – 8.
25 Yoder, *For the Nations*, p. 35.
26 H. A. Drake, *Constantine and the Bishops: The Politics of Intolerance* (Baltimore, MD: John Hopkins Press, 2000), pp. 158 – 62.
27 The sincerity of his conversion is contested by Alastair Kee in *Constantine versus Christ: The Triumph of Ideology* (London: SCM Press, 1982), but the fact that Constantine was baptised along with his household would have been evidence enough to the ancients. It is a Jamesian idea that inner experience rather than public action is the litmus test of true religion.
28 Drake, *Constantine and the Bishops*, pp. 192 – 3.
29 Eusebius of Caesarea, 'From a Speech on the Dedication of the Holy Sepulchre Church', translated in Oliver O'Donovan and Joan Lockwood O'Donovan (eds.), *From Irenaeus to Grotius: A Sourcebook of Christian Political Thought* (Grand Rapids, MI: Eerdmans, 1999), pp. 58 – 9.
30 O'Donovan, 'Eusebius of Caesarea', in O'Donovan and O'Donovan (eds.), *Irenaeus to Grotius*, p. 57.
31 Drake, *Constantine and the Bishops*, pp. 297 and 376.
32 Kee, *Constantine versus Christ*, pp. 37 – 48.
33 Eusebius of Caesarea, *Jubilee Oration* cited Kee, *Constantine versus Christ*, pp. 39 – 40.
34 Yoder, *Politics of Jesus*, p. 78.
35 Yoder, *Politics of Jesus*, p. 84.
36 See further my account of the ecological meaning of the covenant in Michael S. Northcott, *The Environment and Christian Ethics* (Cambridge: Cambridge University Press, 1996), chapter 5.
37 John Howard Yoder, *For the Nations: Essays Public and Evangelical* (Grand Rapids, MI: Eerdmans, 1997), p. 244.
38 See also Walter Wink, *Engaging the Powers*.
39 Augustine, *City of God*, XIX, 12, Eng. Trans. (Harmondsworth: Penguin, 1977).
40 St. Thomas Aquinas, *Summa Theologiae* II, II, ae, 40, 1.
41 The just-war position has been much developed and complexified since the Middle Ages: see John Howard Yoder, *When War Is Unjust: Being Honest in Just War Thinking* (New York: Wipf and Stock, 2001) for a full exposition of the many permutations and varieties of just-war thinking.
42 Jean Bethke Elshtain, *Just War Against Terror: The Burden of American Power in a Violent World* (New York: Basic Books, 2003), p. 61.
43 Neil MacKay, 'US Forces Use of Depleted Uranium is Illegal', *The Sunday Herald* (Scotland), 30 March, 2003.

44 Ross B. Mirkarimi, 'The Environmental and Human Health Impacts of the Gulf Region with Special Reference to Iraq', The Arms Control Research Centre, May 1992 at http://www.web-light.nl/VISIE/extremedeformities.html.
45 Sara Flounders, *Metal of Dishonor: How the Pentagon Radiates Soldiers and Civilians with DU Weapons* (New York: International Action Center, 1997), p. 3.
46 Caldicott, *The New Nuclear Danger*, p. 153.
47 Siegwart Horst-Gunther, 'Gulf War Syndrome – A Parallel to Chernobyl: Documentation of the Aftermath of the Gulf War', Vienna, 1995, http://www.firethistime.org/guntheressay.htm.
48 Rita Nakashima Brock, 'The Cross and Communities of Life Restored' Plenary paper, 2003 meeting of the Society for the Study of Theology, Newcastle University.
49 Anselm of Canterbury, *Why God Became Man* (London: Religious Tract Society, 1887).
50 Strozier, *Apocalypse*, p. 79.
51 J. Denny Weaver, *The Nonviolent Atonement* (Grand Rapids, MI: Eerdmans, 2001), p. 48.
52 Weaver, *The Nonviolent Atonement*, p. 48.
53 See further Stanley Hauerwas, 'Out of the Silence' in *First Things* No. 120, February 2002.
54 Yoder, *Politics of Jesus*, p. 234.
55 Yoder, *Politics of Jesus*, p. 236.
56 Yoder, *Politics of Jesus*, p. 238.
57 Yoder, *Politics of Jesus*, p. 244.
58 See further John Howard Yoder, *Body Politics: Five Practices of the Christian Community before the Watching World* (Scottdale, PN: Herald Press, 1999).
59 Yoder, *Body Politics*, p. 29.
60 Yoder, *Politics of Jesus*, p. 245.
61 Yoder, *Politics of Jesus*, p. 247.
62 Samuel P. Huntington, 'The Clash of Civilizations?, *Foreign Affairs*, Vol. 72, No. 3 (Summer, 1993), pp. 22 – 50.
63 See for example Paul Berman, 'Terror and Liberalism', *The American Prospect*, Vol. 12, No. 18, 22 October, 2001.
64 The last theologian to achieve this accolade was, strangely enough, Reinhold Niebuhr.
65 Stanley Hauerwas has now resigned from the Editorial Board of *First Things*.
66 George W. Bush, Address to Congress, 20 September, 2003 cited 'In a Time of War', *First Things* No. 118, December 2001.
67 'In a Time of War'.
68 'In a Time of War'.
69 Stanley Hauerwas, 'Out of the Silence', *First Things* No. 119, February 2002.

70 Hauerwas, 'Out of the Silence'.
71 John Howard Yoder, *For the Nations: Essays Evangelical and Public* (Grand Rapids, MI: Eerdmans, 1997), pp. 57 – 8.
72 Yoder, *For the Nations*, p. 69.
73 Yoder, 'Epilogue', in Yoder, *The Politics of Jesus* (Second Edition, Grand Rapids, MI: Eerdmans, 1994).
74 Yoder, 'Epilogue'.
75 See the account of the Mennonite Central Committee's conciliation work in R. Scott Appleby, *The Ambivalence of the Sacred: Religion, Violence and Reconciliation* (Lanham, MA: Rowman and Littlefield, 2000), pp. 143 – 50.
76 Yoder, 'Epilogue'.
77 Duncan B. Forrester, 'The Church and the Concentration Camp: Some Reflections on Moral Community', in Mark Thiessen Nation (ed.), *Faithfulness and Fortitude: In conversation with the Theological Ethics of Stanley Hauerwas* (Edinburgh: T. and T. Clark, 2000), pp. 189 – 207.
78 See Benjamin Franklin's speech at http://www.jmu.edu/madison/prayers.htm.

Epilogue

1 Michael Welker, 'Angels and God's Presence in Creation' in his *Creation and Reality*, Eng. Trans. John F. Hoffmeyer (Minneapolis, MN: Fortress Press, 1999), pp. 45 – 59.
2 Gabriel Fakre, 'Angels Heard and Demons Seen', *Theology Today*, Vol. 51, No. 3 (October 1994), pp. 345 – 58.
3 I am grateful to Alastair McIntosh for his insightful exposition of the temptations of Christ at an address to an away weekend of St James' Church, Leith, in May 2003.
4 Fakre, 'Angels Heard and Demons Seen', p. 357.

Index